FREE Test Taking Tips Video/DVD Offer

To better serve you, we created videos covering test taking tips that we want to give you for FREE. **These videos cover world-class tips that will help your child or student succeed on their test.**

We just ask that you send us feedback about this product. Please let us know what you thought about it—whether good, bad, or indifferent.

To get your **FREE videos**, you can use the QR code below or email freevideos@studyguideteam.com with "Free Videos" in the subject line and the following information in the body of the email:

- a. The title of your product

- b. Your product rating on a scale of 1-5, with 5 being the highest

- c. Your feedback about the product

If you have any questions or concerns, please don't hesitate to contact us at info@studyguideteam.com.

Thank you!

ISEE Lower Level Test Prep 2024 and 2025
4 Practice Exams and ISEE Book
[7th Edition]

Lydia Morrison

Interested in buying more than 10 copies of our product? Contact us about bulk discounts:
bulkorders@studyguideteam.com

ISBN 13: 9781637754139

Table of Contents

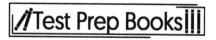

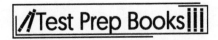

Welcome

Dear Reader,

Welcome to your new Test Prep Books study guide! We are pleased that you chose us to help you prepare for your exam. There are many study options to choose from, and we appreciate you choosing us. Studying can be a daunting task, but we have designed a smart, effective study guide to help prepare you for what lies ahead.

Whether you're a parent helping your child learn and grow, a high school student working hard to get into your dream college, or a nursing student studying for a complex exam, we want to help give you the tools you need to succeed. We hope this study guide gives you the skills and the confidence to thrive, and we can't thank you enough for allowing us to be part of your journey.

In an effort to continue to improve our products, we welcome feedback from our customers. We look forward to hearing from you. Suggestions, success stories, and criticisms can all be communicated by emailing us at info@studyguideteam.com.

Sincerely,
Test Prep Books Team

FREE Videos/DVD OFFER

Doing well on your exam requires both knowing the test content and understanding how to use that knowledge to do well on the test. We offer completely FREE test taking tip videos. **These videos cover world-class tips that you can use to succeed on your test.**

To get your **FREE videos**, you can use the QR code below or email freevideos@studyguideteam.com with "Free Videos" in the subject line and the following information in the body of the email:

    a. The title of your product
    b. Your product rating on a scale of 1-5, with 5 being the highest
    c. Your feedback about the product

If you have any questions or concerns, please don't hesitate to contact us at info@studyguideteam.com.

1

Quick Overview

As you draw closer to taking your exam, effective preparation becomes more and more important. Thankfully, you have this study guide to help you get ready. Use this guide to help keep your studying on track and refer to it often.

This study guide contains several key sections that will help you be successful on your exam. The guide contains tips for what you should do the night before and the day of the test. Also included are test-taking tips. Knowing the right information is not always enough. Many well-prepared test takers struggle with exams. These tips will help equip you to accurately read, assess, and answer test questions.

A large part of the guide is devoted to showing you what content to expect on the exam and to helping you better understand that content. In this guide are practice test questions so that you can see how well you have grasped the content. Then, answer explanations are provided so that you can understand why you missed certain questions.

Don't try to cram the night before you take your exam. This is not a wise strategy for a few reasons. First, your retention of the information will be low. Your time would be better used by reviewing information you already know rather than trying to learn a lot of new information. Second, you will likely become stressed as you try to gain a large amount of knowledge in a short amount of time. Third, you will be depriving yourself of sleep. So be sure to go to bed at a reasonable time the night before. Being well-rested helps you focus and remain calm.

Be sure to eat a substantial breakfast the morning of the exam. If you are taking the exam in the afternoon, be sure to have a good lunch as well. Being hungry is distracting and can make it difficult to focus. You have hopefully spent lots of time preparing for the exam. Don't let an empty stomach get in the way of success!

When travelling to the testing center, leave earlier than needed. That way, you have a buffer in case you experience any delays. This will help you remain calm and will keep you from missing your appointment time at the testing center.

Be sure to pace yourself during the exam. Don't try to rush through the exam. There is no need to risk performing poorly on the exam just so you can leave the testing center early. Allow yourself to use all of the allotted time if needed.

Remain positive while taking the exam even if you feel like you are performing poorly. Thinking about the content you should have mastered will not help you perform better on the exam.

Once the exam is complete, take some time to relax. Even if you feel that you need to take the exam again, you will be well served by some down time before you begin studying again. It's often easier to convince yourself to study if you know that it will come with a reward!

2

Test-Taking Strategies

1. Predicting the Answer

When you feel confident in your preparation for a multiple-choice test, try predicting the answer before reading the answer choices. This is especially useful on questions that test objective factual knowledge. By predicting the answer before reading the available choices, you eliminate the possibility that you will be distracted or led astray by an incorrect answer choice. You will feel more confident in your selection if you read the question, predict the answer, and then find your prediction among the answer choices. After using this strategy, be sure to still read all of the answer choices carefully and completely. If you feel unprepared, you should not attempt to predict the answers. This would be a waste of time and an opportunity for your mind to wander in the wrong direction.

2. Reading the Whole Question

Too often, test takers scan a multiple-choice question, recognize a few familiar words, and immediately jump to the answer choices. Test authors are aware of this common impatience, and they will sometimes prey upon it. For instance, a test author might subtly turn the question into a negative, or he or she might redirect the focus of the question right at the end. The only way to avoid falling into these traps is to read the entirety of the question carefully before reading the answer choices.

3. Looking for Wrong Answers

Long and complicated multiple-choice questions can be intimidating. One way to simplify a difficult multiple-choice question is to eliminate all of the answer choices that are clearly wrong. In most sets of answers, there will be at least one selection that can be dismissed right away. If the test is administered on paper, the test taker could draw a line through it to indicate that it may be ignored; otherwise, the test taker will have to perform this operation mentally or on scratch paper. In either case, once the obviously incorrect answers have been eliminated, the remaining choices may be considered. Sometimes identifying the clearly wrong answers will give the test taker some information about the correct answer. For instance, if one of the remaining answer choices is a direct opposite of one of the eliminated answer choices, it may well be the correct answer. The opposite of obviously wrong is obviously right! Of course, this is not always the case. Some answers are obviously incorrect simply because they are irrelevant to the question being asked. Still, identifying and eliminating some incorrect answer choices is a good way to simplify a multiple-choice question.

4. Don't Overanalyze

Anxious test takers often overanalyze questions. When you are nervous, your brain will often run wild, causing you to make associations and discover clues that don't actually exist. If you feel that this may be a problem for you, do whatever you can to slow down during the test. Try taking a deep breath or counting to ten. As you read and consider the question, restrict yourself to the particular words used by the author. Avoid thought tangents about what the author *really* meant, or what he or she was *trying* to say. The only things that matter on a multiple-choice test are the words that are actually in the question. You must avoid reading too much into a multiple-choice question, or supposing that the writer meant something other than what he or she wrote.

3

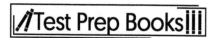

5. No Need for Panic

It is wise to learn as many strategies as possible before taking a multiple-choice test, but it is likely that you will come across a few questions for which you simply don't know the answer. In this situation, avoid panicking. Because most multiple-choice tests include dozens of questions, the relative value of a single wrong answer is small. As much as possible, you should compartmentalize each question on a multiple-choice test. In other words, you should not allow your feelings about one question to affect your success on the others. When you find a question that you either don't understand or don't know how to answer, just take a deep breath and do your best. Read the entire question slowly and carefully. Try rephrasing the question a couple of different ways. Then, read all of the answer choices carefully. After eliminating obviously wrong answers, make a selection and move on to the next question.

6. Confusing Answer Choices

When working on a difficult multiple-choice question, there may be a tendency to focus on the answer choices that are the easiest to understand. Many people, whether consciously or not, gravitate to the answer choices that require the least concentration, knowledge, and memory. This is a mistake. When you come across an answer choice that is confusing, you should give it extra attention. A question might be confusing because you do not know the subject matter to which it refers. If this is the case, don't

 eliminate the answer before you have affirmatively settled on another. When you come across an answer choice of this type, set it aside as you look at the remaining choices. If you can confidently assert that one of the other choices is correct, you can leave the confusing answer aside. Otherwise, you will need to take a moment to try to better understand the confusing answer choice. Rephrasing is one way to tease out the sense of a confusing answer choice.

7. Your First Instinct

Many people struggle with multiple-choice tests because they overthink the questions. If you have studied sufficiently for the test, you should be prepared to trust your first instinct once you have carefully and completely read the question and all of the answer choices. There is a great deal of research suggesting that the mind can come to the correct conclusion very quickly once it has obtained all of the relevant information. At times, it may seem to you as if your intuition is working faster even than your reasoning mind. This may in fact be true. The knowledge you obtain while studying may be retrieved from your subconscious before you have a chance to work out the associations that support it. Verify your instinct by working out the reasons that it should be trusted.

8. Key Words

Many test takers struggle with multiple-choice questions because they have poor reading comprehension skills. Quickly reading and understanding a multiple-choice question requires a mixture of skill and experience. To help with this, try jotting down a few key words and phrases on a piece of scrap paper. Doing this concentrates the process of reading and forces the mind to weigh the relative importance of the question's parts. In selecting words and phrases to write down, the test taker thinks

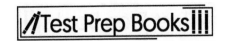

about the question more deeply and carefully. This is especially true for multiple-choice questions that are preceded by a long prompt.

9. Subtle Negatives

One of the oldest tricks in the multiple-choice test writer's book is to subtly reverse the meaning of a question with a word like *not* or *except*. If you are not paying attention to each word in the question, you can easily be led astray by this trick. For instance, a common question format is, "Which of the following is…?" Obviously, if the question instead is, "Which of the following is not…?," then the answer will be quite different. Even worse, the test makers are aware of the potential for this mistake and will include one answer choice that would be correct if the question were not negated or reversed. A test taker who misses the reversal will find what he or she believes to be a correct answer and will be so confident that he or she will fail to reread the question and discover the original error. The only way to avoid this is to practice a wide variety of multiple-choice questions and to pay close attention to each and every word.

10. Reading Every Answer Choice

It may seem obvious, but you should always read every one of the answer choices! Too many test takers fall into the habit of scanning the question and assuming that they understand the question because they recognize a few key words. From there, they pick the first answer choice that answers the question they believe they have read. Test takers who read all of the answer choices might discover that one of the latter answer choices is actually *more* correct. Moreover, reading all of the answer choices can remind you of facts related to the question that can help you arrive at the correct answer. Sometimes, a misstatement or incorrect detail in one of the latter answer choices will trigger your memory of the subject and will enable you to find the right answer. Failing to read all of the answer choices is like not reading all of the items on a restaurant menu: you might miss out on the perfect choice.

11. Spot the Hedges

One of the keys to success on multiple-choice tests is paying close attention to every word. This is never truer than with words like *almost*, *most*, *some*, and *sometimes*. These words are called "hedges" because they indicate that a statement is not totally true or not true in every place and time. An absolute statement will contain no hedges, but in many subjects, the answers are not always straightforward or absolute. There are always exceptions to the rules in these subjects. For this reason,

you should favor those multiple-choice questions that contain hedging language. The presence of qualifying words indicates that the author is taking special care with his or her words, which is certainly important when composing the right answer. After all, there are many ways to be wrong, but there is only one way to be right! For this reason, it is wise to avoid answers that are absolute when taking a multiple-choice test. An absolute answer is one that says things are either all one way or all another. They often include words like *every*, *always*, *best*, and *never*. If you are taking a multiple-choice test in a subject that doesn't lend itself to absolute answers, be on your guard if you see any of these words.

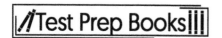
12. Long Answers

 In many subject areas, the answers are not simple. As already mentioned, the right answer often requires hedges. Another common feature of the answers to a complex or subjective question are qualifying clauses, which are groups of words that subtly modify the meaning of the sentence. If the question or answer choice describes a rule to which there are exceptions or the subject matter is complicated, ambiguous, or confusing, the correct answer will require many words in order to be expressed clearly and accurately. In essence, you should not be deterred by answer choices that seem excessively long. Oftentimes, the author of the text will not be able to write the correct answer without offering some qualifications and modifications. Your job is to read the answer choices thoroughly and completely and to select the one that most accurately and precisely answers the question.

13. Restating to Understand

Sometimes, a question on a multiple-choice test is difficult not because of what it asks but because of how it is written. If this is the case, restate the question or answer choice in different words. This process serves a couple of important purposes. First, it forces you to concentrate on the core of the question. In order to rephrase the question accurately, you have to understand it well. Rephrasing the question will concentrate your mind on the key words and ideas. Second, it will present the information to your mind in a fresh way. This process may trigger your memory and render some useful scrap of information picked up while studying.

14. True Statements

Sometimes an answer choice will be true in itself, but it does not answer the question. This is one of the main reasons why it is essential to read the question carefully and completely before proceeding to the answer choices. Too often, test takers skip ahead to the answer choices and look for true statements. Having found one of these, they are content to select it without reference to the question above. The savvy test taker will always read the entire question before turning to the answer choices. Then, having settled on a correct answer choice, he or she will refer to the original question and ensure that the selected answer is relevant. The mistake of choosing a correct-but-irrelevant answer choice is especially common on questions related to specific pieces of objective knowledge.

15. No Patterns

One of the more dangerous ideas that circulates about multiple-choice tests is that the correct answers tend to fall into patterns. These erroneous ideas range from a belief that B and C are the most common right answers, to the idea that an unprepared test-taker should answer "A-B-A-C-A-D-A-B-A." It cannot be emphasized enough that pattern-seeking of this type is exactly the WRONG way to approach a multiple-choice test. To begin with, it is highly unlikely that the test maker will plot the correct answers according to some predetermined pattern. The questions are scrambled and delivered in a random order. Furthermore, even if the test maker was following a pattern in the assignation of correct answers, there is no reason why the test taker would know which pattern he or she was using. Any attempt to discern a pattern in the answer choices is a waste of time and a distraction from the real work of taking the test. A test taker would be much better served by extra preparation before the test than by reliance on a pattern in the answers.

Bonus Content

We host multiple bonus items online, including all 4 practice tests in digital format. Scan the QR code or go to this link to access this content:

testprepbooks.com/bonus/isee-lower

The first time you access the tests, you will need to register as a "new user" and verify your email address.

If you have any issues, please email support@testprepbooks.com.

Introduction to the ISEE Lower Exam

Function of the Test

The Lower Level ISEE (Independent School Entrance Exam) is a test, offered by the Educational Records Bureau (ERB), that is designed to be used for admission assessment at independent schools for entrance to fifth and sixth grades. Two other ISEE exams cover students seeking to enter other grades. Accordingly, the typical test taker is usually a prospective fifth or sixth grade student at a private school in the United States. The test is also used by a few international schools, primarily those catering to American parents.

ISEE scores are available to the test taker and to schools the test taker is seeking admission to. They are typically used only by such schools, and only as part of the admissions process.

Test Administration

The test is available in both computer and paper versions. The computer version can be taken online, allowing it to be administered at any time and date. The test may also be administered at ERB member schools, ERB offices, and any of 400 plus Prometric testing sites.

Upon arrival at the testing site, test takers present a verification letter or identification and get checked in. Test takers are encouraged to ask questions for clarification before the exam begins, as administrators are not permitted to discuss the test questions once testing begins. Test takers are asked to bring four #2 pencils and two pens.

Test takers may register for the Lower Level ISEE no more than three times during a given year, once each in any or all of three testing seasons. The testing seasons are fall (August through November), winter (December through March), and spring/summer (April through July). Reasonable accommodations are available for test takers with documented disabilities under the Americans with Disabilities Act.

ERB recently set the limit on retakes at one per testing season.

Test Format

The content of the Lower Level ISEE is based on standards prepared by organizations including the National Council of Teachers of English, the International Reading Association, and the National Council of Teachers of Mathematics. The test consists of four multiple-choice sections and one essay section. A test taker's ISEE score is based on their performance on the four multiple choice sections. The essay is

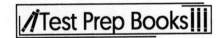

not graded, but is included with the scores when they are sent to a school. A breakdown of the sections is as follows:

Section	Content	Questions	Time
Verbal Reasoning	Multiple choice, scored	34	20
Quantitative Reasoning	Multiple choice, scored	38	35
Reading Comprehension	Multiple choice, scored	25	25
Mathematics Achievement	Multiple choice, scored	30	30
Essay	Written, unscored	N/A	30

Scoring

Scores are based only on the number of correct answers provided. There is no penalty for guessing incorrectly, aside from the missed opportunity to provide another correct answer. That total number of correct answers becomes a raw score, which is then converted to a scaled score between 760 and 940. There is no set passing score on the exam. Instead, scores are reviewed by schools in conjunction with other factors in determining admissions decisions.

Scores are first provided to the test taker's family. The family may then decide whether to release the report to schools, and to which schools to release it. Scores may be received as soon as a couple days after completion of an exam.

Study Prep Plan for the ISEE Lower Test

1 **Schedule -** Use one of our study schedules below or come up with one of your own.

2 **Relax -** Test anxiety can hurt even the best students. There are many ways to reduce stress. Find the one that works best for you.

3 **Execute -** Once you have a good plan in place, be sure to stick to it.

One Week Study Schedule	
Day 1	Verbal Reasoning
Day 2	Quantitative Reasoning and Math Achievement
Day 3	Geometry
Day 4	Quantitative Reasoning Practice Quiz
Day 5	Practice Test #1
Day 6	Practice Test #2
Day 7	Take Your Exam!

Two Week Study Schedule			
Day 1	Verbal Reasoning	Day 8	Quantitative Reasoning Practice Quiz
Day 2	Sentence Completion	Day 9	Organization/Logic
Day 3	Quantitative Reasoning and Math Achievement	Day 10	Practice Test #1
Day 4	Strategies and Algorithms to PerforM...	Day 11	Practice Test #2
Day 5	Algebraic Concepts	Day 12	Practice Test #3
Day 6	Geometry	Day 13	Practice Test #4
Day 7	Data Analysis and Probability	Day 14	Take Your Exam!

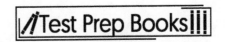

One Month Study Schedule					
Day 1	Verbal Reasoning	Day 11	Geometry	Day 21	Take a Break!
Day 2	Adjective Suffixes	Day 12	Data Analysis and Probability	Day 22	Practice Test #1
Day 3	Verbal Reasoning Practice Quiz	Day 13	Graphical Representation of Data	Day 23	Answer Explanations #1
Day 4	Quantitative Reasoning and Math Achievement	Day 14	Quantitative Reasoning Practice Quiz	Day 24	Practice Test #2
Day 5	Rounding Multi-Digit Numbers	Day 15	Mathematics Achievement Practice Quiz	Day 25	Answer Explanations #2
Day 6	Strategies and Algorithms to Perform...	Day 16	Reading Comprehension	Day 26	Take a Break!
Day 7	Properties of Operations	Day 17	Organization/Logic	Day 27	Practice Test #3
Day 8	Comparing, Classifying, and Ordering Rational...	Day 18	Reading Comprehension Practice Quiz	Day 28	Answer Explanations #3
Day 9	Algebraic Concepts	Day 19	Writing the Essay	Day 29	Practice Test #4
Day 10	Multistep One-Variable Linear...	Day 20	Practice Essay Question	Day 30	Take Your Exam!

Build your own prep plan by visiting:

testprepbooks.com/prep

11

As you study for your test, we'd like to take the opportunity to remind you that you are capable of great things! With the right tools and dedication, you truly can do anything you set your mind to. The fact that you are holding this book right now shows how committed you are. In case no one has told you lately, you've got this! Our intention behind including this coloring page is to give you the chance to take some time to engage your creative side when you need a little brain-break from studying. As a company, we want to encourage people like you to achieve their dreams by providing good quality study materials for the tests and certifications that improve careers and change lives. As individuals, many of us have taken such tests in our careers, and we know how challenging this process can be. While we can't come alongside you and cheer you on personally, we can offer you the space to recall your purpose, reconnect with your passion, and refresh your brain through an artistic practice. We wish you every success, and happy studying!

Verbal Reasoning

Synonyms

Synonyms are words that mean the same or nearly the same if given a list of words in the same language. When presented with several words and asked to choose the synonym, more than one word may be similar to the original. However, one word is generally the strongest match. Synonyms should always share the same part of speech. For instance, *shy* and *timid* are both adjectives and hold similar meanings. The words *shy* and *loner* are similar, but shy is an adjective, while loner is a noun. Another way to test for the best synonym is to reread the question with each possible word and determine which one makes the most sense. Consider the words: adore, sweet, kind, and nice.

Now consider the following sentence: *He will love you forever.*

> He will adore you forever.
> He will sweet you forever.
> He will kind you forever.
> He will nice you forever.

In the first sentence, the word *love* is used as a verb. The best synonym from the list that shares the same part of speech is *adore*. Adore is a verb, and when substituted in the sentence, it is the only substitution that makes grammatical and semantic sense.

Synonyms can be found for nouns, adjectives, verbs, adverbs, and prepositions. Here are some examples of synonyms from different parts of speech:

- Nouns: clothes, wardrobe, attire, apparel
- Verbs: run, spring, dash
- Adjectives: fast, quick, rapid, swift
- Adverbs: slowly, nonchalantly, leisurely
- Prepositions: near, proximal, neighboring, close

Here are several more examples of synonyms in the English language:

Word	Synonym	Meaning
smart	intelligent	having or showing a high level of intelligence
exact	specific	clearly identified
almost	nearly	not quite but very close
to annoy	to bother	to irritate
to answer	to reply	to form a written or verbal response
building	edifice	a structure that stands on its own with a roof and four walls
business	commerce	the act of purchasing, negotiating, trading, and selling
defective	faulty	when a device is not working or not working well

15

Vocabulary

In order to understand synonyms, one must have a good foundation of vocabulary. *Vocabulary* is the words a person uses on a daily basis. Having a good vocabulary is important. It's important in writing and also when you talk to people. Many of the questions on the test may have words that you don't know. Therefore, it's important to learn ways to find out a word's meaning.

It's hard to use vocabulary correctly. Imagine being thrust into a foreign country. If you didn't know right words to use to ask for the things you need, you could run into trouble! Asking for help from people who don't share the same vocabulary is hard. Language helps us understand each other. The more vocabulary words a person knows, the easier they can ask for things they need. This section of the study guide focuses on getting to know vocabulary through basic grammar.

Prefixes and Suffixes

In this section, we will look at the *meaning* of various prefixes and suffixes when added to a root word. A *prefix* is a combination of letters found at the beginning of a word. A *suffix* is a combination of letters found at the end. A *root word* is the word that comes after the prefix, before the suffix, or between them both. Sometimes a root word can stand on its own without either a prefix or a suffix. More simply:

Prefix + Root Word = Word
Root Word + Suffix = Word
Prefix + Root Word + Suffix = Word
Root Word = Word

Knowing the definitions of common prefixes and suffixes is helpful. It's helpful when you are trying to find out the meaning of a word you don't know. Also, knowing prefixes can help you find out the number of things, the negative of something, or the time and space of an object! Understanding suffixes can help when trying to find out the meaning of an adjective, noun, or verb.

The following charts look at some of the most common prefixes, what they mean, and how they're used to find out a word's meaning:

Number and Quantity Prefixes

Prefix	Definition	Example
bi-	two	bicycle, bilateral
mono-	one, single	monopoly, monotone
poly-	many	polygamy, polygon
semi-	half, partly	semiannual, semicircle
uni-	one	unicycle, universal

Here's an example of a number prefix:

The girl rode on a *bicycle* to school.

Look at the word *bicycle*. The root word (*cycle*) comes from the Greek and means *wheel*. The prefix *bi-* means *two*. The word *bicycle* means two wheels! When you look at any bicycles, they all have two wheels. If you had a unicycle, your bike would only have one wheel, because *uni-* means *one*.

16

Negative Prefixes

Prefix	Definition	Example
a-	without, lack of	amoral, atypical
in-	not, opposing	inability, inverted
non-	not	nonexistent, nonstop
un-	not, reverse	unable, unspoken

Here's an example of a negative prefix:

> The girl was *insensitive* to the boy who broke his leg.

Look at the word *insensitive.* In the chart above, the prefix *in-* means *not* or *opposing*. Replace the prefix with *not*. Now place *not* in front of the word *sensitive.* Now we see that the girl was "not sensitive" to the boy who broke his leg. In simpler terms, she showed that she did not care. These are easy ways to use prefixes and suffixes in order to find out what a word means.

Time and Space Prefixes

Prefix	Definition	Example
a-	in, on, of, up, to	aloof, associate
ab-	from, away, off	abstract, absent
ad-	to, towards	adept, adjacent
ante-	before, previous	antebellum, antenna
anti-	against, opposing	anticipate, antisocial
cata-	down, away, thoroughly	catacomb, catalogue
circum-	around	circumstance, circumvent
com-	with, together, very	combine, compel
contra-	against, opposing	contraband, contrast
de-	from	decrease, descend
dia-	through, across, apart	diagram, dialect
dis-	away, off, down, not	disregard, disrespect
epi-	upon	epidemic, epiphany
ex-	out	example, exit
hypo-	under, beneath	hypoallergenic, hypothermia
inter-	among, between	intermediate, international
intra-	within	intrapersonal, intravenous
ob-	against, opposing	obtain, obscure
per-	through	permanent, persist
peri-	around	periodontal, periphery
post-	after, following	postdate, postoperative
pre-	before, previous	precede, premeditate
pro-	forward, in place of	program, propel
retro-	back, backward	retroactive, retrofit
sub-	under, beneath	submarine, substantial
super-	above, extra	superior, supersede
trans-	Across, beyond, or over	transform, transmit
ultra-	beyond, excessively	ultraclean, ultralight

Here's an example of a space prefix:

> The teacher's motivational speech helped *propel* her students toward greater academic achievement.

Look at the word *propel*. The prefix *pro-* means *forward*. *Forward* means something related to time and space. *Propel* means to drive or move in a forward direction. Therefore, knowing the prefix *pro-* helps interpret that the students are moving forward *toward greater academic achievement*.

18

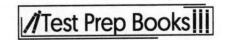

Miscellaneous Prefixes

Prefix	Definition	Example
belli-	war, warlike	bellied, belligerent
bene-	well, good	benediction, beneficial
equi-	equal	equidistant, equinox
for-	away, off, from	forbidden, forsaken
fore-	previous	forecast, forebode
homo-	same, equal	homogeneous, homonym
hyper-	excessive, over	hyperextend, hyperactive
in-	in, into	insignificant, invasive
magn-	large	magnetic, magnificent
mal-	bad, poorly, not	maladapted, malnourished
mis-	bad, poorly, not	misplace, misguide
mor-	death	mortal, morgue
neo-	new	neoclassical, neonatal
omni-	all, everywhere	omnipotent, omnipresent
ortho-	right, straight	orthodontist, orthopedic
over-	above	overload, overstock,
pan-	all, entire	panacea, pander
para-	beside, beyond	paradigm, parameter
phil-	love, like	philanthropy, philosophic
prim-	first, early	primal, primer
re-	backward, again	reload, regress
sym-	with, together	symmetry, symbolize
vis-	to see	visual, visibility

Here's another prefix example:

The computer was *primitive*; it still had a floppy disk drive!

The word *primitive* has the prefix *prim-*. The prefix *prim-* indicates being *first* or *early*. *Primitive* refers to the historical development of something. Therefore, the sentence is saying that the computer is an older model, because it still has a floppy disk drive.

The charts that follow review some of the most common suffixes. They also include examples of how the suffixes that are used to determine the meaning of a word. Remember, suffixes are added to the *end* of a root word:

Adjective Suffixes

Suffix	Definition	Example
-able (-ible)	capable of being	teachable, accessible
-esque	in the style of, like	humoresque, statuesque
-ful	filled with, marked by	helpful, deceitful
-ic	having, containing	manic, elastic
-ish	suggesting, like	malnourish, tarnish
-less	lacking, without	worthless, fearless
-ous	marked by, given to	generous, previous

Here's an example of an adjective suffix:

> The live model looked so *statuesque* in the window display; she didn't even move!

Look at the word *statuesque*. The suffix *-esque* means *in the style of* or *like*. If something is *statuesque*, it's *like a statue*. In this sentence, the model looks like a statue.

Noun Suffixes

Suffix	Definition	Example
-acy	state, condition	literacy, legacy
-ance	act, condition, fact	distance, importance
-ard	one that does	leotard, billiard
-ation	action, state, result	legislation, condemnation
-dom	state, rank, condition	freedom, kingdom
-er (-or)	office, action	commuter, spectator
-ess	feminine	caress, princess
-hood	state, condition	childhood, livelihood
-ion	action, result, state	communion, position
-ism	act, manner, doctrine	capitalism, patriotism
-ist	worker, follower	stylist, activist
-ity (-ty)	state, quality, condition	community, dirty
-ment	result, action	empowerment, segment
-ness	quality, state	fitness, rudeness
-ship	position	censorship, leadership
-sion (-tion)	state, result	tension, transition
-th	act, state, quality	twentieth, wealth
-tude	quality, state, result	attitude, latitude

Look at the following example of a noun suffix:

> The *spectator* cheered when his favorite soccer team scored a goal.

Look at the word *spectator*. The suffix *-or* means *action*. In this sentence, the *action* is to *spectate* (watch something). Therefore, a *spectator* is someone involved in watching something.

Verb Suffixes

Suffix	Definition	Example
-ate	having, showing	facilitate, integrate
-en	cause to be, become	frozen, written
-fy	make, cause to have	modify, rectify
-ize	cause to be, treat with	realize, sanitize

Here's an example of a verb suffix:

> The preschool had to *sanitize* the toys every Tuesday and Thursday.

In the word *sanitize*, the suffix *-ize* means *cause to be* or *treat with*. By adding the suffix *-ize* to the root word *sanitary*, the meaning of the word becomes active: *cause to be sanitary*.

Sentence Completion

Context Clues

It's common to find words that aren't familiar in writing. When you don't know a word, there are some "tricks" that can be used to find out its meaning. *Context clues* are words or phrases in a sentence or paragraph that provide hints about a word and what it means. For example, if an unknown word is attached to a noun with other surrounding words as clues, these can help you figure out the word's meaning. Consider the following example:

> After the treatment, Grandma's natural rosy cheeks looked *wan* and ghostlike.

The word we don't know is *wan*. The first clue to its meaning is in the phrase *After the treatment,* which tells us that something happened after a procedure (possibly medical). A second clue is the word *rosy*, which describes Grandma's natural cheek color that changed after the treatment. Finally, the word *ghostlike* infers that Grandma's cheeks now look white. By using the context clues in the sentence, we can figure out that the meaning of the word *wan* means *pale*.

Below are more ways to use context clues to find out the meaning of a word we don't know:

Contrasts

Look for context clues that *contrast* the unknown word. When reading a sentence with a word we don't know, look for an opposite word or idea. Here's an example:

> Since Mary didn't cite her research sources, she lost significant points for *plagiarizing* the content of her report.

In this sentence, *plagiarizing* is the word we don't know. Notice that when Mary *didn't cite her research sources,* it resulted in her losing points for *plagiarizing the content of her report*. These contrasting ideas tell us that Mary did something wrong with the content. This makes sense because the definition of *plagiarizing* is "taking the work of someone else and passing it off as your own."

21

Contrasts often use words like *but, however, although,* or phrases like *on the other hand.* For example:

The *gargantuan* television won't fit in my car, but it will cover the entire wall in the den.

The word we don't know is *gargantuan*. Notice that the television is too big to fit in a car, <u>but *it will cover the entire wall in the den*</u>. This tells us that the television is extremely large. The word *gargantuan* means *enormous*.

Synonyms

Another way to find out a word you don't know is to think of synonyms for that word. *Synonyms* are words with the same meaning. To do this, replace synonyms one at a time. Then read the sentence after each synonym to see if the meaning is clear. By replacing a word we don't know with a word we do know, it's easier to uncover its meaning. For example:

Gary's clothes were *saturated* after he fell into the swimming pool.

In this sentence, we don't know the word *saturated*. To brainstorm synonyms for *saturated*, think about what happens to Gary's clothes after falling into the swimming pool. They'd be *soaked* or *wet*. These both turn out to be good synonyms to try. The actual meaning of *saturated* is "thoroughly soaked."

Antonyms

Sometimes sentences contain words or phrases that oppose each other. Opposite words are known as *antonyms*. An example of an antonym is *hot* and *cold*. For example:

Although Mark seemed *tranquil*, you could tell he was actually nervous as he paced up and down the hall.

The word we don't know is *tranquil*. The sentence says that Mark was in fact not *tranquil*. He was *actually nervous*. The opposite of the word *nervous* is *calm*. *Calm* is the meaning of the word *tranquil*.

Explanations or Descriptions

Explanations or descriptions of other things in the sentence can also provide clues to an unfamiliar word. Take the following example:

Golden Retrievers, Great Danes, and Pugs are the top three *breeds* competing in the dog show.

We don't know the word *breeds*. Look at the sentence for a clue. The subjects (*Golden Retrievers, Great Danes,* and *Pugs*) describe different types of dogs. This description helps uncover the meaning of the word *breeds*. The word *breeds* means "a particular type of animal."

Inferences

Inferences are clues to an unknown word that tell us its meaning. These inferences can be found within the sentence where the word appears. Or, they can be found in a sentence before the word or after the word. Look at the following example:

The *wretched* old lady was kicked out of the restaurant. She was so mean and nasty to the waiter!

Here, we don't know the word *wretched*. The first sentence says that the *old lady was kicked out of the restaurant*, but it doesn't say why. The sentence after tells us why: *She was so mean and nasty to the waiter!* This infers that the old lady was *kicked out* because she was *so mean and nasty* or, in other words, *wretched*.

When you prepare for a vocabulary test, try reading harder materials to learn new words. If you don't know a word on the test, look for prefixes and suffixes to find out what the word means and get rid of wrong answers. If two answers both seem right, see if there are any differences between them. Then select the word that best fits. Context clues in the sentence or paragraph can also help you find the meaning of a word you don't know. By learning new words, a person can expand their knowledge. They can also improve the quality of their writing.

Practice Quiz

Synonyms

Directions: Each question has one word, followed by four other words. Please select one answer whose meaning is closest to the word in capital letters.

1. WEARY
    a. Tired
    b. Clothing
    c. Happy
    d. Whiny

2. VAST
    a. Rapid
    b. Expansive
    c. Small
    d. Ocean

Sentence Completion

Directions: Select the word or phrase that most correctly completes the sentence.

3. Driving across the United States, the two friends became _____ each time they arrived in a new state. They shared many good memories on that trip they would remember for the rest of their lives.
    a. closer
    b. distant
    c. suffering
    d. irritable

4. After Kira wrote her first book, she _____ her fans the sequel would be just as exciting as the first.
    a. denied
    b. promised
    c. invigorated
    d. germinated

5. Ever since the bus changed its route from Anna's house to the other side of town, _____
    a. Anna started receiving better grades.
    b. Anna became afraid of the rain.
    c. Anna began riding her bike to school.
    d. Anna proved to her friend she could beat her in Ping-Pong.

See answers on the next page.

Answer Explanations

1. A: Weary most closely means tired. Someone who is weary and tired may be whiny, but they do not necessarily mean the same thing.

2. B: Something that is vast is big and expansive. Choice *D*, ocean, may be described as vast. However, the word itself does not mean vast. The heavens or skies may also be described as vast. Someone's imagination or vocabulary can also be vast.

3. A: The two friends became closer. For this question, it's important to look at the context of the sentence. The second sentence says the friends shared good memories on the trip, which would not make the friends distant or irritable, Choices *B* and *D*. Choice *C* does not grammatically fit within the sentence: "became suffering" is incorrect usage. Therefore, Choice *A* is correct.

4. B: She promised her fans the sequel would be just as exciting as the first. Choice *A*, denied, is the opposite of the word *promised* and does not fit with the word *excited*. Choice *C*, invigorated, means energized, and might fit the tone of the sentence with the word *excited*. However, *promised* is the better word to use here. Choice *D*, germinated, means to grow.

5. C: Anna began riding her bike to school. This question determines whether or not you can understand the nature of cause and effect. Choices *A*, *B*, and *D* could possibly be in a chain of events of effects from the bus taking a different route. However, the most direct cause is Choice *C*.

Quantitative Reasoning and Math Achievement

Introduction

While the Quantitative Reasoning and Math Achievement sections are separate on the official ISEE Lower Level exam, they both draw from the same six "strands" of the NCTM (National Council of Teachers of Mathematics). These six strands are Numbers and Operations with Whole Numbers; Numbers and Operations with Decimals, Percents, and Fractions; Algebraic Concepts; Geometry; Measurement; and Data Analysis and Probability.

Numbers and Operations

Base-10 Numerals, Number Names, and Expanded Form

Numbers used in everyday life are constituted in a *base-10 system*. Each digit in a number, depending on its location, represents some multiple of 10, or quotient of 10 when dealing with decimals. Each digit to the left of the decimal point represents a higher multiple of 10. Each digit to the right of the decimal point represents a quotient of a higher multiple of 10 for the divisor. For example, consider the number 7,631.42. The digit one represents simply the number one. The digit 3 represents 3×10. The digit 6 represents:

$$6 \times 10 \times 10 \text{ (or } 6 \times 100)$$

The digit 7 represents:

$$7 \times 10 \times 10 \times 10 \text{ (or } 7 \times 1000)$$

The digit 4 represents $4 \div 10$. The digit 2 represents $(2 \div 10) \div 10$, or $2 \div (10 \times 10)$ or $2 \div 100$.

A number is written in *expanded form* by expressing it as the sum of the value of each of its digits. The expanded form in the example above, which is written with the highest value first down to the lowest value, is expressed as:

$$7,000 + 600 + 30 + 1 + 0.4 + 0.02$$

When verbally expressing a number, the integer part of the number (the numbers to the left of the decimal point) resembles the expanded form without the addition between values. In the above example, the numbers read "seven thousand six hundred thirty-one." When verbally expressing the decimal portion of a number, the number is read as a whole number, followed by the place value of the furthest digit (non-zero) to the right. In the above example, 0.42 is read "forty-two hundredths." Reading the number 7,631.42 in its entirety is expressed as "seven thousand six hundred thirty-one and forty-two hundredths." The word *and* is used between the integer and decimal parts of the number.

Composing and Decomposing Multi-Digit Numbers

Composing and decomposing numbers aids in conceptualizing what each digit of a multi-digit number represents. The standard, or typical, form in which numbers are written consists of a series of digits representing a given value based on their place value. Consider the number 592.7. This number is composed of 5 hundreds, 9 tens, 2 ones, and 7 tenths.

26

Composing a number requires adding the given numbers for each place value and writing the numbers in standard form. For example, composing 4 thousands, 5 hundreds, 2 tens, and 8 ones consists of adding as follows: $4,000 + 500 + 20 + 8$, to produce 4,528 (standard form).

Decomposing a number requires taking a number written in standard form and breaking it apart into the sum of each place value. For example, the number 83.17 is decomposed by breaking it into the sum of 4 values (for each of the 4 digits): 8 tens, 3 ones, 1 tenth, and 7 hundredths. The decomposed or "expanded" form of 83.17 is:

$$80 + 3 + 0.1 + 0.07$$

Place Value of a Given Digit

The number system that is used consists of only ten different digits or characters. However, this system is used to represent an infinite number of values. The *place value system* makes this infinite number of values possible. The position in which a digit is written corresponds to a given value. Starting from the decimal point (which is implied, if not physically present), each subsequent place value to the left represents a value greater than the one before it. Conversely, starting from the decimal point, each subsequent place value to the right represents a value less than the one before it.

The names for the place values to the left of the decimal point are as follows:

...	Billions	Hundred-Millions	Ten-Millions	Millions	Hundred-Thousands	Ten-Thousands	Thousands	Hundreds	Tens	Ones

*Note that this table can be extended infinitely further to the left.

The names for the place values to the right of the decimal point are as follows:

Decimal Point (.)	Tenths	Hundredths	Thousandths	Ten-Thousandths	...

*Note that this table can be extended infinitely further to the right.

When given a multi-digit number, the value of each digit depends on its place value. Consider the number 682,174.953. Referring to the chart above, it can be determined that the digit 8 is in the ten-thousands place. It is in the fifth place to the left of the decimal point. Its value is 8 ten-thousands or 80,000. The digit 5 is two places to the right of the decimal point. Therefore, the digit 5 is in the hundredths place. Its value is 5 hundredths or $\frac{5}{100}$ (equivalent to .05).

Base-10 System

Value of Digits

In accordance with the *base-10 system*, the value of a digit increases by a factor of ten each place it moves to the left. For example, consider the number 7. Moving the digit one place to the left (70), increases its value by a factor of:

$$10 \ (7 \times 10 = 70)$$

Moving the digit two places to the left (700) increases its value by a factor of 10 twice:

$$(7 \times 10 \times 10 = 700)$$

27

Moving the digit three places to the left (7,000) increases its value by a factor of 10 three times $(7 \times 10 \times 10 \times 10 = 7,000)$, and so on.

Conversely, the value of a digit decreases by a factor of ten each place it moves to the right. (Note that multiplying by $\frac{1}{10}$ is equivalent to dividing by 10). For example, consider the number 40. Moving the digit one place to the right (4) decreases its value by a factor of 10 $(40 \div 10 = 4)$. Moving the digit two places to the right (0.4), decreases its value by a factor of 10 twice:

$$40 \div 10 \div 10 = 0.4 \text{ or } 40 \times \frac{1}{10} \times \frac{1}{10} = 0.4$$

Moving the digit three places to the right (0.04) decreases its value by a factor of 10 three times $(40 \div 10 \div 10 \div 10 = 0.04)$ or $(40 \times \frac{1}{10} \times \frac{1}{10} \times \frac{1}{10} = 0.04)$, and so on.

Exponents to Denote Powers of 10

The value of a given digit of a number in the base-10 system can be expressed utilizing powers of 10. A power of 10 refers to 10 raised to a given exponent such as 10^0, 10^1, 10^2, 10^3, etc. For the number 10^3, 10 is the base and 3 is the exponent. A base raised by an exponent represents how many times the base is multiplied by itself. Therefore:

$$10^1 = 10$$

$$10^2 = 10 \times 10 = 100$$

$$10^3 = 10 \times 10 \times 10 = 1,000$$

$$10^4 = 10 \times 10 \times 10 \times 10 = 10,000$$

Any base with a zero exponent equals one.

Powers of 10 are utilized to decompose a multi-digit number without writing all the zeroes. Consider the number 872,349. This number is decomposed to:

$$800,000 + 70,000 + 2,000 + 300 + 40 + 9$$

When utilizing powers of 10, the number 872,349 is decomposed to:

$$(8 \times 10^5) + (7 \times 10^4) + (2 \times 10^3) + (3 \times 10^2) + (4 \times 10^1) + (9 \times 10^0)$$

The power of 10 by which the digit is multiplied corresponds to the number of zeroes following the digit when expressing its value in standard form. For example, 7×10^4 is equivalent to 70,000 or 7 followed by four zeros.

Rounding Multi-Digit Numbers

Rounding numbers changes the given number to a simpler and less accurate number than the exact given number. Rounding allows for easier calculations which estimate the results of using the exact

given number. The accuracy of the estimate and ease of use depends on the place value to which the number is rounded. Rounding numbers consists of:

- Determining what place value the number is being rounded to
- Examining the digit to the right of the desired place value to decide whether to round up or keep the digit
- Replacing all digits to the right of the desired place value with zeros

To round 746,311 to the nearest ten thousands, the digit in the ten thousands place should be located first. In this case, this digit is 4 (7<u>4</u>6,311). Then, the digit to its right is examined. If this digit is 5 or greater, the number will be rounded up by increasing the digit in the desired place by one. If the digit to the right of the place value being rounded is 4 or less, the number will be kept the same. For the given example, the digit being examined is a 6, which means that the number will be rounded up by increasing the digit to the left by one. Therefore, the digit 4 is changed to a 5. Finally, to write the rounded number, any digits to the left of the place value being rounded remain the same and any to its right are replaced with zeros.

For the given example, rounding 746,311 to the nearest ten thousand will produce 750,000. To round 746,311 to the nearest hundred, the digit to the right of the three in the hundreds place is examined to determine whether to round up or keep the same number. In this case, that digit is a one, so the number will be kept the same and any digits to its right will be replaced with zeros. The resulting rounded number is 746,300.

Rounding place values to the right of the decimal follows the same procedure, but digits being replaced by zeros can simply be dropped. To round 3.752891 to the nearest thousandth, the desired place value is located (3.75<u>2</u>891) and the digit to the right is examined. In this case, the digit 8 indicates that the number will be rounded up, and the 2 in the thousandths place will increase to a 3. Rounding up and replacing the digits to the right of the thousandths place produces 3.753000 which is equivalent to 3.753. Therefore, the zeros are not necessary, and the rounded number should be written as 3.753.

When rounding up, if the digit to be increased is a 9, the digit to its left is increased by 1 and the digit in the desired place value is changed to a zero. For example, the number 1,598 rounded to the nearest ten is 1,600. Another example shows the number 43.72961 rounded to the nearest thousandth is 43.730 or 43.73.

Solving Multistep Mathematical and Real-World Problems

Problem Situations for Operations

Addition and subtraction are *inverse operations*. Adding a number and then subtracting the same number will cancel each other out, resulting in the original number, and vice versa. For example, $8 + 7 - 7 = 8$ and $137 - 100 + 100 = 137$. Similarly, multiplication and division are inverse operations. Therefore, multiplying by a number and then dividing by the same number results in the original number, and vice versa. For example, $8 \times 2 \div 2 = 8$ and $12 \div 4 \times 4 = 12$. Inverse operations are used to work backwards to solve problems. In the case that 7 and a number add to 18, the inverse operation of subtraction is used to find the unknown value ($18 - 7 = 11$). If a school's entire 4th grade was divided evenly into 3 classes each with 22 students, the inverse operation of multiplication is used to determine the total students in the grade ($22 \times 3 = 66$). Additional scenarios involving inverse operations are included in the tables below.

There are a variety of real-world situations in which one or more of the operators is used to solve a problem. The tables below display the most common scenarios.

Addition & Subtraction

	Unknown Result	Unknown Change	Unknown Start
Adding to	5 students were in class. 4 more students arrived. How many students are in class? $5 + 4 =?$	8 students were in class. More students arrived late. There are now 18 students in class. How many students arrived late? $8+? = 18$ Solved by inverse operations $18- 8 =?$	Some students were in class early. 11 more students arrived. There are now 17 students in class. How many students were in class early? $? +11 = 17$ Solved by inverse operations $17- 11 =?$
Taking from	**15** students were in class. 5 students left class. How many students are in class now? $15- 5 =?$	12 students were in class. Some students left class. There are now 8 students in class. How many students left class? $12-? = 8$ Solved by inverse operations $8+? = 12 \rightarrow 12- 8 =?$	Some students were in class. 3 students left class. Then there were 13 students in class. How many students were in class before? $?- 3 = 13$ Solved by inverse operations $13 + 3 =?$

	Unknown Total	Unknown Addends (Both)	Unknown Addends (One)
Putting together/ taking apart	The homework assignment is 10 addition problems and 8 subtraction problems. How many problems are in the homework assignment? $10 + 8 =?$	Bobby has $9. How much can Bobby spend on candy and how much can Bobby spend on toys? $9 =? +?$	Bobby has 12 pairs of pants. 5 pairs of pants are shorts, and the rest are long. How many pairs of long pants does he have? $12 = 5+?$ Solved by inverse operations $12- 5 =?$

	Unknown Difference	Unknown Larger Value	Unknown Smaller Value
Comparing	Bobby has 5 toys. Tommy has 8 toys. How many more toys does Tommy have than Bobby? $5 + ? = 8$ Solved by inverse operations $8 - 5 = ?$ Bobby has $6. Tommy has $10. How many fewer dollars does Bobby have than Tommy? $10 - 6 = ?$	Tommy has 2 more toys than Bobby. Bobby has 4 toys. How many toys does Tommy have? $2 + 4 = ?$ Bobby has 3 fewer dollars than Tommy. Bobby has $8. How many dollars does Tommy have? $? - 3 = 8$ Solved by inverse operations $8 + 3 = ?$	Tommy has 6 more toys than Bobby. Tommy has 10 toys. How many toys does Bobby have? $? + 6 = 10$ Solved by inverse operations $10 - 6 = ?$ Bobby has $5 less than Tommy. Tommy has $9. How many dollars does Bobby have? $9 - 5 = ?$

Multiplication and Division

	Unknown Product	Unknown Group Size	Unknown Number of Groups
Equal groups	There are 5 students, and each student has 4 pieces of candy. How many pieces of candy are there in all? $5 \times 4 = ?$	14 pieces of candy are shared equally by 7 students. How many pieces of candy does each student have? $7 \times ? = 14$ Solved by inverse operations $14 \div 7 = ?$	If 18 pieces of candy are to be given out 3 to each student, how many students will get candy? $? \times 3 = 18$ Solved by inverse operations $18 \div 3 = ?$

	Unknown Product	Unknown Factor	Unknown Factor
Arrays	There are 5 rows of students with 3 students in each row. How many students are there? $5 \times 3 = ?$	If 16 students are arranged into 4 equal rows, how many students will be in each row? $4 \times ? = 16$ Solved by inverse operations $16 \div 4 = ?$	If 24 students are arranged into an array with 6 columns, how many rows are there? $? \times 6 = 24$ Solved by inverse operations $24 \div 6 = ?$

31

	Larger Unknown	Smaller Unknown	Multiplier Unknown
Comparing	A small popcorn costs $1.50. A large popcorn costs 3 times as much as a small popcorn. How much does a large popcorn cost? $1.50 \times 3 = ?$	A large soda costs $6 and that is 2 times as much as a small soda costs. How much does a small soda cost? $2 \times ? = 6$ Solved by inverse operations $6 \div 2 = ?$	A large pretzel costs $3 and a small pretzel costs $2. How many times as much does the large pretzel cost as the small pretzel? $? \times 2 = 3$ Solved by inverse operations $3 \div 2 = ?$

Remainders in Division Problems

If a given total cannot be divided evenly into a given number of groups, the amount left over is the *remainder*. Consider the following scenario: 32 textbooks must be packed into boxes for storage. Each box holds 6 textbooks. How many boxes are needed? To determine the answer, 32 is divided by 6, resulting in 5 with a remainder of 2. A remainder may be interpreted three ways:

- Add 1 to the quotient
  How many boxes will be needed? Six boxes will be needed because five will not be enough.

- Use only the quotient
  How many boxes will be full? Five boxes will be full.

- Use only the remainder
  If you only have 5 boxes, how many books will not fit? Two books will not fit.

Strategies and Algorithms to Perform Operations on Rational Numbers

A *rational number* is any number that can be written in the form of a ratio or fraction. Integers can be written as fractions with a denominator of 1 ($5 = \frac{5}{1}$; $-342 = \frac{-342}{1}$; etc.).

Decimals that terminate and/or repeat can also be written as fractions ($47 = \frac{47}{100}$; $.\overline{33} = \frac{1}{3}$).

When adding or subtracting fractions, the numbers must have the same denominators. In these cases, numerators are added or subtracted, and denominators are kept the same. For example,

$$\frac{2}{7} + \frac{3}{7} = \frac{5}{7} \text{ and } \frac{4}{5} - \frac{3}{5} = \frac{1}{5}$$

If the fractions to be added or subtracted do not have the same denominator, a common denominator must be found. This is accomplished by changing one or both fractions to a different but equivalent fraction. Consider the example $\frac{1}{6} + \frac{4}{9}$. First, a common denominator must be found. One method is to find the least common multiple (LCM) of the denominators 6 and 9. This is the lowest number that both 6 and 9 will divide into evenly. In this case the LCM is 18. Both fractions should be changed to equivalent fractions with a denominator of 18. To obtain the numerator of the new fraction, the old numerator is multiplied by the same number by which the old denominator is multiplied. For the fraction $\frac{1}{6}$, 6 multiplied by 3 will produce a denominator of 18. Therefore, the numerator is multiplied by 3 to

32

produce the new numerator $\left(\frac{1\times3}{6\times3} = \frac{3}{18}\right)$. For the fraction $\frac{4}{9}$, multiplying both the numerator and denominator by 2 produces $\frac{8}{18}$. Since the two new fractions have common denominators, they can be added:

$$\frac{3}{18} + \frac{8}{18} = \frac{11}{18}$$

When multiplying or dividing rational numbers, these numbers may be converted to fractions and multiplied or divided accordingly. When multiplying fractions, all numerators are multiplied by each other and all denominators are multiplied by each other. For example:

$$\frac{1}{3} \times \frac{6}{5} = \frac{1 \times 6}{3 \times 5} = \frac{6}{\mathbf{15}}$$

and

$$\frac{-1}{2} \times \frac{3}{1} \times \frac{11}{100} = \frac{-1\times3\times11}{2\times1\times100} = \frac{-33}{200}$$

When dividing fractions, the problem is converted by multiplying by the reciprocal of the divisor. This is done by changing division to multiplication and "flipping" the second fraction, or divisor. For example,

$$\frac{1}{2} \div \frac{3}{5} \rightarrow \frac{1}{2} \times \frac{5}{3} \text{ and } \frac{5}{1} \div \frac{1}{3} \rightarrow \frac{5}{1} \times \frac{3}{1}$$

To complete the problem, the rules for multiplying fractions should be followed.

Note that when adding, subtracting, multiplying, and dividing mixed numbers (ex. $4\frac{1}{2}$), it is easiest to convert these to improper fractions (larger numerator than denominator). To do so, the denominator is kept the same. To obtain the numerator, the whole number is multiplied by the denominator and added to the numerator. For example, $4\frac{1}{2} = \frac{9}{2}$ and $7\frac{2}{3} = \frac{23}{3}$. Also, note that answers involving fractions should be converted to the simplest form.

Rational Numbers and Their Operations

Composing and Decomposing Fractions

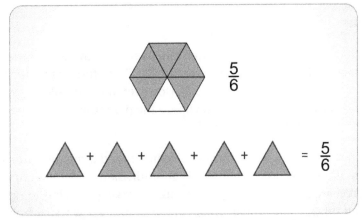

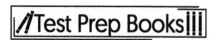

Fractions can be broken apart into sums of fractions with the same denominator. For example, the fraction $\frac{5}{6}$ can be *decomposed* into sums of fractions with all denominators equal to 6 and the numerators adding to 5. The fraction $\frac{5}{6}$ is decomposed as:

$$\frac{3}{6} + \frac{2}{6}; \text{ or } \frac{2}{6} + \frac{2}{6} + \frac{1}{6}; \text{ or } \frac{3}{6} + \frac{1}{6} + \frac{1}{6}; \text{ or } \frac{1}{6} + \frac{1}{6} + \frac{1}{6} + \frac{2}{6}; \text{ or } \frac{1}{6} + \frac{1}{6} + \frac{1}{6} + \frac{1}{6} + \frac{1}{6}$$

A unit fraction is a fraction in which the numerator is 1. If decomposing a fraction into unit fractions, the sum will consist of a unit fraction added the number of times equal to the numerator. For example:

$$\frac{3}{4} = \frac{1}{4} + \frac{1}{4} + \frac{1}{4} \text{ (unit fractions } \frac{1}{4} \text{ added 3 times)}$$

Composing fractions is simply the opposite of decomposing. It is the process of adding fractions with the same denominators to produce a single fraction. For example, $\frac{3}{7} + \frac{2}{7} = \frac{5}{7}$ and $\frac{1}{5} + \frac{1}{5} + \frac{1}{5} = \frac{3}{5}$.

Decrease in Value of a Unit Fraction

A *unit fraction* is one in which the numerator is 1 $(\frac{1}{2}, \frac{1}{3}, \frac{1}{8}, \frac{1}{20},$ etc.). The denominator indicates the number of *equal pieces* that the whole is divided into. The greater the number of pieces, the smaller each piece will be. Therefore, the greater the denominator of a unit fraction, the smaller it is in value. Unit fractions can also be compared by converting them to decimals. For example, $\frac{1}{2} = 0.5, \frac{1}{3} = 0.\overline{3}, \frac{1}{8} = 0.125, \frac{1}{20} = 0.05$, etc.

Use of the Same Whole when Comparing Fractions

Fractions all represent parts of the same whole. Fractions may have different denominators, but they represent parts of the same one whole, like a pizza. For example, the fractions $\frac{5}{7}$ and $\frac{2}{3}$ can be difficult to compare because they have different denominators. The first fraction may represent a whole divided into seven parts, where five parts are used. The second fraction represents the same whole divided into three parts, where two are used. It may be helpful to convert one or more of the fractions so that they have common denominators for converting to equivalent fractions by finding the LCM of the denominator. Comparing is much easier if fractions are converted to the equivalent fractions of $\frac{15}{21}$ and $\frac{14}{21}$. These fractions show a whole divided into 21 parts, where the numerators can be compared because the denominators are the same.

Order of Operations

When reviewing calculations consisting of more than one operation, the order in which the operations are performed affects the resulting answer. Consider $5 \times 2 + 7$. Performing multiplication then addition results in an answer of 17 ($5 \times 2 = 10$; $10 + 7 = 17$). However, if the problem is written $5 \times (2 + 7)$, the order of operations dictates that the operation inside the parentheses must be performed first. The resulting answer is 45 ($2 + 7 = 9$, then $5 \times 9 = 45$).

The *order* in which operations should be performed is remembered using the acronym PEMDAS. **PEMDAS** stands for parentheses, exponents, multiplication/division, and addition/subtraction. Multiplication and division are performed in the same step, working from left to right with whichever comes first. Addition and subtraction are performed in the same step, working from left to right with whichever comes first.

Consider the following example:

$$8 \div 4 + 8(7 - 7)$$

Performing the operation inside the parentheses produces $8 \div 4 + 8(0)$ or $8 \div 4 + 8 \times 0$. There are no exponents, so multiplication and division are performed next from left to right resulting in: $2 + 8 \times 0$, then $2 + 0$. Finally, addition and subtraction are performed to obtain an answer of 2. Now consider the following example: $6 \times 3 + 3^2 - 6$. Parentheses are not applicable. Exponents are evaluated first, $6 \times 3 + 9 - 6$. Then multiplication/division forms $18 + 9 - 6$. At last, addition/subtraction leads to the final answer of 21.

Properties of Operations

Properties of operations exist that make calculations easier and solve problems for missing values. The following table summarizes commonly used properties of real numbers.

Property	Addition	Multiplication
Commutative	$a + b = b + a$	$a \times b = b \times a$
Associative	$(a + b) + c = a + (b + c)$	$(a \times b) \times c = a \times (b \times c)$
Identity	$a + 0 = a; \ 0 + a = a$	$a \times 1 = a; \ 1 \times a = a$
Inverse	$a + (-a) = 0$	$a \times \dfrac{1}{a} = 1; \ a \neq 0$
Distributive	$a(b + c) = ab + ac$	

The commutative property of addition states that the order in which numbers are added does not change the sum. Similarly, the commutative property of multiplication states that the order in which numbers are multiplied does not change the product. The associative property of addition and multiplication state that the grouping of numbers being added or multiplied does not change the sum or product, respectively. The commutative and associative properties are useful for performing calculations. For example, $(47 + 25) + 3$ is equivalent to $(47 + 3) + 25$, which is easier to calculate.

The identity property of addition states that adding zero to any number does not change its value. The identity property of multiplication states that multiplying a number by one does not change its value. The inverse property of addition states that the sum of a number and its opposite equals zero. Opposites are numbers that are the same with different signs (ex. 5 and -5; $-\frac{1}{2}$ and $\frac{1}{2}$). The inverse property of multiplication states that the product of a number (other than zero) and its reciprocal equals one. Reciprocal numbers have numerators and denominators that are inverted (ex. $\frac{2}{5}$ and $\frac{5}{2}$). Inverse properties are useful for canceling quantities to find missing values (see algebra content). For example, $a + 7 = 12$ is solved by adding the inverse of 7 (which is -7) to both sides in order to isolate a.

The distributive property states that multiplying a sum (or difference) by a number produces the same result as multiplying each value in the sum (or difference) by the number and adding (or subtracting) the products. Consider the following scenario: You are buying three tickets for a baseball game. Each ticket costs $18. You are also charged a fee of $2 per ticket for purchasing the tickets online. The cost is calculated:

$$3 \times 18 + 3 \times 2$$

Using the distributive property, the cost can also be calculated $3(18 + 2)$.

Representing Rational Numbers and Their Operations

Concrete Models

Concrete objects are used to develop a tangible understanding of operations of rational numbers. Tools such as tiles, blocks, beads, and hundred charts are used to model problems. For example, a hundred chart (10×10) and beads can be used to model multiplication. If multiplying 5 by 4, beads are placed across 5 rows and down 4 columns producing a product of 20. Similarly, tiles can be used to model division by splitting the total into equal groups. If dividing 12 by 4, 12 tiles are placed one at a time into 4 groups. The result is 4 groups of 3. This is also an effective method for visualizing the concept of remainders.

Representations of objects can be used to expand on the concrete models of operations. Pictures, dots, and tallies can help model these concepts. Utilizing concrete models and representations creates a foundation upon which to build an abstract understanding of the operations.

Rational Numbers on a Number Line

A *number line* typically consists of integers (...3,2,1,0,-1,-2,-3...), and is used to visually represent the value of a rational number. Each rational number has a distinct position on the line determined by comparing its value with the displayed values on the line. For example, if plotting -1.5 on the number line below, it is necessary to recognize that the value of -1.5 is .5 less than -1 and .5 greater than -2. Therefore, -1.5 is plotted halfway between -1 and -2.

Number lines can also be useful for visualizing sums and differences of rational numbers. Adding a value indicates moving to the right (values increase to the right), and subtracting a value indicates moving to the left (numbers decrease to the left). For example, $5 - 7$ is displayed by starting at 5 and moving to the left 7 spaces, if the number line is in increments of 1. This will result in an answer of -2.

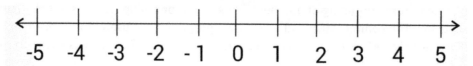

Multiplication and Division Problems

Multiplication and division are *inverse* operations that can be represented by using rectangular arrays, area models, and equations. Rectangular arrays include an arrangement of rows and columns that correspond to the factors and display product totals.

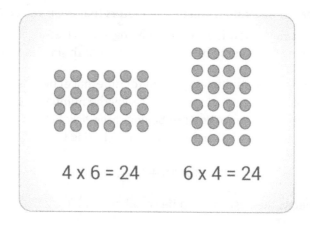

$4 \times 6 = 24$ $6 \times 4 = 24$

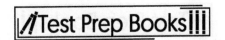

Another method of multiplication can be done with the use of an *area model*. An area model is a rectangle that is divided into rows and columns that match up to the number of place values within each number. Take the example 29×65. These two numbers can be split into simpler numbers:

$$29 = 25 + 4 \text{ and } 65 = 60 + 5$$

The products of those 4 numbers are found within the rectangle and then summed up to get the answer. The entire process is:

$$(60 \times 25) + (5 \times 25) + (60 \times 4) + (5 \times 4)$$

$$1,500 + 240 + 125 + 20 = 1,885$$

Here is the actual area model:

	25	**4**
60	60x25 1,500	60x4 240
5	5x25 125	5x4 20

```
    1 , 5 0 0
        2 4 0
        1 2 5
  +        2 0
    1 , 8 8 5
```

Multiplying decimals involves the same procedure as multiplying whole numbers, but including the decimal places in the end result. The problem involves multiplying the two numbers together, ignoring the decimal places, and then inserting the total number of decimal places in the original numbers into the result. For example, given the problem 87.5×0.45, the answer is found by multiplying 875×45 to obtain 39,375 and then inputting a decimal point three places to the left because there are three total decimal places in the original problem. Therefore, the answer is 39.375.

Dividing a number by a single digit or two digits can be turned into repeated subtraction problems. An area model can be used throughout the problem that represents multiples of the divisor. For example, the answer to $8580 \div 55$ can be found by subtracting 55 from 8580 one at a time and counting the total number of subtractions necessary.

However, a simpler process involves using larger multiples of 55. First, $100 \times 55 = 5,500$ is subtracted from 8,580, and 3,080 is leftover. Next, $50 \times 55 = 2,750$ is subtracted from 3,080 to obtain 380. $5 \times 55 = 275$ is subtracted from 330 to obtain 55, and finally, $1 \times 55 = 55$ is subtracted from 55 to obtain zero. Therefore, there is no remainder, and the answer is:

$$100 + 50 + 5 + 1 = \mathbf{156}$$

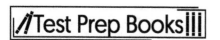

Here is a picture of the area model and the repeated subtraction process:

$$8580 \div 55$$

	55
100	5500
50	2750
5	275
1	55

```
    55 | 8580
         -5500   (100 x 55)
          3080
         -2750   (50 x 55)
           330
          -275    (5 x 55)
            55
           -55    (1 x 55)
             0
```

Checking the answer to a division problem involves multiplying the answer—the quotient—times the divisor to see if the dividend is obtained. If there is a remainder, the same process is computed, but the remainder is added on at the end to try to match the dividend. In the previous example, $156 \times 55 = 8580$ would be the checking procedure. Dividing decimals involves the same repeated subtraction process. The only difference would be that the subtractions would involve numbers that include values in the decimal places. Lining up decimal places is crucial in this type of problem.

Comparing, Classifying, and Ordering Rational Numbers

A **rational number** is any number that can be written as a fraction or ratio. Within the set of rational numbers, several subsets exist that are referenced throughout the mathematics topics. Counting numbers are the first numbers learned as a child. Counting numbers consist of 1,2,3,4, and so on. Whole numbers include all counting numbers and zero (0,1,2,3,4,...). Integers include counting numbers, their opposites, and zero (...,-3,-2,-1,0,1,2,3,...). Rational numbers are inclusive of integers, fractions, and decimals that terminate, or end (1.7, 0.04213) or repeat (0.136$\overline{5}$).

When comparing or ordering numbers, the numbers should be written in the same format (decimal or fraction), if possible. For example, $\sqrt{49}$, 7.3, and $\frac{15}{2}$ are easier to order if each one is converted to a decimal, such as 7, 7.3, and 7.5 (converting fractions and decimals is covered in the following section). A number line is used to order and compare the numbers. Any number that is to the right of another number is greater than that number. Conversely, a number positioned to the left of a given number is less than that number.

Converting Between Fractions, Decimals, and Percent

To convert a fraction to a decimal, the numerator is divided by the denominator. For example, $\frac{3}{8}$ can be converted to a decimal by dividing 3 by 8 ($\frac{3}{8} = 0.375$). To convert a decimal to a fraction, the decimal point is dropped, and the value is written as the numerator. The denominator is the place value farthest to the right with a digit other than zero. For example, to convert .48 to a fraction, the numerator is 48,

and the denominator is 100 (the digit 8 is in the hundredths place). Therefore, $.48 = \frac{48}{100}$. Fractions should be written in the simplest form, or reduced. To reduce a fraction, the numerator and denominator are divided by the largest common factor. In the previous example, 48 and 100 are both divisible by 4. Dividing the numerator and denominator by 4 results in a reduced fraction of $\frac{12}{25}$.

To convert a decimal to a percent, the number is multiplied by 100. To convert .13 to a percent, .13 is multiplied by 100 to get 13 percent. To convert a fraction to a percent, the fraction is converted to a decimal and then multiplied by 100. For example, $\frac{1}{5} = 0.20$ and 0.20 multiplied by 100 produces 20 percent.

To convert a percent to a decimal, the value is divided by 100. For example, 125% is equal to 1.25 ($\frac{125}{100}$). To convert a percent to a fraction, the percent sign is dropped, and the value is written as the numerator with a denominator of 100. For example, $80\% = \frac{80}{100}$. This fraction can be reduced ($\frac{80}{100} = \frac{4}{5}$).

Percent

The word *percent* means per hundred. Similar to a unit rate in which the second quantity is always one unit, a percent is a rate where the second quantity is always 100 units. If the results of a poll state that 47% of people support a given policy, this indicates that 47 out of every 100 individuals polled were in support. In other words, 47 per 100 support the policy. If an upgraded model of a car costs 110% of the cost of the base model, for every $100 that is spent for the base model, $110 must be spent to purchase the upgraded model. In other words, the upgraded model costs $110 per $100 for the cost of the base model.

When dealing with percentages, the numbers can be evaluated as a value in hundredths. For example, 15% is expressed as fifteen hundredths and is written as $\frac{15}{100}$ or 0.15.

Unit-Rate Problems

A rate is a ratio in which two terms are in different units. When rates are expressed as a quantity of one, they are considered *unit rates*. To determine a unit rate, the first quantity is divided by the second. Knowing a unit rate makes calculations easier than simply having a rate. For example, suppose a 3 pound bag of onions costs $1.77. To calculate the price of 5 pounds of onions, a proportion could show:

$$\frac{3}{1.77} = \frac{5}{x}$$

However, by knowing the unit rate, the value of pounds of onions is multiplied by the unit price. The unit price is calculated:

$$\$1.77/3 \text{ lb} = \$0.59/\text{lb}$$

Multiplying the weight of the onions by the unit price yields:

$$5 \text{ lb} \times \frac{\$0.59}{\text{lb}} = \$2.95$$

The *lb.* units cancel out.

Similar to unit-rate problems, *unit conversions* appear in real-world scenarios including cooking, measurement, construction, and currency. Given the conversion rate, unit conversions are written as a fraction (ratio) and multiplied by a quantity in one unit to convert it to the corresponding unit. To determine how many minutes are in $3\frac{1}{2}$ hours, the conversion rate of 60 minutes to 1 hour is written as $\frac{60\ min}{1h}$. Multiplying the quantity by the conversion rate results in:

$$3\frac{1}{2}\ \text{h} \times \frac{60\ \text{min}}{1\ \text{h}} = 210\ \text{min (The h unit is canceled.)}$$

To convert a quantity in minutes to hours, the fraction for the conversion rate is flipped to cancel the *min* unit. To convert 195 minutes to hours, $195\ \text{min}\ \times\ \frac{1\ \text{h}}{60\ \text{min}}$ is multiplied. The result is $\frac{195\ h}{60}$ which reduces to $3\frac{1}{4}$ h.

Converting units may require more than one multiplication. The key is to set up conversion rates so that units cancel each other out and the desired unit is left. To convert 3.25 yards to inches, given that 1 yd = 3 ft and 12 in = 1 ft, the calculation is performed by multiplying:

$$3.25\ \text{yd}\ \times \frac{3\ \text{ft}}{1\ \text{yd}} \times \frac{12\ \text{in}}{1\ \text{ft}}$$

The *yd* and *ft* units will cancel, resulting in 117 in.

Using Proportional Relationships

A proportion is a statement consisting of two equal ratios. Proportions will typically give three of four quantities and require solving for the missing value. The key to solving proportions is to set them up properly. Consider the following: 7 gallons of gas costs $14.70. How many gallons can you get for $20? The information is written as equal ratios with a variable representing the missing quantity:

$$\left(\frac{\text{gallons}}{\text{cost}} = \frac{\text{gallons}}{\text{cost}}\right) : \frac{7}{14.70} = \frac{x}{20}$$

To solve for x, the proportion is cross-multiplied. This means the numerator of the first ratio is multiplied by the denominator of the second, and vice versa. The resulting products are shown equal to each other. Cross-multiplying results in:

$$(7)(20) = (14.7)(x)$$

By solving the equation for x (see the algebra content), the answer is that 9.5 gallons of gas may be purchased for $20.

Percent problems can also be solved by setting up proportions. Examples of common percent problems are:

a. What is 15% of 25?
b. What percent of 45 is 3?
c. 5 is $\frac{1}{2}$% of what number?

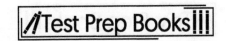

Setting up the proper proportion is made easier by following the format:

$$\frac{is}{of} = \frac{\%}{100}$$

A variable is used to represent the missing value. The proportions for each of the three examples are set up as follows:

a. $\frac{x}{25} = \frac{15}{100}$

b. $\frac{3}{45} = \frac{x}{100}$

c. $\frac{5}{x} = \frac{\frac{1}{2}}{100}$

By cross-multiplying and solving the resulting equation for the variable, the missing values are determined to be:

a. 3.75

b. $6.\overline{6}\%$

c. 1,000

Basic Concepts of Number Theory

Prime and Composite Numbers

Whole numbers are classified as either prime or composite. A *prime number* can only be divided evenly by itself and one. For example, the number 11 can only be divided evenly by 11 and one; therefore, 11 is a prime number. A helpful way to visualize a prime number is to use concrete objects and try to divide them into equal piles. If dividing 11 coins, the only way to divide them into equal piles is to create 1 pile of 11 coins or to create 11 piles of 1 coin each. Other examples of prime numbers include 2, 3, 5, 7, 13, 17, and 19.

A *composite number* is any whole number that is not a prime number. A composite number is a number that can be divided evenly by one or more numbers other than itself and one. For example, the number 6 can be divided evenly by 2 and 3. Therefore, 6 is a composite number. If dividing 6 coins into equal piles, the possibilities are 1 pile of 6 coins, 2 piles of 3 coins, 3 piles of 2 coins, or 6 piles of 1 coin. Other examples of composite numbers include 4, 8, 9, 10, 12, 14, 15, 16, 18, and 20.

To determine if a number is a prime or composite number, the number is divided by every whole number greater than one and less than its own value. If it divides evenly by any of these numbers, then the number is composite. If it does not divide evenly by any of these numbers, then the number is prime. For example, when attempting to divide the number 5 by 2, 3, and 4, none of these numbers divide evenly. Therefore, 5 must be a prime number.

Factors and Multiples of Numbers

The *factors* of a number are all integers that can be multiplied by another integer to produce the given number. For example, 2 is multiplied by 3 to produce 6. Therefore, 2 and 3 are both factors of 6. Similarly, $1 \times 6 = 6$ and $2 \times 3 = 6$, so 1, 2, 3, and 6 are all factors of 6. Another way to explain a factor

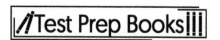
is to say that a given number divides evenly by each of its factors to produce an integer. For example, 6 does not divide evenly by 5. Therefore, 5 is not a factor of 6.

Multiples of a given number are found by taking that number and multiplying it by any other whole number. For example, 3 is a factor of 6, 9, and 12. Therefore, 6, 9, and 12 are multiples of 3. The multiples of any number are an infinite list. For example, the multiples of 5 are 5, 10, 15, 20, and so on. This list continues without end. A list of multiples is used in finding the least common multiple, or LCM, for fractions when a common denominator is needed. The denominators are written down and their multiples listed until a common number is found in both lists. This common number is the LCM.

Prime factorization breaks down each factor of a whole number until only prime numbers remain. All composite numbers can be factored into prime numbers. For example, the prime factors of 12 are 2, 2, and 3 ($2 \times 2 \times 3 = 12$). To produce the prime factors of a number, the number is factored, and any composite numbers are continuously factored until the result is the product of prime factors only. A factor tree, such as the one below, is helpful when exploring this concept.

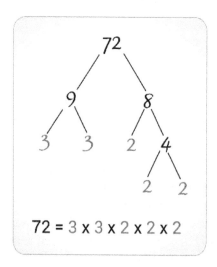

$$72 = 3 \times 3 \times 2 \times 2 \times 2$$

Determining the Reasonableness of Results

When solving math word problems, the solution obtained should make sense within the given scenario. The step of checking the solution will reduce the possibility of a calculation error or a solution that may be *mathematically* correct but not applicable in the real world. Consider the following scenarios:

A problem states that Lisa got 24 out of 32 questions correct on a test and asks to find the percentage of correct answers. To solve the problem, a student divided 32 by 24 to get 1.33, and then multiplied by 100 to get 133 percent. By examining the solution within the context of the problem, the student should recognize that getting all 32 questions correct will produce a perfect score of 100 percent. Therefore, a score of 133% with 8 incorrect answers does not make sense, and the calculations should be checked.

A problem states that the maximum weight on a bridge cannot exceed 22,000 pounds. The problem asks to find the maximum number of cars that can be on the bridge at one time if each car weighs 4,000 pounds. To solve this problem, a student divided 22,000 by 4,000 to get an answer of 5.5. By examining the solution within the context of the problem, the student should recognize that although the calculations are mathematically correct, the solution does not make sense. Half of a car on a bridge is

not possible, so the student should determine that a maximum of 5 cars can be on the bridge at the same time.

Mental Math Estimation

Once a result is determined to be logical within the context of a given problem, the result should be evaluated by its nearness to the expected answer. This is performed by approximating given values to perform mental math. Numbers should be rounded to the nearest value possible to check the initial results.

Consider the following example: A problem states that a customer is buying a new sound system for their home. The customer purchases a stereo for $435, 2 speakers for $67 each, and the necessary cables for $12. The customer chooses an option that allows him to spread the costs over equal payments for 4 months. How much will the monthly payments be?

After making calculations for the problem, a student determines that the monthly payment will be $145.25. To check the accuracy of the results, the student rounds each cost to the nearest ten ($440 + 70 + 70 + 10$) and determines that the total is approximately $590. Dividing by 4 months gives an approximate monthly payment of $147.50. Therefore, the student can conclude that the solution of $145.25 is very close to what should be expected.

When rounding, the place-value that is used in rounding can make a difference. Suppose the student had rounded to the nearest hundred for the estimation. The result ($400 + 100 + 100 + 0 = 600; \ 600 \div 4 = 150$) will show that the answer is reasonable but not as close to the actual value as rounding to the nearest ten.

Algebraic Concepts

Algebraic Expressions and Equations

An *algebraic expression* is a statement about an unknown quantity expressed in mathematical symbols. A variable is used to represent the unknown quantity, usually denoted by a letter. An equation is a statement in which two expressions (at least one containing a variable) are equal to each other. An algebraic expression can be thought of as a mathematical phrase and an equation can be thought of as a mathematical sentence.

Algebraic expressions and equations both contain numbers, variables, and mathematical operations. The following are examples of algebraic expressions: $5x + 3$, $7xy - 8(x^2 + y)$, and $\sqrt{a^2 + b^2}$. An expression can be simplified or evaluated for given values of variables. The following are examples of equations: $2x + 3 = 7$, $a^2 + b^2 = c^2$, and $2x + 5 = 3x - 2$. An equation contains two sides separated by an equal sign. *Equations* can be solved to determine the value(s) of the variable for which the statement is true.

Adding and Subtracting Linear Algebraic Expressions

An algebraic expression is simplified by combining like terms. A term is a number, variable, or product of a number and variables separated by addition and subtraction. For the algebraic expression $3x^2 - 4x + 5 - 5x^2 + x - 3$, the terms are $3x^2$, -4x, 5, $-5x^2$, x, and -3. Like terms have the same variables raised to the same powers (exponents). The like terms for the previous example are $3x^2$ and $-5x^2$, -4x and x, 5 and -3. To combine like terms, the coefficients (numerical factor of the term including sign) are added,

43

and the variables and their powers are kept the same. Note that if a coefficient is not written, it is an implied coefficient of 1 ($x = 1x$). The previous example will simplify to:

$$-2x^2 - 3x + 2$$

When adding or subtracting algebraic expressions, each expression is written in parentheses. The negative sign is distributed when necessary, and like terms are combined. Consider the following: add $2a + 5b - 2$ to $a - 2b + 8c - 4$. The sum is set as follows:

$$(a - 2b + 8c - 4) + (2a + 5b - 2)$$

In front of each set of parentheses is an implied positive one, which, when distributed, does not change any of the terms. Therefore, the parentheses are dropped and like terms are combined:

$$a - 2b + 8c - 4 + 2a + 5b - 2$$

$$3a + 3b + 8c - 6$$

Consider the following problem: Subtract $2a + 5b - 2$ from $a - 2b + 8c - 4$. The difference is set as follows:

$$(a - 2b + 8c - 4) - (2a + 5b - 2)$$

The implied one in front of the first set of parentheses will not change those four terms. However, distributing the implied -1 in front of the second set of parentheses will change the sign of each of those three terms:

$$a - 2b + 8c - 4 - 2a - 5b + 2$$

Combining like terms yields the simplified expression:

$$-a - 7b + 8c - 2$$

Distributive Property

The *distributive property* states that multiplying a sum (or difference) by a number produces the same result as multiplying each value in the sum (or difference) by the number and adding (or subtracting) the products. Using mathematical symbols, the distributive property states:

$$a(b + c) = ab + ac$$

The expression $4(3 + 2)$ is simplified using the order of operations. Simplifying inside the parentheses first produces 4×5, which equals 20. The expression $4(3 + 2)$ can also be simplified using the distributive property:

$$4(3 + 2) = 4 \times 3 + 4 \times 2 = 12 + 8 = 20$$

Consider the following example: $4(3x - 2)$. The expression cannot be simplified inside the parentheses because $3x$ and -2 are not like terms and therefore cannot be combined. However, the expression can be simplified by using the distributive property and multiplying each term inside of the parentheses by the term outside of the parentheses: $12x - 8$. The resulting equivalent expression contains no like terms, so it cannot be further simplified.

Consider the expression:

$$(3x + 2y + 1) - (5x - 3) + 2(3y + 4)$$

Again, there are no like terms, but the distributive property is used to simplify the expression. Note there is an implied one in front of the first set of parentheses and an implied -1 in front of the second set of parentheses. Distributing the 1, -1, and 2 produces:

$$1(3x) + 1(2y) + 1(1) - 1(5x) - 1(-3) + 2(3y) + 2(4)$$

$$3x + 2y + 1 - 5x + 3 + 6y + 8$$

This expression contains like terms that are combined to produce the simplified expression:

$$-2x + 8y + 12$$

Algebraic expressions are tested to be equivalent by choosing values for the variables and evaluating both expressions. For example, $4(3x - 2)$ and $12x - 8$ are tested by substituting 3 for the variable x and calculating to determine if equivalent values result.

Simple Expressions for Given Values

An algebraic expression is a statement written in mathematical symbols, typically including one or more unknown values represented by variables. For example, the expression $2x + 3$ states that an unknown number (x) is multiplied by 2 and added to 3. If given a value for the unknown number, or variable, the value of the expression is determined. For example, if the value of the variable x is 4, the value of the expression 4 is multiplied by 2, and 3 is added. This results in a value of 11 for the expression.

When given an algebraic expression and values for the variable(s), the expression is evaluated to determine its numerical value. To evaluate the expression, the given values for the variables are substituted (or replaced), and the expression is simplified using the order of operations. Parentheses should be used when substituting. Consider the following: Evaluate $a - 2b + ab$ for $a = 3$ and $b = -1$. To evaluate, any variable a is replaced with 3 and any variable b with -1, producing:

$$(3) - 2(-1) + (3)(-1)$$

Next, the order of operations is used to calculate the value of the expression, which is 2.

Parts of Expressions

Algebraic expressions consist of variables, numbers, and operations. A term of an expression is any combination of numbers and/or variables, and terms are separated by addition and subtraction. For example, the expression $5x^2 - 3xy + 4 - 2$ consists of 4 terms: $5x^2$, -3xy, 4y, and -2. Note that each term includes its given sign (+ or −). The variable part of a term is a letter that represents an unknown quantity. The coefficient of a term is the number by which the variable is multiplied. For the term $4y$, the variable is y, and the coefficient is 4. Terms are identified by the power (or exponent) of its variable.

A number without a variable is referred to as a constant. If the variable is to the first power (x^1 or simply x), it is referred to as a linear term. A term with a variable to the second power (x^2) is quadratic, and a term to the third power (x^3) is cubic. Consider the expression $x^3 + 3x - 1$. The constant is -1. The linear term is 3x. There is no quadratic term. The cubic term is x^3.

An algebraic expression can also be classified by how many terms exist in the expression. Any like terms should be combined before classifying. A monomial is an expression consisting of only one term. Examples of monomials are: 17, $2x$, and $-5ab^2$. A binomial is an expression consisting of two terms separated by addition or subtraction. Examples include $2x - 4$ and $-3y^2 + 2y$. A trinomial consists of 3 terms. For example, $5x^2 - 2x + 1$ is a trinomial.

Verbal Statements and Algebraic Expressions

An algebraic expression is a statement about unknown quantities expressed in mathematical symbols. The statement *five times a number added to forty* is expressed as $5x + 40$. An equation is a statement in which two expressions (with at least one containing a variable) are equal to one another. The statement *five times a number added to forty is equal to ten* is expressed as:

$$5x + 40 = 10$$

Real world scenarios can also be expressed mathematically. Suppose a job pays its employees $300 per week and $40 for each sale made. The weekly pay is represented by the expression $40x + 300$ where x is the number of sales made during the week.

Consider the following scenario: Bob had $20 and Tom had $4. After selling 4 ice cream cones to Bob, Tom has as much money as Bob. The cost of an ice cream cone is an unknown quantity and can be represented by a variable (x). The amount of money Bob has after his purchase is four times the cost of an ice cream cone subtracted from his original

$$\$20 \rightarrow 20 - 4x$$

The amount of money Tom has after his sale is four times the cost of an ice cream cone added to his original:

$$\$4 \rightarrow 4x + 4$$

After the sale, the amount of money that Bob and Tom have is equal:

$$20 - 4x = 4x + 4$$

When expressing a verbal or written statement mathematically, it is vital to understand words or phrases that can be represented with symbols. The following are examples:

Symbol	Phrase
+	Added to; increased by; sum of; more than
−	Decreased by; difference between; less than; take away
×	Multiplied by; 3(4,5...) times as large; product of
÷	Divided by; quotient of; half (third, etc.) of
=	Is; the same as; results in; as much as; equal to
x, t, n, etc.	A number; unknown quantity; value of; variable

Use of Formulas

Formulas are mathematical expressions that define the value of one quantity, given the value of one or more different quantities. Formulas look like equations because they contain variables, numbers,

operators, and an equal sign. All formulas are equations, but not all equations are formulas. A formula must have more than one variable. For example, $2x + 7 = y$ is an equation and a formula (it relates the unknown quantities x and y). However, $2x + 7 = 3$ is an equation but not a formula (it only expresses the value of the unknown quantity x).

Formulas are typically written with one variable alone (or isolated) on one side of the equal sign. This variable can be thought of as the *subject* in that the formula is stating the value of the *subject* in terms of the relationship between the other variables. Consider the distance formula: $distance = rate \times time$ or $d = rt$. The value of the subject variable d (distance) is the product of the variable r and t (rate and time). Given the rate and time, the distance traveled can easily be determined by substituting the values into the formula and evaluating.

The formula $P = 2l + 2w$ expresses how to calculate the perimeter of a rectangle (P) given its length (l) and width (w). To find the perimeter of a rectangle with a length of 3ft and a width of 2ft, these values are substituted into the formula for l and w:

$$P = 2(3 \text{ ft}) + 2(2 \text{ ft})$$

Following the order of operations, the perimeter is determined to be 10ft. When working with formulas such as these, including units is an important step.

Given a formula expressed in terms of one variable, the formula can be manipulated to express the relationship in terms of any other variable. In other words, the formula can be rearranged to change which variable is the *subject*. To solve for a variable of interest by manipulating a formula, the equation may be solved as if all other variables were numbers. The same steps for solving are followed, leaving operations in terms of the variables instead of calculating numerical values. For the formula $P = 2l + 2w$, the perimeter is the subject expressed in terms of the length and width. To write a formula to calculate the width of a rectangle, given its length and perimeter, the previous formula relating the three variables is solved for the variable w. If P and l were numerical values, this is a two-step linear equation solved by subtraction and division. To solve the equation $P = 2l + 2w$ for w, $2l$ is first subtracted from both sides:

$$P - 2l = 2w$$

Then both sides are divided by 2:

$$\frac{P - 2l}{2} = w$$

Dependent and Independent Variables

A variable represents an unknown quantity and, in the case of a formula, a specific relationship exists between the variables. Within a given scenario, variables are the quantities that are changing. If two variables exist, one is dependent and one is independent. The value of one variable depends on the other variable. If a scenario describes distance traveled and time traveled at a given speed, distance is *dependent* and time is *independent*. The distance traveled depends on the time spent traveling. If a scenario describes the cost of a cab ride and the distance traveled, the cost is dependent and the distance is independent. The cost of a cab ride depends on the distance travelled. Formulas often contain more than two variables and are typically written with the dependent variable alone on one side of the equation. This lone variable is the *subject* of the statement. If a formula contains three or more

variables, one variable is dependent and the rest are independent. The values of all independent variables are needed to determine the value of the dependent variable.

The formula $P = 2l + 2w$ expresses the dependent variable P in terms of the independent variables, l and w. The perimeter of a rectangle depends on its length and width. The formula $d = rt$ ($distance = rate \times time$) expresses the dependent variable d in terms of the independent variables, r and t. The distance traveled depends on the rate (or speed) and the time traveled.

Multistep One-Variable Linear Equations and Inequalities

Linear equations and linear inequalities are both comparisons of two algebraic expressions. However, unlike equations in which the expressions are equal, linear inequalities compare expressions that may be unequal. Linear equations typically have one value for the variable that makes the statement true. Linear inequalities generally have an infinite number of values that make the statement true.

When solving a *linear equation*, the desired result requires determining a numerical value for the unknown variable. If given a linear equation involving addition, subtraction, multiplication, or division, working backwards isolates the variable. Addition and subtraction are inverse operations, as are multiplication and division. Therefore, they can be used to cancel each other out.

The first steps to solving linear equations are distributing, if necessary, and combining any like terms on the same side of the equation. Sides of an equation are separated by an *equal* sign. Next, the equation is manipulated to show the variable on one side. Whatever is done to one side of the equation must be done to the other side of the equation to remain equal. Inverse operations are then used to isolate the variable and undo the order of operations backwards. Addition and subtraction are undone, then multiplication and division are undone.

For example, solve $4(t - 2) + 2t - 4 = 2(9 - 2t)$

Distributing: $4t - 8 + 2t - 4 = 18 - 4t$

Combining like terms: $6t - 12 = 18 - 4t$

Adding $4t$ to each side to move the variable: $10t - 12 = 18$

Adding 12 to each side to isolate the variable: $10t = 30$

Dividing each side by 10 to isolate the variable: $t = 3$

The answer can be checked by substituting the value for the variable into the original equation, ensuring that both sides calculate to be equal.

Linear inequalities express the relationship between unequal values. More specifically, they describe in what way the values are unequal. A value can be greater than (>), less than (<), greater than or equal to (≥), or less than or equal to (≤) another value. $5x + 40 > 65$ is read as *five times a number added to forty is greater than sixty-five.*

When solving a linear inequality, the solution is the set of all numbers that make the statement true. The inequality $x + 2 \geq 6$ has a solution set of 4 and every number greater than 4 (4.01; 5; 12; 107; etc.). Adding 2 to 4 or any number greater than 4 results in a value that is greater than or equal to 6. Therefore, $x \geq 4$ is the solution set.

To algebraically solve a linear inequality, follow the same steps as those for solving a linear equation. The inequality symbol stays the same for all operations *except* when multiplying or dividing by a negative number. If multiplying or dividing by a negative number while solving an inequality, the relationship reverses (the sign flips). In other words, > switches to < and vice versa. Multiplying or dividing by a positive number does not change the relationship, so the sign stays the same. An example is shown below.

Solve $-2x - 8 \leq 22$ for the value of x.

Add 8 to both sides to isolate the variable:

$$-2x \leq 30$$

Divide both sides by -2 to solve for x:

$$x \geq -15$$

Solutions of a linear equation or a linear inequality are the values of the variable that make a statement true. In the case of a linear equation, the solution set (list of all possible solutions) typically consists of a single numerical value. To find the solution, the equation is solved by isolating the variable. For example, solving the equation $3x - 7 = -13$ produces the solution $x = -2$. The only value for x which produces a true statement is -2. This can be checked by substituting -2 into the original equation to check that both sides are equal. In this case, $3(-2) - 7 = -13 \rightarrow -13 = -13$; therefore, -2 is a solution.

Although linear equations generally have one solution, this is not always the case. If there is no value for the variable that makes the statement true, there is no solution to the equation. Consider the equation:

$$x + 3 = x - 1$$

There is no value for x in which adding 3 to the value produces the same result as subtracting one from the value. Conversely, if any value for the variable makes a true statement, the equation has an infinite number of solutions. Consider the equation:

$$3x + 6 = 3(x + 2)$$

Any number substituted for x will result in a true statement (both sides of the equation are equal).

By manipulating equations like the two above, the variable of the equation will cancel out completely. If the remaining constants express a true statement (ex. $6 = 6$), then all real numbers are solutions to the equation. If the constants left express a false statement (ex. $3 = -1$), then no solution exists for the equation.

Solving a linear inequality requires all values that make the statement true to be determined. For example, solving $3x - 7 \geq -13$ produces the solution $x \geq -2$. This means that -2 and any number greater than -2 produces a true statement. Solution sets for linear inequalities will often be displayed using a number line. If a value is included in the set ($\geq$ or $\leq$), a shaded dot is placed on that value and an arrow extending in the direction of the solutions. For a variable > or $\geq$ a number, the arrow will point right on a number line, the direction where the numbers increase. If a variable is < or $\leq$ a number, the arrow will point left on a number line, which is the direction where the numbers decrease. If the value is not included in the set (> or <), an open (unshaded) circle on that value is used with an arrow in the appropriate direction.

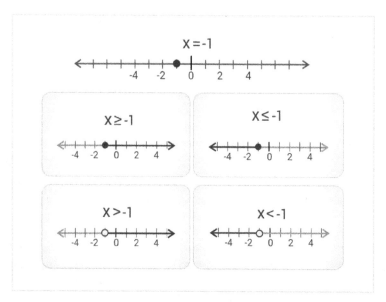

Similar to linear equations, a linear inequality may have a solution set consisting of all real numbers, or can contain no solution. When solved algebraically, a linear inequality in which the variable cancels out and results in a true statement (ex. $7 \geq 2$) has a solution set of all real numbers. A linear inequality in which the variable cancels out and results in a false statement (ex. $7 \leq 2$) has no solution.

Linear Relationships

Linear relationships describe the way two quantities change with respect to each other. The relationship is defined as linear because a line is produced if all the sets of corresponding values are graphed on a coordinate grid. When expressing the linear relationship as an equation, the equation is often written in the form $y = mx + b$ (slope-intercept form) where m and b are numerical values and x and y are variables (for example, $y = 5x + 10$). Given a linear equation and the value of either variable (x or y), the value of the other variable can be determined.

Suppose a teacher is grading a test containing 20 questions with 5 points given for each correct answer, adding a curve of 10 points to each test. This linear relationship can be expressed as the equation $y = 5x + 10$ where x represents the number of correct answers, and y represents the test score. To determine the score of a test with a given number of correct answers, the number of correct answers is substituted into the equation for x and evaluated. For example, for 10 correct answers, 10 is substituted for x:

$$y = 5(10) + 10 \rightarrow y = 60$$

50

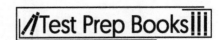

Therefore, 10 correct answers will result in a score of 60. The number of correct answers needed to obtain a certain score can also be determined. To determine the number of correct answers needed to score a 90, 90 is substituted for y in the equation (y represents the test score) and solved:

$$90 = 5x + 10$$

$$80 = 5x$$

$$16 = x$$

Therefore, 16 correct answers are needed to score a 90.

Linear relationships may be represented by a table of 2 corresponding values. Certain tables may determine the relationship between the values and predict other corresponding sets. Consider the table below, which displays the money in a checking account that charges a monthly fee:

Month	0	1	2	3	4
Balance	$210	$195	$180	$165	$150

An examination of the values reveals that the account loses $15 every month (the month increases by one and the balance decreases by 15). This information can be used to predict future values. To determine what the value will be in month 6, the pattern can be continued, and it can be concluded that the balance will be $120. To determine which month the balance will be $0, $210 is divided by $15 (since the balance decreases $15 every month), resulting in month 14.

Similar to a table, a graph can display corresponding values of a linear relationship.

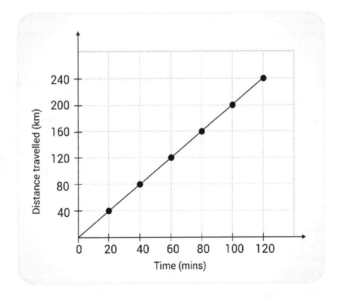

The graph above represents the relationship between distance traveled and time. To find the distance traveled in 80 minutes, the mark for 80 minutes is located at the bottom of the graph. By following this mark directly up on the graph, the corresponding point for 80 minutes is directly across from the 160 kilometer mark. This information indicates that the distance travelled in 80 minutes is 160 kilometers. To predict information not displayed on the graph, the way in which the variables change with respect

to one another is determined. In this case, distance increases by 40 kilometers as time increases by 20 minutes. This information can be used to continue the data in the graph or convert the values to a table.

Number and Shape Patterns

Patterns within a sequence can come in 2 distinct forms: the items (shapes, numbers, etc.) either repeat in a constant order, or the items change from one step to another in some consistent way. The core is the smallest unit, or number of items, that repeats in a repeating pattern. For example, the pattern ○○▲○○▲○... has a core that is ○○▲. Knowing only the core, the pattern can be extended. Knowing the number of steps in the core allows the identification of an item in each step without drawing/writing the entire pattern out. For example, suppose the tenth item in the previous pattern must be determined. Because the core consists of three items (○○▲), the core repeats in multiples of 3. In other words, steps 3, 6, 9, 12, etc. will be ▲ completing the core with the core starting over on the next step. For the above example, the 9th step will be ▲ and the 10th will be ○.

The most common patterns in which each item changes from one step to the next are arithmetic and geometric sequences. An arithmetic sequence is one in which the items increase or decrease by a constant difference. In other words, the same thing is added or subtracted to each item or step to produce the next. To determine if a sequence is arithmetic, determine what must be added or subtracted to step one to produce step two. Then, check if the same thing is added/subtracted to step two to produce step three. The same thing must be added/subtracted to step three to produce step four, and so on.

Consider the pattern 13, 10, 7, 4 ... To get from step one (13) to step two (10) by adding or subtracting requires subtracting by 3. The next step is checking if subtracting 3 from step two (10) will produce step three (7), and subtracting 3 from step three (7) will produce step four (4). In this case, the pattern holds true. Therefore, this is an arithmetic sequence in which each step is produced by subtracting 3 from the previous step. To extend the sequence, 3 is subtracted from the last step to produce the next. The next three numbers in the sequence are 1, -2, -5.

A geometric sequence is one in which each step is produced by multiplying or dividing the previous step by the same number. To determine if a sequence is geometric, decide what step one must be multiplied or divided by to produce step two. Then check if multiplying or dividing step two by the same number produces step three, and so on. Consider the pattern 2, 8, 32, 128 ... To get from step one (2) to step two (8) requires multiplication by 4. The next step determines if multiplying step two (8) by 4 produces step three (32), and multiplying step three (32) by 4 produces step four (128). In this case, the pattern holds true. Therefore, this is a geometric sequence in which each step is produced by multiplying the previous step by 4. To extend the sequence, the last step is multiplied by 4 and repeated. The next three numbers in the sequence are 512; 2,048; 8,192.

Although arithmetic and geometric sequences typically use numbers, these sequences can also be represented by shapes. For example, an arithmetic sequence could consist of shapes with three sides, four sides, and five sides (add one side to the previous step to produce the next). A geometric sequence could consist of eight blocks, four blocks, and two blocks (each step is produced by dividing the number of blocks in the previous step by 2).

52

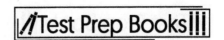

Geometry

Geometry is part of mathematics. It deals with shapes and their properties. Geometry means knowing the names and properties of shapes. It is also similar to measurement and number operations. The basis of geometry involves being able to label and describe shapes and their properties. That knowledge will lead to working with formulas such as area, perimeter, and volume. This knowledge will help to solve word problems involving shapes.

Flat or two-dimensional shapes include circles, triangles, hexagons, and rectangles, among others. Three-dimensional solid shapes, such as spheres and cubes, are also used in geometry. A shape can be classified based on whether it is open like the letter U or closed like the letter O. Further classifications involve counting the number of sides and vertices (corners) on the shapes. This will help you tell the difference between shapes.

Polygons can be drawn by sketching a fixed number of line segments that meet to create a closed shape. In addition, *triangles* can be drawn by sketching a closed space using only three line segments. *Quadrilaterals* are closed shapes with four line segments. Note that a triangle has three vertices, and a quadrilateral has four vertices.

To draw circles, one curved line segment must be drawn that has only one endpoint. This creates a closed shape. Given such direction, every point on the line would be the same distance away from its center. The radius of a circle goes from an endpoint on the center of the circle to an endpoint on the circle. The diameter is the line segment created by placing an endpoint on the circle, drawing through the radius, and placing the other endpoint on the circle. A **compass** can be used to draw circles of a more precise size and shape.

Area and Perimeter

Area relates to two-dimensional geometric shapes. Basically, a figure is divided into two-dimensional units. The number of units needed to cover the figure is counted. Area is measured using square units, such as square inches, feet, centimeters, or kilometers.

Perimeter is the length of all its sides. The perimeter of a given closed sided figure would be found by first measuring the length of each side and then calculating the sum of all sides.

Formulas can be used to calculate area and perimeter. The area of a rectangle is found by multiplying its length, *l*, times its width, *w*. Therefore, the formula for area is $A = l \times w$. An equivalent expression is found by using the term base, *b*, instead of length, to represent the horizontal side of the shape. In this case, the formula is $A = b \times h$. This same formula can be used for all parallelograms. Here is a visualization of a rectangle with its labeled sides:

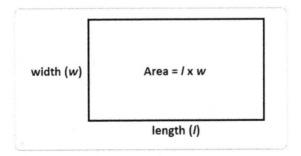

53

A square has four equal sides with the length s. Its length is equal to its width. The formula for the area of a square is $A = s \times s$. Finally, the area of a triangle is calculated by dividing the area of the rectangle that would be formed by the base, the altitude, and height of the triangle. Therefore, the area of a triangle is:

$$A = \frac{1}{2} \times b \times h$$

Formulas for perimeter are derived by adding length measurements of the sides of a figure. The perimeter of a rectangle is the result of adding the length of the four sides. Therefore, the formula for perimeter of a rectangle is $P = 2 \times l + 2 \times w$, and the formula for perimeter of a square is $P = 4 \times s$. The perimeter of a triangle would be the sum of the lengths of the three sides.

Volume

Volume is a measurement of the amount of space that in a 3-dimensional figure. Volume is measured using cubic units, such as cubic inches, feet, centimeters, or kilometers.

Say you have 10 playing die that are each one cubic centimeter. Say you placed these along the length of a rectangle. Then 8 die are placed along its width. The remaining area is filled in with die. There would be 80 die in total. This would equal a volume of 80 cubic centimeters. Say the shape is doubled so that its height consists of two cube lengths. There would be 160 cubes. Also, its volume would be 160 cubic centimeters. Adding another level of cubes would mean that there would be $3 \times 80 = 240$ cubes. This idea shows that volume is calculated by multiplying area times height. The actual formula for volume of a three-dimensional rectangular solid is $V = l \times w \times h$. In this formula *l* represents length, *w* represents width, and *h* represents height. Volume can also be thought of as area of the base times the height. The base in this case would be the entire rectangle formed by *l* and *w*. Here is an example of a rectangular solid with labeled sides:

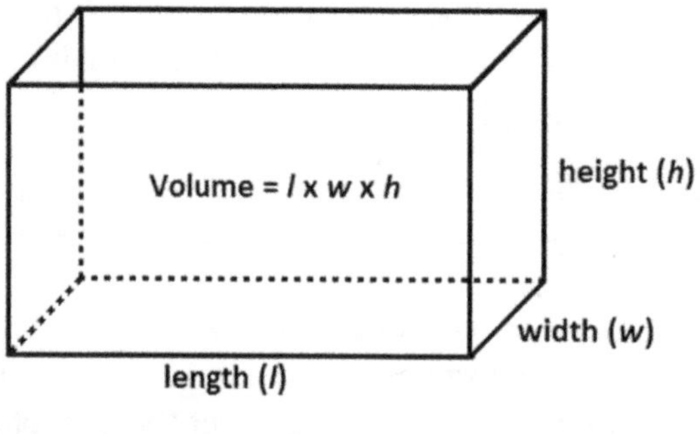

A *cube* is a special type of rectangular solid in which its length, width, and height are the same. If this length is *s*, then the formula for the volume of a cube is:

$$V = s \times s \times s$$

Lines and Angles

In geometry, a *line* connects two points, has no thickness, and extends indefinitely in both directions beyond the points. If it does end at two points, it is known as a *line segment*. It is important to distinguish between a line and a line segment.

An *angle* can be visualized as a corner. It is defined as the formation of two rays connecting at a vertex that extend indefinitely. Angles are measured in degrees. Their measurement is a measure of rotation. A

full rotation equals 360 degrees and represents a circle. Half of a rotation equals 180 degrees and represents a half-circle. Subsequently, 90 degrees represents a quarter-circle. Similar to the hands on a clock, an angle begins at the center point, and two lines extend indefinitely from that point in two different directions.

A clock can be useful when learning how to measure angles. At 3:00, the big hand is on the 12 and the small hand is on the 3. The angle formed is 90 degrees and is known as a *right angle*. Any angle less than 90 degrees, such as the one formed at 2:00, is known as an *acute angle*. Any angle greater than 90 degrees is known as an *obtuse angle*. The entire clock represents 360 degrees, and each clockwise increment on the clock represents an addition of 30 degrees. Therefore, 6:00 represents 180 degrees, 7:00 represents 210 degrees, etc. Angle measurement is additive. An angle can be broken into two non-overlapping angles. The total measure of the larger angle is equal to the sum of the measurements of the two smaller angles.

A *ray* is a straight path that has an endpoint on one end and extends indefinitely in the other direction. Lines are known as being *coplanar* if they are located in the same plane. Coplanar lines exist within the same two-dimensional surface. Two lines are *parallel* if they are coplanar, extend in the same direction, and never cross. They are known as being *equidistant* because they are always the same distance from each other. If lines do cross, they are known as *intersecting lines*. As discussed previously, angles are utilized throughout geometry, and their measurement can be seen through the use of an analog clock. An angle is formed when two rays begin at the same endpoint. *Adjacent angles* can be formed by forming two angles out of one shared ray. They are two side-by-side angles that also share an endpoint.

Perpendicular lines are coplanar lines that form a right angle at their point of intersection. A triangle that contains a right angle is known as a *right triangle*. The sum of the angles within any triangle is always 180 degrees. Therefore, in a right triangle, the sum of the two angles that are not right angles is 90 degrees. Any two angles that sum up to 90 degrees are known as *complementary angles*. A triangle that contains an obtuse angle is known as an *obtuse triangle*. A triangle that contains three acute angles is known as an *acute triangle*. Here is an example of a 180-degree angle, split up into an acute and obtuse angle:

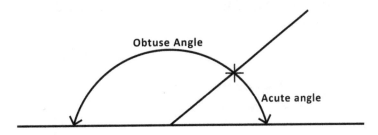

The vocabulary regarding many two-dimensional shapes is important to understand and use appropriately. Many four-sided figures can be identified using properties of angles and lines. A *quadrilateral* is a closed shape with four sides. A *parallelogram* is a specific type of quadrilateral that has two sets of parallel lines having the same length. A *trapezoid* is a quadrilateral having only one set of parallel sides. A *rectangle* is a parallelogram that has four right angles. A *rhombus* is a parallelogram with four equal sides and sometimes two acute angles and two obtuse angles. The acute angles are of equal measure, and the obtuse angles are of equal measure. Finally, a *square* is a rhombus consisting of four right angles. It is important to note that some of these shapes share common attributes. For instance, all four-sided shapes are quadrilaterals. All squares are rectangles, but not all rectangles are squares.

Symmetry is another concept in geometry. If a two-dimensional shape can be folded along a straight line and the halves line up exactly, the figure is *symmetric*. The line is known as a *line of symmetry*. Circles, squares, and rectangles are examples of symmetric shapes.

Measurement

Measuring Lengths of Objects

The length of an object can be measured using standard tools such as rulers, yard sticks, meter sticks, and measuring tapes. The following image depicts a yardstick:

Choosing the right tool to perform the measurement requires determining whether United States customary units or metric units are desired, and having a grasp of the approximate length of each unit and the approximate length of each tool. The measurement can still be performed by trial and error without the knowledge of the approximate size of the tool.

For example, to determine the length of a room in feet, a United States customary unit, various tools can be used for this task. These include a ruler (typically 12 inches/1 foot long), a yardstick (3 feet/1 yard long), or a tape measure displaying feet (typically either 25 feet or 50 feet). Because the length of a room is much larger than the length of a ruler or a yardstick, a tape measure should be used to perform the measurement.

When the correct measuring tool is selected, the measurement is performed by first placing the tool directly above or below the object (if making a horizontal measurement) or directly next to the object (if making a vertical measurement). The next step is aligning the tool so that one end of the object is at the mark for zero units, then recording the unit of the mark at the other end of the object. To give the length of a paperclip in metric units, a ruler displaying centimeters is aligned with one end of the paper clip to the mark for zero centimeters.

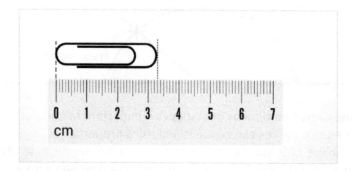

Directly down from the other end of the paperclip is the mark that measures its length. In this case, that mark is two small dashes past the 3 centimeter mark. Each small dash is 1 millimeter (or .1 centimeters). Therefore, the length of the paper clip is 3.2 centimeters.

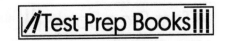

To compare the lengths of objects, each length must be expressed in the same unit. If possible, the objects should be measured with the same tool or with tools utilizing the same units. For example, a ruler and a yardstick can both measure length in inches. If the lengths of the objects are expressed in different units, these different units must be converted to the same unit before comparing them. If two lengths are expressed in the same unit, the lengths may be compared by subtracting the smaller value from the larger value. For example, suppose the lengths of two gardens are to be compared. Garden A has a length of 4 feet, and garden B has a length of 2 yards. 2 yards is converted to 6 feet so that the measurements have similar units. Then, the smaller length (4 feet) is subtracted from the larger length (6ft): 6ft – 4ft = 2ft. Therefore, garden B is 2 feet larger than garden A.

Relative Sizes of United States Customary Units and Metric Units

The United States customary system and the metric system each consist of distinct units to measure lengths and volume of liquids. The US customary units for length, from smallest to largest, are inch (in), foot (ft), yard (yd), and mile (mi). The metric units for length, from smallest to largest, are: millimeter (mm), centimeter (cm), decimeter (dm), meter (m), and kilometer (km). The relative size of each unit of length is shown below.

US Customary	Metric	Conversion
12 in = 1 ft	10 mm = 1 cm	1 in = 2.54 cm
36 in = 3 ft = 1 yd	10 cm = 1 dm (decimeter)	1 m ≈ 3.28 ft ≈ 1.09 yd
5,280 ft = 1,760 yd = 1mi	100 cm = 10 dm = 1 m	1 mi ≈ 1.6 km
	1000 m = 1 km	

The US customary units for volume of liquids, from smallest to largest, are fluid ounces (fl oz), cup (c), pint (pt), quart (qt), and gallon (gal). The metric units for volume of liquids, from smallest to largest, are: milliliter (mL), centiliter (cL), deciliter (dL), liter (L), and kiloliter (kL). The relative size of each unit of liquid volume is shown below.

US Customary	Metric	Conversion
8 fl oz = 1 c	10 mL = 1 cL	1 pt ≈ 0.473 L
2 c = 1 pt	10 cL = 1 dL	1 L ≈ 1.057 qt
4 c = 2 pt = 1 qt	1,000 mL = 100 cL = 10 dL = 1 L	1 gal ≈ 3.785 L
4 qt = 1 gal	1,000 L = 1 kL	

The US customary system measures weight (how strongly Earth is pulling on an object) in the following units, from least to greatest: ounce (oz), pound (lb), and ton. The metric system measures mass (the quantity of matter within an object) in the following units, from least to greatest: milligram (mg), centigram (cg), gram (g), kilogram (kg), and metric ton (MT). The relative sizes of each unit of weight and mass are shown below.

US Measures of Weight	Metric Measures of Mass
16 oz = 1 lb	10 mg = 1 cg
2,000 lb = 1 ton	100 cg = 1 g
	1,000 g = 1 kg
	1,000 kg = 1 MT

Note that weight and mass DO NOT measure the same thing.

Time is measured in the following units, from shortest to longest: second (sec), minute (min), hour (h), day (d), week (wk), month (mo), year (yr), decade, century, millennium. The relative sizes of each unit of time is shown below.

- 60 sec = 1 min
- 60 min = 1 h
- 24 hr = 1 d
- 7 d = 1 wk
- 52 wk = 1 yr
- 12 mo = 1 yr
- 10 yrs = 1 decade
- 100 yrs = 1 century
- 1,000 yrs = 1 millennium

Conversion of Units

When working with different systems of measurement, conversion from one unit to another may be necessary. The conversion rate must be known to convert units. One method for converting units is to write and solve a proportion. The arrangement of values in a proportion is extremely important. Suppose that a problem requires converting 20 fluid ounces to cups. To do so, a proportion can be written using the conversion rate of 8 fl oz = 1 c with x representing the missing value. The proportion can be written in any of the following ways:

$$\frac{1}{8} = \frac{x}{20} \left(\frac{\text{c for conversion}}{\text{fl oz for conversion}} = \frac{\text{unknown c}}{\text{fl oz given}} \right)$$

$$\frac{8}{1} = \frac{20}{x} \left(\frac{\text{fl oz for conversion}}{\text{c for conversion}} = \frac{\text{fl oz given}}{\text{unknown c}} \right)$$

$$\frac{1}{x} = \frac{8}{20} \left(\frac{\text{c for conversion}}{\text{unknown c}} = \frac{\text{fl oz for conversion}}{\text{fl oz given}} \right)$$

$$\frac{x}{1} = \frac{20}{8} \left(\frac{\text{unknown c}}{\text{c for conversion}} = \frac{\text{fl oz given}}{\text{fl oz for conversion}} \right)$$

To solve a proportion, the ratios are cross-multiplied and the resulting equation is solved. When cross-multiplying, all four proportions above will produce the same equation:

$$(8)(x) = (20)(1) \rightarrow 8x = 20$$

Divide by 8 to isolate the variable x, the result is $x = 2.5$. The variable x represented the unknown number of cups. Therefore, the conclusion is that 20 fluid ounces converts (is equal) to 2.5 cups.

Sometimes converting units requires writing and solving more than one proportion. Suppose an exam question asks to determine how many hours are in 2 weeks. Without knowing the conversion rate between hours and weeks, this can be determined knowing the conversion rates between weeks and

days, and between days and hours. First, weeks are converted to days, then days are converted to hours. To convert from weeks to days, the following proportion can be written:

$$\frac{7}{1} = \frac{x}{2} \left(\frac{\text{days conversion}}{\text{weeks conversion}} = \frac{unknown \text{ days}}{\text{weeks given}} \right)$$

Cross-multiplying produces:

$$(7)(2) = (x)(1) \rightarrow 14 = x$$

Therefore, 2 weeks is equal to 14 days. Next, a proportion is written to convert 14 days to hours:

$$\frac{24}{1} = \frac{x}{14} \left(\frac{\text{conversion hours}}{\text{conversion days}} = \frac{unknown \text{ hours}}{\text{given days}} \right)$$

Cross-multiplying produces:

$$(24)(14) = (x)(1) \rightarrow 336 = x$$

Therefore, the answer is that there are 336 hours in 2 weeks.

Data Analysis and Probability

Measures of Center and Range

The *center* of a set of data (statistical values) can be represented by its mean, median, or mode. These are sometimes referred to as measures of central tendency. The *mean* is the average of the data set. The mean can be calculated by adding the data values and dividing by the sample size (the number of data points). Suppose a student has test scores of 93, 84, 88, 72, 91, and 77. To find the mean, or average, the scores are added and the sum is divided by 6 because there are 6 test scores:

$$\frac{93 + 84 + 88 + 72 + 91 + 77}{6} = \frac{505}{6} = 84.17$$

Given the mean of a data set and the sum of the data points, the sample size can be determined by dividing the sum by the mean. Suppose you are told that Kate averaged 12 points per game and scored a total of 156 points for the season. The number of games that she played (the sample size or the number of data points) can be determined by dividing the total points (sum of data points) by her average (mean of data points): $\frac{156}{12} = 13$. Therefore, Kate played in 13 games this season.

If given the mean of a data set and the sample size, the sum of the data points can be determined by multiplying the mean and sample size. Suppose you are told that Tom worked 6 days last week for an average of 5.5 hours per day. The total number of hours worked for the week (sum of data points) can be determined by multiplying his daily average (mean of data points) by the number of days worked (sample size): $5.5 \times 6 = 33$. Therefore, Tom worked a total of 33 hours last week.

The median of a data set is the value of the data point in the middle when the sample is arranged in numerical order. To find the median of a data set, the values are written in order from least to greatest. The lowest and highest values are simultaneously eliminated, repeating until the value in the middle remains. Suppose the salaries of math teachers are: $35,000; $38,500; $41,000; $42,000; $42,000;

$44,500; $49,000. The values are listed from least to greatest to find the median. The lowest and highest values are eliminated until only the middle value remains. Repeating this step three times reveals a median salary of $42,000. If the sample set has an even number of data points, two values will remain after all others are eliminated. In this case, the mean of the two middle values is the median. Consider the following data set: 7, 9, 10, 13, 14, 14. Eliminating the lowest and highest values twice leaves two values, 10 and 13, in the middle. The mean of these values $\left(\frac{10+13}{2}\right)$ is the median. Therefore, the set has a median of 11.5.

The mode of a data set is the value that appears most often. A data set may have a single mode, multiple modes, or no mode. If different values repeat equally as often, multiple modes exist. If no value repeats, no mode exists. Consider the following data sets:

- A: 7, 9, 10, 13, 14, 14
- B: 37, 44, 33, 37, 49, 44, 51, 34, 37, 33, 44
- C: 173, 154, 151, 168, 155

Set A has a mode of 14. Set B has modes of 37 and 44. Set C has no mode.

The *range* of a data set is the difference between the highest and the lowest values in the set. The range can be considered the span of the data set. To determine the range, the smallest value in the set is subtracted from the largest value. The ranges for the data sets A, B, and C above are calculated as follows:

A: $14 - 7 = 7$

B: $51 - 33 = 18$

C: $173 - 151 = 22$

Describing a Set of Data

A set of data can be described in terms of its center, spread, shape and any unusual features. The center of a data set can be measured by its mean, median, or mode. The spread of a data set refers to how far the data points are from the center (mean or median). The spread can be measured by the range or by the quartiles and interquartile range. A data set with all its data points clustered around the center will have a small spread. A data set covering a wide range of values will have a large spread.

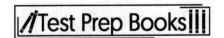

When a data set is displayed as a histogram or frequency distribution plot, the shape indicates if a sample is normally distributed, symmetrical, or has measures of skewness or kurtosis. When graphed, a data set with a normal distribution will resemble a bell curve.

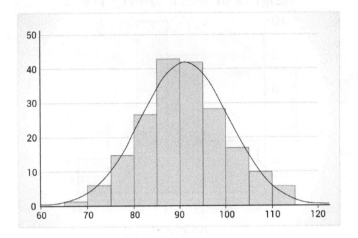

If the data set is symmetrical, each half of the graph when divided at the center is a mirror image of the other. If the graph has fewer data points to the right, the data is skewed right. If it has fewer data points to the left, the data is skewed left.

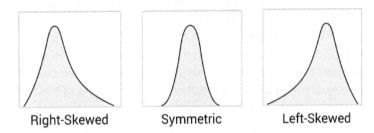

Right-Skewed   Symmetric   Left-Skewed

Kurtosis is a measure of whether the data is heavy-tailed with a high number of outliers, or light-tailed with a low number of outliers.

A description of a data set should include any unusual features such as gaps or outliers. A gap is a span within the range of the data set containing no data points. An outlier is a data point with a value either extremely large or extremely small when compared to the other values in the set.

Interpreting Displays of Data

A set of data can be visually displayed in various forms allowing for quick identification of characteristics of the set. *Histograms*, such as the one shown below, display the number of data points (vertical axis) that fall into given intervals (horizontal axis) across the range of the set. The histogram below displays the heights of black cherry trees in a certain city park. Each rectangle represents the number of trees with heights between a given five-point span. For example, the furthest bar to the right indicates that

61

two trees are between 85 and 90 feet. Histograms can describe the center, spread, shape, and any unusual characteristics of a data set.

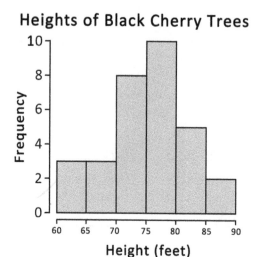

A *scatter plot* is a mathematical diagram that visually displays the relationship or connection between two variables. The independent variable is placed on the *x*-axis, or horizontal axis, and the dependent variable is placed on the *y*-axis, or vertical axis. When visually examining the points on the graph, if the points model a linear relationship, or if a line of best-fit can be drawn through the points with the points relatively close on either side, then a correlation exists. If the line of best-fit has a positive slope (rises from left to right), then the variables have a positive correlation. If the line of best-fit has a negative slope (falls from left to right), then the variables have a negative correlation. If a line of best-fit cannot be drawn, then no correlation exists. A positive or negative correlation can be categorized as strong or weak, depending on how closely the points are graphed around the line of best-fit.

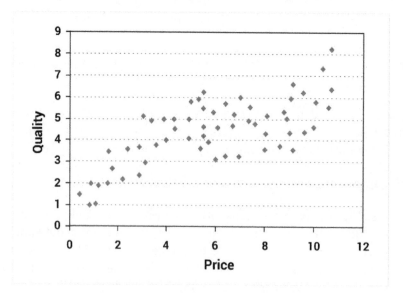

Graphical Representation of Data

Various graphs can be used to visually represent a given set of data. Each type of graph requires a different method of arranging data points and different calculations of the data. To construct a

62

histogram, the range of the data points is divided into equal intervals. The frequency for each interval is then determined, which reveals how many points fall into each interval. A graph is constructed with the vertical axis representing the frequency and the horizontal axis representing the intervals. The lower value of each interval should be labeled along the horizontal axis. Finally, for each interval, a bar is drawn from the lower value of each interval to the lower value of the next interval with a height equal to the frequency of the interval. Because of the intervals, histograms do not have any gaps between bars along the horizontal axis.

A scatter plot displays the relationship between two variables. Values for the independent variable, typically denoted by *x*, are paired with values for the dependent variable, typically denoted by *y*. Each set of corresponding values are written as an ordered pair (*x*, *y*). To construct the graph, a coordinate grid is labeled with the *x*-axis representing the independent variable and the *y*-axis representing the dependent variable. Each ordered pair is graphed.

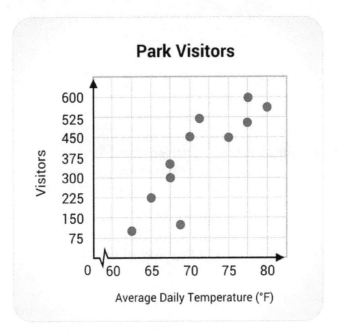

Like a scatter plot, a *line graph* compares variables that change continuously, typically over time. Paired data values (ordered pairs) are plotted on a coordinate grid with the x- and y-axis representing the

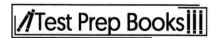
variables. A line is drawn from each point to the next, going from left to right. The line graph below displays cell phone use for given years (two variables) for men, women, and both (three data sets).

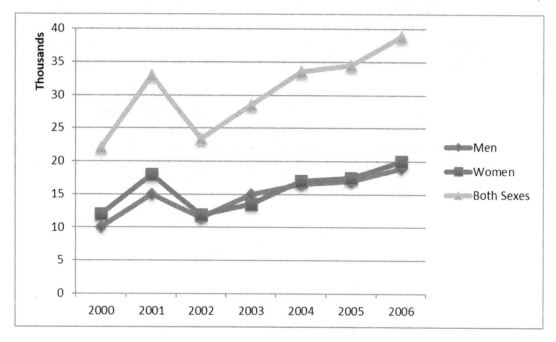

A *line plot*, also called dot plot, displays the frequency of data (numerical values) on a number line. To construct a line plot, a number line is used that includes all unique data values. It is marked with x's or dots above the value the number of times that the value occurs in the data set.

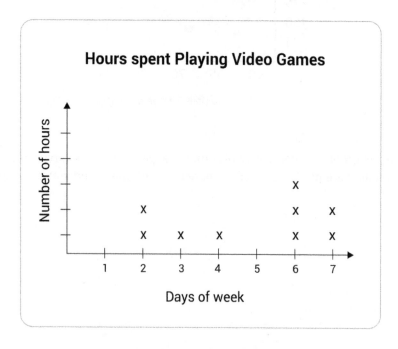

A *bar graph* looks similar to a histogram but displays categorical data. The horizontal axis represents each category and the vertical axis represents the frequency for the category. A bar is drawn for each category (often different colors) with a height extending to the frequency for that category within the data set. A double bar graph displays two sets of data that contain data points consisting of the same

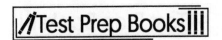

categories. The double bar graph below indicates that two girls and four boys like Pad Thai the most out of all the foods, two boys and five girls like pizza, and so on.

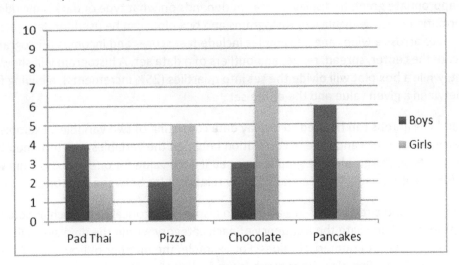

A *circle graph*, also called a pie chart, displays categorical data with each category representing a percentage of the whole data set. To construct a circle graph, the percent of the data set for each category must be determined. To do so, the frequency of the category is divided by the total number of data points and converted to a percent. For example, if 80 people were asked their favorite pizza topping and 20 responded cheese, then cheese constitutes 25% of the data:

$$\frac{20}{80} = 0.25 = 25\%$$

Each category in a data set is represented by a *slice* of the circle proportionate to its percentage of the whole.

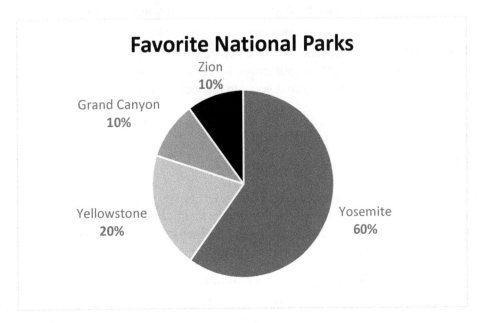

Favorite National Parks

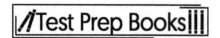

Choice of Graphs to Display Data

Choosing the appropriate graph to display a data set depends on what type of data is included in the set and what information must be displayed. Histograms and box plots can be used for data sets consisting of individual values across a wide range. Examples include test scores and incomes. Histograms and box plots will indicate the center, spread, range, and outliers of a data set. A histogram will show the shape of the data set, while a box plot will divide the set into quartiles (25% increments), allowing for comparison between a given value and the entire set.

Scatter plots and line graphs can be used to display data consisting of two variables. Examples include height and weight, or distance and time. A correlation between the variables is determined by examining the points on the graph. Line graphs are used if each value for one variable pairs with a distinct value for the other variable. Line graphs show relationships between variables.

Line plots, bar graphs, and circle graphs are all used to display categorical data, such as surveys. Line plots and bar graphs both indicate the frequency of each category within the data set. A line plot is used when the categories consist of numerical values. For example, the number of hours of TV watched by individuals is displayed on a line plot. A bar graph is used when the categories consists of words. For example, the favorite ice cream of individuals is displayed with a bar graph. A circle graph can be used to display either type of categorical data. However, unlike line plots and bar graphs, a circle graph does not indicate the frequency of each category. Instead, the circle graph represents each category as its percentage of the whole data set.

Probabilities Relative to Likelihood of Occurrence

Probability is a measure of how likely an event is to occur. Probability is written as a fraction between zero and one. If an event has a probability of zero, the event will never occur. If an event has a probability of one, the event will definitely occur. If the probability of an event is closer to zero, the event is unlikely to occur. If the probability of an event is closer to one, the event is more likely to occur. For example, a probability of $\frac{1}{2}$ means that the event is equally as likely to occur as it is not to occur. An example of this is tossing a coin. The probability of an event can be calculated by dividing the number of favorable outcomes by the number of total outcomes. For example, suppose you have 2 raffle tickets out of 20 total tickets sold. The probability that you win the raffle is calculated:

$$\frac{\text{number of favorable outcomes}}{\text{total number of outcomes}} = \frac{2}{20} = \frac{1}{10} \text{ (always reduce fractions)}$$

Therefore, the probability of winning the raffle is $\frac{1}{10}$ or 0.1.

Chance is the measure of how likely an event is to occur, written as a percent. If an event will never occur, the event has a 0% chance. If an event will certainly occur, the event has a 100% chance. If an event will sometimes occur, the event has a chance somewhere between 0% and 100%. To calculate chance, probability is calculated, and the fraction is converted to a percent.

The probability of multiple events occurring can be determined by multiplying the probability of each event. For example, suppose you flip a coin with heads and tails, and roll a six-sided die numbered one through six. To find the probability that you will flip heads AND roll a two, the probability of each event is determined, and those fractions are multiplied. The probability of flipping heads is $\frac{1}{2}\left(\frac{1 \text{ side with heads}}{2 \text{ sides total}}\right)$,

66

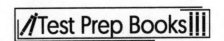

and the probability of rolling a two is $\frac{1}{6}$ $\left(\frac{1 \text{ side with a } 2}{6 \text{ total sides}}\right)$. The probability of flipping heads AND rolling a 2 is:

$$\frac{1}{2} \times \frac{1}{6} = \frac{1}{12}$$

The above scenario with flipping a coin and rolling a die is an example of independent events. Independent events are circumstances in which the outcome of one event does not affect the outcome of the other event. Conversely, dependent events are ones in which the outcome of one event affects the outcome of the second event. Consider the following scenario: a bag contains 5 black marbles and 5 white marbles. What is the probability of picking 2 black marbles without replacing the marble after the first pick?

The probability of picking a black marble on the first pick is:

$$\frac{5}{10} \left(\frac{5 \text{ black marbles}}{10 \text{ total marbles}}\right)$$

Assuming that a black marble was picked, there are now 4 black marbles and 5 white marbles for the second pick. Therefore, the probability of picking a black marble on the second pick is $\frac{4}{9}$:

$$\left(\frac{4 \text{ black marbles}}{9 \text{ total marbles}}\right)$$

To find the probability of picking two black marbles, the probability of each is multiplied:

$$\frac{5}{10} \times \frac{4}{9} = \frac{20}{90} = \frac{2}{9}$$

Quantitative Reasoning Practice Quiz

1. In the following expression, which operation should be completed first? $5 \times 6 + 4 \div 2 - 1$.
   a. Multiplication
   b. Addition
   c. Division
   d. Subtraction

2. Carey bought 50 pounds of fertilizer to use on her lawn. Each segment of her lawn required 11 pounds of fertilizer to do a sufficient job. If we are asked to determine how many segments could be fertilized with the amount purchased, what operation would be necessary to solve this problem?
   a. Multiplication
   b. Division
   c. Addition
   d. Subtraction

3. What unit is used to describe the volume of the following 3-dimensional shape?

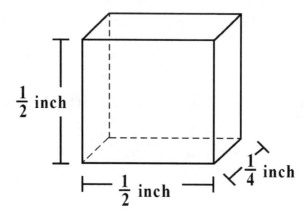

   a. Square inches
   b. Inches
   c. Cubic inches
   d. Squares

4. Brianna has a total of 88 skittles on her table. There are 6 sour skittles for every 5 regular skittles. How many skittles are sour?
   a. 56
   b. 48
   c. 24
   d. 80

5. Riley has 4 red shirts, 5 pink shirts, 2 blue shirts, 4 white shirts, and 1 black shirt. She pulls one out of her closet without looking. What is the probability she will pull out a white shirt?

   a. $\frac{1}{16}$

   b. $\frac{1}{4}$

   c. $\frac{1}{8}$

   d. $\frac{3}{16}$

See answer on the next page.

Quantitative Reasoning Answer Explanations

1. A: Using the order of operations, multiplication and division are computed first from left to right. Multiplication is on the left; therefore, multiplication should be performed first.

2. B: This is a division problem because the original amount needs to be split up into equal amounts. Carey needs to determine how many times 11 goes into 50. This is a division problem:

$$50 \div 11 = 4.55$$

Since this is between 4 and 5, Carey can fertilize 4 full lawn segments.

3. C: The volume of this 3-dimensional figure is calculated using length times width times height. Each of these three measurements is in inches. Therefore, the answer would be labeled in cubic inches.

4. B: Six sour skittle for every five regular skittles can be expressed as a ratio: 6:5. This can be visualized as splitting the skittles into 11 groups: 6 sour skittle groups and 5 regular skittle groups. The number of skittles that are in each group can be found by dividing the total number of skittles by 11:

$$\frac{88 \text{ skittles}}{11 \text{ groups}} = \frac{8 \text{ skittles}}{\text{group}}$$

To find the total number of sour skittles, multiply the number of skittles per group (8) by the number of sour skittle groups (6). This equals 48, Choice *B*.

5. B: There are 16 shirts in all and 4 white shirts, so the probability of randomly choosing a white shirt is one in four:

$$\frac{4}{16} = \frac{1}{4}$$

Mathematics Achievement Practice Quiz

1. What is the sum of $\frac{1}{3}$ and $\frac{2}{5}$?

    a. $\frac{3}{8}$

    b. $\frac{11}{15}$

    c. $\frac{11}{30}$

    d. $\frac{4}{5}$

2. If Danny takes 48 minutes to walk 3 miles, how long should it take him to walk 5 miles maintaining the same speed?

    a. 32 min

    b. 64 min

    c. 80 min

    d. 96 min

3. Which inequality represents the values displayed on the number line?

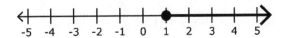

    a. $x < 1$

    b. $x \leq 1$

    c. $x > 1$

    d. $x \geq 1$

4. A group of 25 coworkers were given a choice of three lunch options: a sandwich, a salad, or a hamburger. If 12 employees chose a sandwich and 5 chose a salad, how many employees chose a hamburger?

    a. 17

    b. 8

    c. 13

    d. 5

5. Last year, the New York City area received approximately $27\frac{3}{4}$ inches of snow. The Denver area received approximately three times as much snow as New York City. How much snow fell in Denver?

    a. 60 inches

    b. $27\frac{1}{4}$ inches

    c. $9\frac{1}{4}$ inches

    d. $83\frac{1}{4}$ inches

See answers on the next page.

Mathematics Achievement Answer Explanations

1. B: Fractions must have like denominators to be added. The common denominator is the least common multiple (LCM) of the two original denominators. In this case, the LCM is 15, so both fractions should be changed to equivalent fractions with a denominator of 15. Multiply the bottom of each fraction by whatever number is needed to produce 15, and multiply the top of each fraction by that same number:

$$\frac{1 \times 5}{3 \times 5} = \frac{5}{15} \text{ and } \frac{2 \times 3}{5 \times 3} = \frac{6}{15}$$

Now, add the numerators and keep the denominator the same:

$$\frac{5}{15} + \frac{6}{15} = \frac{11}{15}$$

2. C: To solve the problem, we can write a proportion consisting of ratios comparing distance and time. One way to set up the proportion is:

$$\frac{3}{48} = \frac{5}{x}$$

To solve this proportion, we can cross-multiply: $(3)(x) = (5)(48)$, or $3x = 240$. To isolate the variable, we divide by 3 on both sides, producing $x = 80$.

3. D: The closed dot on 1 indicates that the value is included in the set. The arrow pointing right indicates that numbers greater than 1 (numbers get larger to the right) are included in the set. Therefore, the set includes numbers greater than or equal to 1, which can be written as $x \geq 1$.

4. B: First, the number of employees who did not choose a hamburger must be found. If 5 employees chose a salad and 12 chose a sandwich, then $5 + 12 = 17$ did not choose a hamburger. This number can be subtracted from the total to find out how many employees chose a hamburger:

$$25 - 17 = 8$$

5. D: To find Denver's total snowfall, 3 must be multiplied by $27\frac{3}{4}$. In order to easily do this, the mixed number should be converted into an improper fraction.

$$27\frac{3}{4} = \frac{27 \times 4 + 3}{4} = \frac{111}{4}$$

Therefore, Denver had approximately $\frac{3 \times 111}{4} = \frac{333}{4}$ inches of snow. The improper fraction can be converted back into a mixed number through division.

$$\frac{333}{4} = 83\frac{1}{4} \text{ inches}$$

Reading Comprehension

Main Idea

It is important to know the difference between the topic and the main idea of the passage. Even though these two are similar, they have some differences. A topic is the subject of the text. It can usually be described in a one- to two-word phrase. On the other hand, the main idea is more detailed. It provides the author's central point of the passage. It can be expressed through a complete sentence. It is often found in the beginning, middle, or end of a paragraph. In most nonfiction books, the first sentence of the passage usually states the main idea. Take a look at the passage below to review the topic versus the main idea:

> Cheetahs are one of the fastest mammals on land, reaching up to seventy miles an hour over short distances. Even though cheetahs can run as fast as seventy miles an hour, they usually only have to run half that speed to catch up with their choice of prey. Cheetahs cannot maintain a fast pace over long periods of time because they will overheat their bodies. After a chase, cheetahs need to rest for approximately thirty minutes prior to eating or returning to any other activity.

In the example above, the topic of the passage is Cheetahs because that is the subject of the text. The *main idea* of the text is "Cheetahs are one of the fastest mammals on the land but can only maintain a fast pace for shorter distances." While this covers the topic, it is more detailed. It refers to the text in its entirety. The passage provides more details called supporting details. These will be discussed in the next section.

Supporting Details

Supporting details help you understand the main idea. Supporting details answer questions like *who, what, where, when, why,* and *how.* Supporting details can include examples, facts, statistics, small stories, and visual details.

Persuasive and informative texts often use supporting details. In persuasive texts, authors try to make readers agree with their points of view. In persuasive texts, supporting details are often used as "selling points." If authors say something, they should support it with evidence. This helps to persuade readers. Informative texts use supporting details to inform readers. Take another look at the "Cheetahs" example from the page before to find examples of supporting details.

In the Cheetah example above, supporting details include:

- Cheetahs reach up to seventy miles per hour over short distances.
- Cheetahs usually only have to run half that speed to catch up with their prey.
- Cheetahs will overheat their bodies if they exert a high speed over longer distances.
- They need to rest for thirty minutes after a chase.

Look at the diagram below (applying the cheetah example) to help determine the hierarchy of topic, main idea, and supporting details.

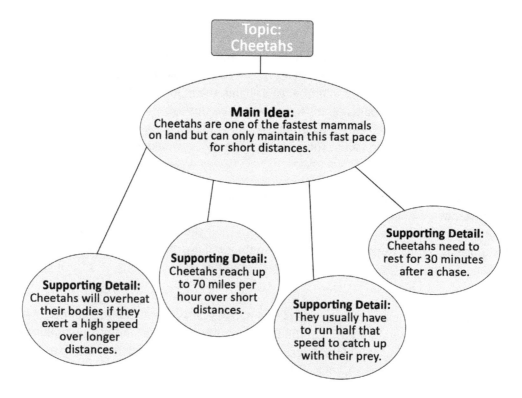

Inferences

When readers put together clues from the writing to "guess" that a certain idea is a fact, it is called making *inferences*. Making inferences helps read "between the lines" of the writing. Readers read "between the lines" to figure out why the author wrote what they wrote.

Inferences are about being able to make wise guesses based on clues from the writing. People make inferences about the world around them every day. However, they may not be aware of what they are doing. For example, a young boy may infer that it is cold outside if he wakes up and his bedroom is chilly. Or, a girl is driving somewhere and she sees a person on the side of the road with a parked car. The girl might think that person's car broke down, and that they are waiting for help. Both of these are examples of how inferences are used every day.

Making inferences is kind of like being a detective. Sometimes clues can be found in the pictures that are inside of a story. For example, a story might show a picture of a school where all the children are in the parking lot. Looking more closely, readers might spot a fire truck parked at the side of the road and might infer that the school had a fire drill or an actual fire.

Vocabulary/Word Choice

Comparison and Contrast
One writing device authors use is comparison and contrast. *Comparison* is when authors take objects and show how they are the same. *Contrast* is when authors take objects and show how they differ.

74

Comparison and contrast essays are mostly written in nonfiction form. There are common words used when authors compare or contrast. The list below will show you some of these words:

Comparison Words:

- Similar to
- Alike
- As well as
- Both

Contrast Words:

- Although
- On the other hand
- Different from
- However
- As opposed to
- More than
- Less than
- On the contrary

Transitional Words and Phrases

There are approximately 200 transitional words and phrases that are commonly used in the English language. Below are lists of common transition words and phrases.

Time	Example	Compare	Contrast	Addition	Logical Relationships	Steps
after	for example	likewise	however	and	if	first
before	in fact	also	yet	also	then	second
during	for instance		but	furthermore	therefore	last
in the middle				moreover	as a result	
					since	

Transitional words and phrases are important writing devices. They connect sentences and paragraphs. Transitional words and phrases help writing to make more sense. They provide clearer meaning to readers.

Interpreting Words and Phrases

Words can have different meaning depending on how they are used in a text. Once a reader knows the correct meaning and how to say a word, they can better understand the context of the word. There are lots of methods for helping readers solve word meanings.

Dictionary: Dictionaries are not allowed on the test. However, readers should know how to use a dictionary and a thesaurus. In dictionaries, there can be more than one meaning for a certain word. Dictionaries also help teach how to say words. A thesaurus teaches words that have the same meanings (synonyms) and words that have opposite meanings (antonyms).

Word Parts: Separating words into their word parts, (root word, prefix, suffix) will help determine the meaning of a word as a whole.

75

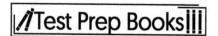

Context Clues: Readers can look at other words in sentences to help them find out the meaning of an unknown word by the way it is used in the same sentence or paragraph. This kind of search provides context clues.

Author's Purpose: Authors use words differently depending on what they want the reader to learn. Some ways writers use words are as follows:

- **Literal**: the exact meaning of the word
- **Figurative**: metaphorical language and figures of speech
- **Technical**: in-depth writing about certain subjects like math or music
- **Connotative**: showing an opinion in the text as a secondary meaning

Organization/Logic

Organization of Text Structures

Text structures are used for different reasons in writing. Each text structure has key words and elements that help identify it. Readers use text structure to help find information within a text. Summarizing requires knowledge of the text structure of a piece of writing. Here are some common text structures that writers use to organize their text:

Chronological Order: Time order or sequence from one point to another. Dates and times might be used, or bullets and numbering. Possible key words: *first, next, then, after, later, finally, before, preceding, following*

Cause and Effect: Showing how causes lead to effects. Possible key words: *cause, effect, consequently, as a result, due to, in order to, because of, therefore, so, leads to, if/then*

Problem and Solution: Talks about a problem in detail and gives solutions to the problem. Possible key words: *difficulty, problem, solve, solution, possible, therefore, if/then, challenge*

Compare and Contrast: Talks about how objects, people, places, and ideas might be the same or different from each other. Possible key words: *like, unlike, similar to, in contrast, on the other hand, whereas, while, although, either or, opposed to, different from, instead*

Description: Explains a topic with the main idea and details. Possible key words: *for example, such as, for instance, most importantly, another, such as, next to, on top of, besides*

Tone/Style/Figurative Language

Tone

The words authors choose to use must always be well thought out. Although words carry specific meanings, they also carry *connotations*—emotional feelings that are evoked by the words. Connotation creates the tone of the writing. Some words can be said to be loaded words or trigger words that ignite strong emotional responses in readers. These two sentences offer examples:

My grandfather is a robust, elderly man.

My grandfather is a chubby, old man.

In the first sentence, the adjectives used to describe the grandfather instill positive emotions in the reader. However, in the second sentence, the adjectives instill negative emotions. The *mood* of a writing piece refers to the emotions—positive or negative—the reader feels during and after reading. *Tone* refers to the author's purposeful choice of words, designed to evoke those feelings.

Style

Style can include any number of technical writing choices. A few examples of style choices include:

- Sentence Construction: When presenting facts, does the writer use shorter sentences to create a quicker sense of the supporting evidence, or do they use longer sentences to elaborate and explain the information?

- Technical Language: Does the writer use jargon to demonstrate their expertise in the subject, or do they use ordinary language to help the reader understand things in simple terms?

- Formal Language: Does the writer refrain from using contractions such as *won't* or *can't* to create a more formal tone, or do they use a colloquial, conversational style to connect to the reader?

- Formatting: Does the writer use a series of shorter paragraphs to help the reader follow a line of argument, or do they use longer paragraphs to examine an issue in great detail and demonstrate their knowledge of the topic?

Figurative Language

Figurative language is a specific style of speaking or writing that uses tools for a variety of effects. It entertains readers, ignites imagination, and promotes creativity. Instead of writing in realistic terms or literal terms, figurative language plays with words and prompts readers to infer the underlying meaning.

There are seven types of figurative language:

Type	Definition	Example
Personification	Giving animate qualities to an inanimate object	The tree stood tall and still, staring up at the sky.
Simile	The comparison of two unlike things using connecting words	Your eyes are as blue as the ocean.
Metaphor	The comparison of two unlike things without the use of connecting words	She was in the twilight of her years.
Hyperbole	An over-exaggeration	I could eat a million of these cookies!
Alliteration	The patterned repetition of an initial consonant sound	The bunnies are bouncing in baskets.
Onomatopoeia	Words that are formed by using the very sound associated with the word itself	"Drip, drip, drip" went the kitchen faucet.

77

Type	Definition	Example
Idioms	Common sayings that carry a lesson or meaning that must be inferred	That math work was a piece of cake!

Interpretation

Since idioms and hyperboles are commonly used in everyday speech, educators may wish to introduce them early.

> I'm so tired that I could sleep forever!—Hyperbole

> He's not playing with a full deck!—Idiom

Other forms of figurative language can be found in poetry and in children's stories. As educators come across figurative speech, they can prompt children's critical thinking skills by asking what they think the author meant by those words or that particular sentence. Giving concrete examples of each style and challenging children to attempt writing their very own creative sentences will strengthen their understanding and application of figurative language.

Reading Comprehension Practice Quiz

The next five questions are based on the following passage.

The Myth of Head Heat Loss

It has recently been brought to my attention that most people believe that 75% of your body heat is lost through your head. I had certainly heard this before, and I'm not going to attempt to say I didn't believe it when I first heard it. It is natural to be gullible to anything said with enough authority. But the "fact" that the majority of your body heat is lost through your head is a lie.

Let me explain. Heat loss is proportional to surface area exposed. An elephant loses a great deal more heat than an anteater because it has a much greater surface area than an anteater. Each cell has mitochondria that produce energy in the form of heat, and it takes a lot more energy to run an elephant than an anteater.

So, each part of your body loses its proportional amount of heat in accordance with its surface area. The human torso probably loses the most heat, though the legs lose a significant amount as well. Some people have asked, "Why does it feel so much warmer when you cover your head than when you don't?" Well, that's because your head loses a lot of heat when it is not clothed, while the clothing on the rest of your body provides insulation. If you went outside with a hat and pants but no shirt, not only would you look silly, but your heat loss would be significantly greater because so much more of you would be exposed. So, if given the choice to cover your chest or your head in the cold, choose the chest. It could save your life.

1. As used in the first paragraph, the word *gullible* most nearly means:
   a. To believe something
   b. To be filled with pride
   c. To give new knowledge
   d. To find something funny

2. Based on the passage, which article of clothing would provide the least insulation?
   a. Coat
   b. Pants
   c. Shirt
   d. Gloves

3. Why does the author compare elephants and anteaters?
   a. To express an opinion
   b. To give an example that helps clarify the main point
   c. To show the differences between the two
   d. To persuade why one is better than the other

4. Which of the following best describes the tone of the passage?
   a. Harsh
   b. Angry
   c. Casual
   d. Indifferent

5. What kind of argument does the author make in order to prove their case?
   a.   They present facts and evidence.
   b.   They make an emotional appeal.
   c.   They base their argument on ethics and morals.
   d.   They rely on their stated qualifications as an author.

See answers on the next page.

Reading Comprehension Answer Explanations

1. A: The first paragraph says that the author once believed that most body heat is lost through your head, but they then pointed out that this statement about heat loss is a lie. This suggests that they believed something that wasn't true. When they use the word *gullible* to describe this sort of behavior, the word means that they believe something. The other answer choices do not directly relate to the word *gullible*.

2. D: The passage focuses only on insulation as it relates to surface area. Since gloves would cover the least surface area of the given options, Choice *D* is correct. A coat and shirt, Choices *A* and *C*, would cover the torso, while pants, Choice *B*, would cover the legs; the torso and legs each have more surface area than the hands.

3. B: Choice *B* is correct because the author is trying to demonstrate the main idea, which is that heat loss is proportional to surface area, so they compare two animals with different surface areas to clarify the main point. Choice *A* is incorrect because the author uses elephants and anteaters to prove a point, that heat loss is proportional to surface area, not to express an opinion. Choice *C* is incorrect because though the author does use them to show differences, they do so in order to give examples that prove the above points. Choice *D* is incorrect because there is no language to indicate favoritism between the two animals.

4. C: Because of the way the author addresses the reader and the colloquial language the author uses (e.g., "let me explain," "so," "well," "didn't," "you would look stupid"), Choice *C* is the best answer because it has a much more casual tone than the usual informative article. Choice *A* may be a tempting choice because the author says the "fact" that most of one's heat is lost through their head is a "lie" and that someone who does not wear a shirt in the cold looks stupid. However, this only happens twice within the passage, and the passage does not give an overall tone of harshness. Choice *B* is incorrect because again, while not necessarily nice, the language does not carry an angry charge. The author is clearly not indifferent to the subject because of the passionate language that they use, so Choice *D* is incorrect.

5. A: The author gives logical examples and reasons in order to prove that most of one's heat is not lost through their head; therefore, Choice *A* is correct. Choice *B* is incorrect because there is not much emotionally charged language in this selection, and even the small amount present is greatly outnumbered by the facts and evidence. Choice *C* is incorrect because there is no mention of ethics or morals in this selection. Choice *D* is incorrect because the author never qualifies himself as someone who has the authority to be writing on this topic.

81

This material is provided for exam preparation purposes only and does not indicate an endorsement of any specific scientific, political, or religious point of view. © TPB Publishing. You have been licensed one copy of this document for personal use only. Any other reproduction or redistribution is strictly prohibited. All rights reserved.

Writing the Essay

Test takers are given thirty minutes to write a short essay in response to a prompt. This section gives test takers the opportunity to show their writing ability as well as show more about themselves. Test takers should be sure to organize their thoughts, prepare a short outline, and write a final copy.

Planning should take place after reading the prompt. This brainstorming stage is when writers consider their purpose and think of ideas that they can use in their writing. Drawing pictures like story webs are great tools to use during the planning stage. Drawing pictures can help connect the writing purpose to supporting details. They can also help begin the process of structuring the writing.

POWER Strategy for Writing

The POWER strategy helps all writers focus and do well during the writing process.

The POWER strategy stands for the following:

- Prewriting or Planning
- Organizing
- Writing a first draft
- Editing the writing
- Revising and rewriting

Prewriting and Planning
During the prewriting and planning phase, writers learn to think about their audience and purpose for the writing assignment. Then they gather information they wish to include in the writing. They do this from their background knowledge or new sources.

Organizing
Next, writers decide on the organization of their writing project. There are many types of *organizational structures*, but the common ones are: story/narrative, informative, opinion, persuasive, compare and contrast, explanatory, and problem/solution formats.

Writing
In this step, the writers write a first draft of their project.

Evaluating
In this stage, writers reread the writing and note the sections that are strong or that need improvement.

Revising and Rewriting
Finally, the writer incorporates any changes they wish to make based on what they've read. Then writers rewrite the piece into a final draft.

Elements of Effective Writing

The following are characteristics that make writing readable and effective:

- Ideas
- Organization
- Voice
- Word choice
- Sentence fluency
- Proper Writing Conventions
- Presentation

Ideas

This refers to the content of the writing. Writers should focus on the topic shown in the picture or prompt. They should narrow down and focus their idea, remembering that they only have fifteen minutes to plan and write! Then they learn to develop the idea and choose the details that best shows the idea to others.

Organization

Many writers are inclined to jump into their writing without a clear direction for where it is going. Organization helps plan out the writing so that it's successful. Your writing should have an introduction, a body, and a conclusion.

Introduction (beginning): Writers should invite the reader into their work with a good introduction. They should restate the prompt in their own words so that readers know what they are going to read about.

Body (middle): The body is where the main thoughts and ideas are put together. Thoughtful transitions between ideas and key points help keep readers interested. Writers should create logical and purposeful sequences of ideas.

Conclusion (end): Writers should include a powerful conclusion to their piece that summarizes the information but leaves the reader with something to think about.

Voice

Voice is how the writer uses words and how they use sentence structure to sound like themselves! It shows that the writing is meaningful and that the author cares about it. It is what makes the writing uniquely the author's own. It is how the reader begins to know the author and what they "sound like."

Word Choice

The right word choice helps the author connect with their audience. If the work is narrative, the words tell a story. If the work is descriptive, the words can almost make you taste, touch, and feel what you are reading! If the work is an opinion, the words give new ideas and invite thought. Writers should choose detailed vocabulary and language that is clear and lively.

Sentence Fluency

When sentences are built to fit together and move with one another to create writing that is easy to read aloud, the author has written with fluency. Sentences and paragraphs start and stop in just the right places so that the writing moves well. Sentences should have a lot of different of structures and lengths.

Proper Writing Conventions

Writers should make their writing clear and understandable through the use of proper grammar, spelling, capitalization, and punctuation.

Presentation

Writers should try to make their work inviting to the reader. Writers show they care about their writing when it is neat and readable.

Tips for the Writing Section

1. Use your time well. Thirty minutes can go by quick! Don't spend too much time doing any one thing. Try to brainstorm briefly and then get writing. Leave a few minutes to read it over and correct any spelling mistakes or confusing parts.

2. Be yourself! You are smart and interesting and teachers want to get to know you and your unique ideas. Don't feel pressured to use big vocabulary words if you aren't positive what they mean. You will be more understandable if you use the right word, not the fanciest word.

Practice Essay Question

Select a topic from the list below and write an essay. You may organize your essay on another sheet of paper.

Topic 1: Who is someone you look up to the most in this world? Why?

Topic 2: If you could move anywhere in the world, where would it be and why?

Topic 3: If you could have dinner with anyone in the world, alive or dead, who would it be? Why have you chosen this person?

Verbal Reasoning

Synonyms

1. ORCHARD
    a. Farm
    b. Fruit
    c. Grove
    d. Peach

2. PERMIT
    a. Law
    b. Parking
    c. Crab
    d. Allow

3. DEMONSTRATE
    a. Tell
    b. Show
    c. Build
    d. Complete

4. ABANDON
    a. Find
    b. Replace
    c. Leave
    d. Destroy

5. TEXTILE
    a. Fabric
    b. Knit
    c. Mural
    d. Ornament

6. OFFSPRING
    a. Bounce
    b. Parent
    c. Music
    d. Child

7. INSPIRE
    a. Motivate
    b. Impale
    c. Exercise
    d. Patronize

8. WOMAN
   a. Man
   b. Lady
   c. Women
   d. Mother

9. CONSISTENT
   a. Steady
   b. Contains
   c. Sticky
   d. Texture

10. PRINCIPLE
   a. Principal
   b. Leader
   c. President
   d. Foundation

11. SYMBOL
   a. Drum
   b. Music
   c. Clang
   d. Emblem

12. OPPRESSED
   a. Acclaimed
   b. Helpless
   c. Beloved
   d. Pressured

13. TRIUMPH
   a. Victory
   b. Burial
   c. Animosity
   d. Banter

14. BLAND
   a. Complex
   b. Dull
   c. Novel
   d. Superior

15. SPECTATOR
   a. Assistant
   b. Guardian
   c. Observer
   d. Participant

16. PAMPHLET
   a. Brochure
   b. Letter
   c. Newspaper
   d. Tome

17. ENCHANT
   a. Complicate
   b. Inform
   c. Mesmerize
   d. Suffice

Sentence Completion A

18. When the baseball game was over, the first thing Jackson did was run towards the dugout to grab his water bottle to relieve his _____ throat.
   a. humid
   b. scorched
   c. parched
   d. dusty

19. When I heard the wolf howl from my tent, my hands started _____ and my heart stopped ... hopefully I would make it through this night alive!
   a. dancing
   b. glowing
   c. shaking
   d. throbbing

20. As soon as the shot rang out, the runners _____ toward the finish line.
   a. sprinted
   b. skipped
   c. rejoiced
   d. herded

21. After Colby's mom picked him up from school, they went to the bank to _____ a check.
   a. celebrate
   b. neutralize
   c. eliminate
   d. deposit

22. The sale at the grocery store _____ my dad to buy four avocados instead of two.
   a. intimidated
   b. inspired
   c. dismayed
   d. berated

23. When Lindsay asked me to _____ her party, I immediately began writing a list of the birthday presents she might like to receive.
    a. acclaim
    b. astound
    c. attend
    d. amend

24. Cooking dinner was her favorite activity until she _____ the fire alarm by burning the casserole in the oven.
    a. activated
    b. offended
    c. unplugged
    d. disbanded

25. Before she arrived at the _____ dentist's office to take care of a cavity, she did some breathing exercises and nervously made sure her teeth were clean.
    a. refreshing
    b. creative
    c. rapturous
    d. dreaded

26. The dog ran around in wide circles, disregarding the boy's command because he had not learned yet to be _____.
    a. peaceful
    b. obedient
    c. impudent
    d. reserved

27. When we caught the eels, their bodies _____ out of our hands and back into the water.
    a. exploded
    b. deteriorated
    c. thundered
    d. slithered

28. Even though at the restaurant my mom _____ the eggplant with no cheese, she still received a huge serving of parmesan on top.
    a. requested
    b. directed
    c. mourned
    d. endorsed

Sentence Completion B

29. Unlike Leo, who always played basketball in the park after school, Gabriel _____
    a. ate his lunch in the cafeteria.
    b. rode his bike to school in the morning.
    c. would also play basketball in the park after school.
    d. would usually go to the library and study after school.

30. Determined to get a good score on her paper, LaShonda _____
    a. went to the gym every day for a month.
    b. taught her little brother how to read.
    c. learned how to speak Spanish and French.
    d. began writing it two weeks before it was due.

31. My mom recently started drinking fruit and vegetable smoothies in order to _____
    a. increase the quality of her health.
    b. obtain a raise at her new job.
    c. prove to herself that she could hike the Appalachian trail.
    d. encourage her sister to start working out at the gym with her.

32. After carefully equipping and securing his safety harness, Thomas began to _____
    a. climb the rock wall.
    b. prepare himself for bed.
    c. pour himself a bowl of cereal.
    d. present his science experiment to the class.

33. Despite being picked last in dodgeball, Diego surprised everyone in his gym class by _____
    a. throwing a giant tantrum.
    b. being eliminated immediately.
    c. eliminating all the members of the other team.
    d. trying to hide behind his teammates for the entire game.

34. It was only once he had seen how small the inside of a lunar module actually was that Jason understood why _____
    a. humanity hadn't yet discovered evidence of alien life.
    b. astronauts had to survive on dehydrated food while in space.
    c. it had taken so many years for humanity to finally reach the Moon.
    d. only a few astronauts could travel to the Moon on any single mission.

Quantitative Reasoning

1. Which of the following is the definition of a prime number?
    a. A number whose only factors are itself and 1
    b. A number greater than 1 whose only factors are itself and 1
    c. A number less than 10
    d. A number divisible by 10

2. Which of the following is the correct order of operations?
    a. Parentheses, Exponents, Multiplication and Division, Addition and Subtraction
    b. Exponents, Parentheses, Multiplication and Division, Addition and Subtraction
    c. Parentheses and Exponents, Addition, Multiplication, Division, Subtraction
    d. Parentheses and Exponents, Division, Addition, Subtraction, Multiplication

3. Which four-sided shape is always a rectangle?
   a. Rhombus
   b. Square
   c. Parallelogram
   d. Quadrilateral

4. Which common denominator would be used in order to evaluate $\frac{2}{3} + \frac{4}{5}$?
   a. 15
   b. 3
   c. 5
   d. 10

5. Which calculation below gives the perimeter of a legal-sized piece of paper that is 14 inches long and $8\frac{1}{2}$ inches wide?
   a. $P = 14 + 8\frac{1}{2}$

   b. $P = 14 + 8\frac{1}{2} + 14 + 8\frac{1}{2}$

   c. $P = 14 \times 8\frac{1}{2}$

   d. $P = 14 \times \frac{17}{2}$

6. Which of the following are units in the metric system?
   a. Inches, feet, miles, pounds
   b. Millimeters, centimeters, meters, pounds
   c. Kilograms, grams, kilometers, meters
   d. Teaspoons, tablespoons, ounces

7. The diameter of a circle measures 5 centimeters. What tool could be used to draw such a circle?
   a. Ruler
   b. Meter stick
   c. Compass
   d. Yard stick

8. Which of the following is represented by $6,000 + 400 + 30 + 5$?
   a. 5,346
   b. 6,345
   c. 64,305
   d. 6,435

9. What method is used to convert a fraction to a decimal?
   a. Divide the denominator by the numerator.
   b. Multiply by 100 and reduce the fraction.
   c. Divide the numerator by the denominator.
   d. Divide by 100 and reduce the fraction.

10. In Jim's school, there are a total of 650 students. There are three girls for every two boys. How many students are girls?
   a. 260 girls
   b. 130 girls
   c. 65 girls
   d. 390 girls

11. When evaluating word problems, which of the following phrases represent the division symbol?
   a. More than
   b. Product of
   c. Quotient of
   d. Results in

12. What would be the next term in the following sequence? 1, 3, 9, 27 …
   a. 81
   b. 90
   c. 270
   d. 139

13. Which two measurements of a triangle are needed to calculate the area of a triangle?
   a. Length, width
   b. Base, height
   c. Perimeter, height
   d. Base, width

14. Which of the following is a true statement regarding a line?
   a. A line has thickness.
   b. A line ends at two points.
   c. A line connects two points.
   d. A line and a line segment are the same thing.

15. What is an angle measuring less than 90 degrees called?
   a. Obtuse
   b. Right
   c. Complementary
   d. Acute

16. Which of the following units would be most appropriate to measure the size of a book?
   a. Millimeters
   b. Feet
   c. Yards
   d. Inches

17. Which of the following lists US customary units for volume of liquids from largest to smallest?
   a. Fluid ounces, cup, pint, quart, gallon
   b. Gallon, quart, pint, cup, fluid ounces
   c. Gallon, quart, pint, fluid ounces, cup
   d. Quart, gallon, pint, cup, fluid ounces

18. Morgan wants to exercise at least 3 hours total this week. He exercised 35 minutes on Monday, 22 minutes on Tuesday, 41 minutes on Wednesday, and 1 hour on Thursday. How many more minutes does Morgan need to exercise to reach his goal of 3 hours?
    a. 22
    b. 81
    c. 25
    d. 44

19. Which of the following measures of central tendency is the data point in the middle of the sample when arranged in numerical order?
    a. Mean
    b. Mode
    c. Median
    d. Range

20. What is the mode of the following data set?

22, 18, 46, 37, 46, 25, 18, 33, 46, 25, 41

    a. 18
    b. 25
    c. 46
    d. 33

21. In the following scatter plot, what type of correlation is present?

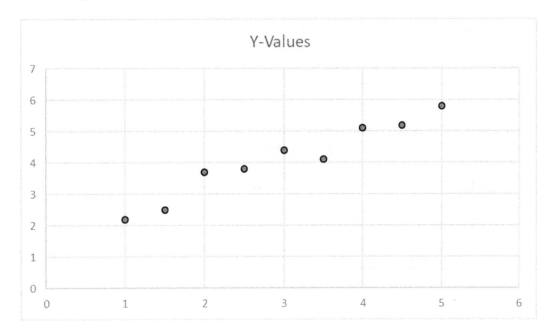

    a. Positive
    b. Negative
    c. Independent
    d. No correlation

22. In the following bar graph, how many children prefer brownies and cake?

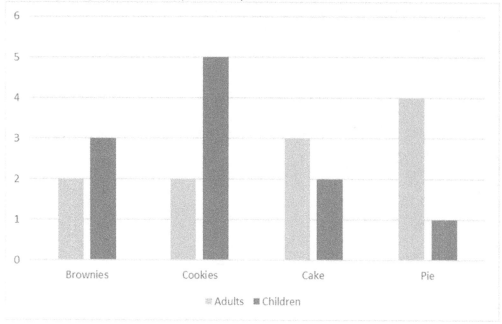

a. 3
b. 4
c. 7
d. 5

23. Which of the following is a three-dimensional shape?
    a. Circle
    b. Triangle
    c. Hexagon
    d. Cube

24. Trevor went to buy school supplies. He spent a total of $18.25. He bought 3 notebooks, 2 packages of paper, and 1 pencil sharpener. How many boxes of pens did he buy?

Item	Cost
Notebook	$2.75
Package of paper	$1.50
Pencil sharpener	$3.00
Box of pens	$2.00

a. 2
b. 3
c. 4
d. 5

25. The teacher has written the following equation on the board: $125 \div 5 + 17 - 3 \times 2(4)$. Using the correct order of operations, what is the solution to this equation?

a. 312
b. 52.63
c. 18
d. 66

26. The cafeteria at Marco Polo Elementary School is a very busy place. There are 300 students who eat lunch every day; 63 of the students bring their lunch to school, and 18 of them go home for lunch. Approximately half of the students share or trade food during lunch, too, and all but 12 students need milk to drink. How many lunches do the cafeteria workers have to cook each day?

a. 300
b. 288
c. 150
d. 219

27. The basketball team is hosting a bake sale to raise money for new uniforms. They want to make sure they have enough desserts to sell. If there are 13 players on the team and the coach asks everyone to make two dozen cookies or brownies to sell, how many cookies and brownies will there be for sale at the bake sale?

a. 26
b. 156
c. 624
d. 312

28. Melody is in the grocery store with her mother. She is trying to estimate how much the groceries will cost. If her mother buys the following items, what is the estimated total cost, rounded to the nearest dollar?

2 gallons of milk: $3.57 each
Half a dozen oranges: $6.00 per dozen
2 pounds of apples: $1.58 per pound
Cereal: $4.28
Bread: $2.73

a. $22
b. $18
c. $25
d. $23

29. Matthew's grandmother gave him $10.00 to spend on anything he wants at the store, but he can't decide what to buy. His choices are anime trading cards ($5.69 per pack), candy bars ($1.59 each), a baseball ($7.99), and a box of sidewalk chalk ($4.25). Which combination of items comes closest to $10.00 without going over?

a. The trading cards and two candy bars
b. The trading cards and the sidewalk chalk
c. The baseball and two candy bars
d. The sidewalk chalk and four candy bars

30. Bobby's teacher, Mrs. Juarez, drew a function machine on the board. She explained that the "In" numbers were the starting point. Then a math rule had to be applied to the number that would result in the "Out" number. The same rule had to be applied to every "In" number for the machine to work. What math rule is being applied to this function machine?

In	Out
2	16
4	
7	21
	26
15	29

a. Multiply by 8.
b. Add 14.
c. Multiply by 3.
d. The "Out" number is prime.

31. Sherika is trying to fill out the function machine that her teacher gave her for homework. She knows she has to figure out the rule first and then apply it to all of the numbers. What should the numbers be for x, y, and z to complete the machine?

In	Out
3	11
5	x
y	18
z	25
23	31

a. $x = 13; y = 10; z = 13$
b. $x = 14; y = 4; z = 14$
c. $x = 8, y = 8$, and $z = 8$
d. $x = 13; y = 10; z = 17$

32. Beth, Charlotte, and Daniel all live on May Street. Albert and Joseph live on Oak Street, which crosses perpendicular to May Street. Amy lives on Apple Tree Lane, which is parallel to May Street and also crosses Oak Street. Which people live in collinear points?

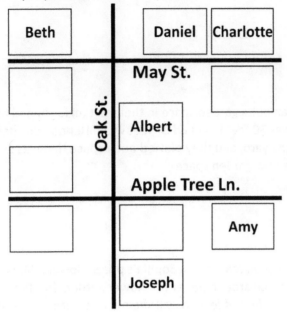

a. Beth, Charlotte, and Daniel
b. Daniel, Albert, and Joseph
c. Beth, Charlotte, and Amy
d. Albert, Amy, and Daniel

33. Mr. McMurtry's class is learning about geometry, and they are working with lines. He has drawn four images on the board and has asked the class to identify the line:

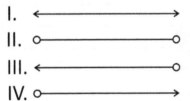

Jackson and Micaela say the correct answer is *II*. Toby thinks the correct answer is *III* and *IV* because they are the same and just point in different directions. Sudipta says the correct answer is *I*, but her friend Marigold thinks the correct answer is *IV*. Who is right?

a. Jackson and Micaela
b. Toby
c. Sudipta
d. Marigold

34. Marietta needs a new hat to go with her witch costume for Halloween. She needs to describe what she wants to her mother so her mom can make her hat. Marietta cannot remember the name for the shape of the hat she wants. She knows it's round at the bottom and then rises up to a point at the top. What shape does she want?
   a. Sphere
   b. Cone
   c. Triangle
   d. Circle

35. Ava is helping her dad plan out a garden space in their rectangle-shaped backyard. They measured the whole backyard, which was 50 feet long and 37 feet wide. Her dad decided to designate a rectangular back section of the yard, and they plotted out a space that was 20 feet long and 15 feet wide. What is the area of the new garden space?
   a. 1850 square feet
   b. 87 square feet
   c. 300 square feet
   d. 35 square feet

36. The deer and rabbits have been feasting on Sophia's prized flowers! She is very upset and has decided that she must put a fence around her entire flower garden. Her flower garden is a square that is 18 feet on each side. How many feet of fencing will she need to enclose the whole garden?
   a. 72
   b. 324
   c. 36
   d. 54

37. Jill, Kai, Jayden, and Alex were having a race to see who could do the most math problems in 30 minutes. According to the graph below, who completed the most problems?

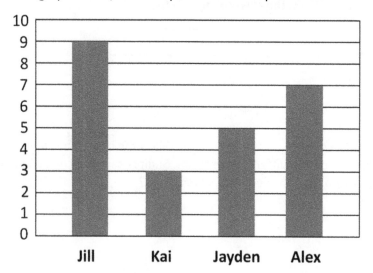

   a. Jill
   b. Kai
   c. Jayden
   d. Alex

38. Four basketball teams competed in the final playoff games. Together, the teams scored 350 points. The teams with the top two scores will get to play in the championship game. According to the bar graph, which two teams will be playing against each other?

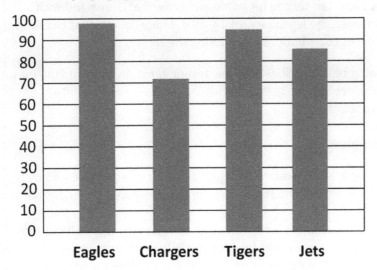

a. Jets vs. Chargers
b. Eagles vs. Chargers
c. Eagles vs. Tigers
d. Tigers vs. Jets

Reading Comprehension

Questions 1 – 5 are based on the following passage.

Christopher Columbus is often credited with discovering America. This is a matter of perspective; America was unknown to fifteenth-century Europe, but bear in mind that the places he "discovered" were already filled with people who had been living there for centuries. What's more, Christopher Columbus was not the first European explorer to reach the Americas! Rather, it was Leif Erikson who first came to the New World and contacted the natives nearly 500 years before Christopher Columbus.

Leif Erikson, the son of Erik the Red (a famous Viking outlaw and explorer in his own right), was born in either 970 or 980, depending on which historian you read. In 999, Leif left Greenland and traveled to Norway, where he would serve as a guard to King Olaf Tryggvason. It was there that he became a convert to Christianity. Leif later tried to return home with the intention of taking supplies and spreading Christianity to Greenland, but his ship was blown off course and he arrived in a strange new land: present-day Newfoundland, Canada.

When he finally returned to his adopted homeland of Greenland, Leif consulted with a merchant who had also seen the shores of this previously unknown land. The son of the legendary Viking explorer then gathered a crew of 35 men and set sail. Leif became the first European to set foot in the New World as he explored present-day Baffin Island and Labrador, Canada. His crew

99

called the land Vinland since it was plentiful with grapes. This happened around 1000, nearly 500 years before Columbus famously sailed the ocean blue.

Eventually, in 1003, Leif set sail for home and arrived at Greenland with a ship full of timber. In 1020, 17 years later, the legendary Viking died. Many believe that Leif Erikson should receive more credit for his contributions in exploring the New World.

1. Which of the following best describes how the author generally presents the information?
    a. Chronological order
    b. Comparison-contrast
    c. Cause-effect
    d. Conclusion-premises

2. Which of the following is an opinion, rather than a historical fact, expressed by the author?
    a. Leif Erikson was definitely the son of Erik the Red; however, historians debate the year of his birth.
    b. Leif Erikson's crew called the land Vinland since it was plentiful with grapes.
    c. Leif Erikson deserves more credit for his contributions in exploring the New World.
    d. Leif Erikson explored the Americas nearly 500 years before Christopher Columbus.

3. Which of the following most accurately describes the author's main conclusion?
    a. Leif Erikson is a legendary Viking explorer.
    b. Leif Erikson deserves more credit for exploring America hundreds of years before Columbus.
    c. Spreading Christianity motivated Leif Erikson's expeditions more than any other factor.
    d. Leif Erikson contacted the natives nearly five hundred years before Columbus.

4. Which of the following best describes the author's intent in the passage?
    a. To entertain
    b. To inform
    c. To alert
    d. To suggest

5. Which of the following can be logically inferred from the passage?
    a. The Vikings disliked exploring the New World.
    b. Leif Erikson's banishment from Iceland led to his exploration of present-day Canada.
    c. Leif Erikson never shared his stories of exploration with the King of Norway.
    d. Historians have difficulty definitively pinpointing events in the Vikings' history.

Questions 6 – 10 are based on the following passage.

Smoking tobacco products is terribly destructive. A single cigarette contains over 4,000 chemicals, including 43 known carcinogens and 400 deadly toxins. Some of the most dangerous ingredients include tar, carbon monoxide, formaldehyde, ammonia, arsenic, and DDT. Smoking can cause numerous types of cancer, including throat, mouth, nasal cavity, esophageal, gastric, pancreatic, renal, bladder, and cervical cancer.

Cigarettes contain a drug called nicotine, one of the most addictive substances known. Addiction is defined as a compulsion to seek the substance despite negative consequences. According to the National Institute on Drug Abuse, nearly 35 million smokers expressed a desire to quit smoking in 2015; however, more than 85% of those who struggle with addiction will not achieve

their goal. Almost all smokers regret picking up that first cigarette. You would be wise to learn from their mistake if you have not yet started smoking.

According to the US Department of Health and Human Services, 16 million people in the United States presently suffer from a smoking-related condition, and nearly nine million suffer from a serious smoking-related illness. According to the Centers for Disease Control and Prevention (CDC), tobacco products cause nearly six million deaths per year. This number is projected to rise to over eight million deaths by 2030. Smokers, on average, die ten years earlier than their nonsmoking peers.

In the United States, local, state, and federal governments typically tax tobacco products, which leads to high prices. Nicotine users who struggle with addiction sometimes pay more for a pack of cigarettes than for a few gallons of gas. Additionally, smokers tend to stink. The smell of smoke is all-consuming and creates a pervasive nastiness. Smokers also risk staining their teeth and fingers with yellow residue from the tar.

Smoking is deadly, expensive, and socially unappealing. Clearly, smoking is not worth the risks.

6. Which of the following statements most accurately summarizes the passage?
   a. Tobacco is less healthy than many alternatives.
   b. Tobacco is deadly, expensive, and socially unappealing, and smokers would be much better off kicking the addiction.
   c. In the United States, local, state, and federal governments typically tax tobacco products, which leads to high prices.
   d. Tobacco products shorten smokers' lives by ten years and kill more than six million people per year.

7. The author would be most likely to agree with which of the following statements?
   a. Smokers should only quit "cold turkey" and avoid any devices that help stop using nicotine.
   b. Other substances are more addictive than tobacco.
   c. Smokers should quit for whatever reason that gets them to stop smoking.
   d. People who want to continue smoking should advocate for a reduction in tobacco product taxes.

8. Which of the following represents an opinion statement on the part of the author?
   a. According to the Centers for Disease Control and Prevention (CDC), tobacco products cause nearly six million deaths per year.
   b. Nicotine users who struggle with addiction sometimes pay more for a pack of cigarettes than for a few gallons of gas.
   c. Smokers also risk staining their teeth and fingers with yellow residue from the tar.
   d. Additionally, smokers tend to stink. The smell of smoke is all-consuming and creates a pervasive nastiness.

9. The primary purpose of this passage is:
   a. To tell a narrative story about smoking
   b. To describe the experience of smoking from the author's perspective
   c. To persuade readers not to smoke
   d. To give facts about smoking without taking sides on the issue

10. According to the passage, which of the following is likely to occur within the next decade?
    a. Smoking and tobacco products will be banned in the United States.
    b. Deaths from tobacco product use will increase by over two million people per year.
    c. Over 1,000 new chemicals will be added to current cigarette formulas.
    d. Most current smokers will stop smoking because it is not healthy for them.

Questions 11 – 15 are based on the following passage:

Children's literature holds a special place in many people's hearts. The stories that delight young readers can be imaginative and educational, and can help foster a love of reading in children. Stories speak to children in a way adults sometimes do not understand. However, everything is not all joy and happy endings in this genre. Many of the stories, tales, and books that are widely recognized within this category feature darker themes. Some of the stories typically associated with children, including fairy tales and fables, contain more serious issues such as child abandonment, violence, and death. Some of the earliest fairy tales come from the Brothers Grimm fairy tale collections. These stories in their original form are surprisingly gruesome. Stories such as *Hansel and Gretel*, *Little Red Riding Hood*, and *Cinderella* all contain elements that many people would consider too dark for children. These early stories often presented these disturbing images and elements in order to serve as a warning for children to induce good behavior.

More recent entries into children's literature, such as *Where the Wild Things Are* and *The Giving Tree*, are less shocking than some of the older tales but still touch on serious issues. When children read about characters in a story dealing with these types of issues, it can help them learn how to process some of the same emotions that occur in their own lives. Whether children are learning a lesson, processing emotions, or just enjoying a good story, reading literature can be an important part of their life's journey.

11. What is the primary topic of this passage?
    a. Children's literature cannot be enjoyed by adults.
    b. Children's literature is universally loved.
    c. Children's literature often contains serious themes.
    d. Children's literature should only have happy endings.

12. What is the meaning of the word *gruesome* in the first paragraph?
    a. Numb
    b. Peculiar
    c. Comfortable
    d. Horrible

13. What does the author mean to do by adding the following description?

These stories in their original form are surprisingly gruesome.

    a. The stories were originally written in another language.
    b. When the stories were first written, they were grimmer than later adaptations.
    c. The original stories have been translated into different formats.
    d. Adults, rather than children, were the intended audience for the early stories.

14. What is meant by the figurative language in the following statement?

Stories speak to children in a way adults sometimes do not understand.

    a. Adults do not care for children's stories.
    b. Children derive meaning from stories that adults do not.
    c. Children's stories should always be read aloud to better understand the story.
    d. Children's lack of life experiences causes them to sometimes misinterpret stories.

15. What type of writing is being used in this passage?
    a. Persuasive
    b. Expository
    c. Descriptive
    d. Narrative

Questions 16 – 20 are based on the following passage.

There are many inventions that we use in our daily lives that we take for granted. One major example is the telephone. We have the ability to communicate with anyone around the world at any time. This is a relatively new phenomenon. The telephone has made significant progress over the years. The first telephone ever invented is very different from the modern cellphone that we are used to.

There is much controversy in the discussion about who invented the telephone. Most people would say it was Alexander Graham Bell in 1876. Although Bell can be credited with the first patented telephone, Johann Phillip Reis created his own version of the telephone in 1861 and even coined the term *telephon*. Thomas Edison credited Reis as the inventor of the telephone. There are other notable people who worked on the development of the telephone, such as Elisha Gray and Antonio Meucci. However, from the perspective of numerous institutions such as Canadian Parliament, Bell is officially known as the inventor.

In the beginning of the telephone's history, it was not widely used by the public. The Stock Exchange, railway stations, government buildings, and some of the larger corporations all used telephones for their business. These telephones were connected directly by wires. You would first speak with a telephone operator before connecting with the person you wished to speak with. As technology advanced, telephones became commonplace in people's homes, and operators were no longer needed. Around the 1970s, these wildly popular phones were attached to the wall and were known as rotary phones. Slowly, the telephone became more and more mobile.

The cellular telephone or cellphone was developed in the 1980s. These phones could be used anywhere. They were very large and heavy, so they were not practical at first. It took around 20 years for the cellphone to become pocket-sized, but once it was it became a huge hit. People were riveted with the idea of talking to their friends and family on the go. New features such as a camera, text messaging, and games were added. The cellphone had taken the idea of the telephone and morphed it into so much more.

In the 2010s, the cellphone advanced into the smartphone. The smartphone can do tasks that were never thought possible for the original telephone. It can connect to the internet, take high-resolution videos, give directions via GPS, and more. Whenever you use your smartphone, try to

103

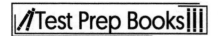

remember the decades of hard work and innovation that went into making it. And when you think of the future, try to imagine all of the ways that the smartphone can evolve next!

16. What point of view is this passage written in?
   a. First person
   b. Second person
   c. Third person
   d. Fourth person

17. Based on the information provided in this passage, what did Alexander Graham Bell do that the other inventors did not?
   a. He obtained a patent for the telephone.
   b. He sabotaged the other inventors so that he would be recognized first.
   c. He paid more for the patent than other inventors.
   d. He worked harder than the other inventors.

18. Which of the following types of telephone was created in the 1980s?
   a. Smartphone
   b. Cellular telephone
   c. Rotary telephone
   d. Touch-tone telephone

19. What does the word *riveted* in this passage most nearly mean?
   a. Uninterested
   b. Captivated
   c. Sympathetic
   d. Overjoyed

20. Which form of technology has undergone the most similar history of advancement to the telephone?
   a. Blender
   b. Radio
   c. Television
   d. Microwave

Questions 21 – 25 are based on the following passage.

There are many different types of penguins. Taxonomists (a type of biologist that categorizes species of animals) believe that there are anywhere from 16 to 22 different species of penguins. These species live in many different parts of the world. Not all penguins live in cold climates! However, it is true that all penguins are aquatic and flightless.

The emperor penguin is the species that most people imagine in their mind when penguins are mentioned. They are the largest penguin species in the world, standing up to 48 inches tall. They can weigh anywhere from 50 to 100 pounds. Emperor penguins live in Antarctica in large colonies of up to 10,000 penguins! They eat a diet of fish and crustaceans. Emperor penguins live for about 15 to 20 years in the wild.

African penguins live in South Africa and Namibia. They are small penguins standing at 24 to 28 inches tall and weighing up to 8 pounds. They are known for having pink skin above their eyes.

104

They feed on fish, shrimp, and squid. They are hunted by hostile sharks and seals. Their lifespan is anywhere from 10 to 25 years.

Little blue fairy penguins live on the coasts of New Zealand. Their scientific name is *Eudyptula*, which means "good little diver." They hunt for their food in the shallow waters when it is dark outside. Little blue fairy penguins enjoy a diet of small fish like anchovies and sardines. They are known for having blue feathers and eyes. They are also known as the smallest penguins in the world at around 12 inches tall and weighing under 4 pounds. They live about 6.5 years on average.

Macaroni penguins are unique penguins that live on a number of different islands that span from South America to Antarctica. At an estimated population of 24 million, macaroni penguins are the most populous species of penguin. They are known for having bright yellow feathers on their head. They are 28 inches tall on average and weigh anywhere from 7 to 14 pounds. A fun fact is that their name comes from a fashion term from the 18th century rather than the macaroni noodle. Macaroni penguins eat krill, fish, and crustaceans. They live for about 8 to 15 years.

21. What is the purpose of this passage?
    a. To persuade readers to donate to penguin conservation
    b. To educate readers about a few different species of penguins
    c. To compare penguins to decide which is the best species
    d. To question why penguins live in different regions of the world

22. What information is provided about macaroni penguins?
    a. Predators
    b. Conservation status
    c. Scientific name
    d. Geographic location

23. What is the main difference between the emperor penguin and the little blue fairy penguin?
    a. Colony size
    b. Feather color
    c. Size
    d. Diet

24. What does the word *hostile* in this passage most nearly mean?
    a. Friendly
    b. Aggressive
    c. Fast
    d. Fearful

25. Which of the following statements is true?
    a. Macaroni penguins are named after the macaroni and cheese dish.
    b. Little blue fairy penguins have the longest lifespans out of the species mentioned in this passage.
    c. African penguins are known for their bright yellow feathers.
    d. Emperor penguins are the largest species of penguins.

Mathematics Achievement

1. Which of the following whole numbers is NOT a multiple of 8?
   a. 80
   b. 2
   c. 32
   d. 48

2. Find the value of the following: $233 + 592$.
   a. 725
   b. 835
   c. 815
   d. 825

3. Find the value of $2 + 8 \times 3 - 4 \div 2$.
   a. 13
   b. 24
   c. 26
   d. 18

4. Calculate the remainder in the following division problem: $603 \div 5$.
   a. 0.6
   b. 5
   c. 3
   d. 120

5. Calculate the equivalent to the expression $5(9 - 4)$.
   a. $45 - 20$
   b. $45 + 20$
   c. $5(-5)$
   d. $14 + 1$

6. Which of the following is between $\frac{1}{3}$ and $\frac{2}{5}$?
   a. $\frac{1}{4}$
   b. $\frac{2}{3}$
   c. $\frac{3}{8}$
   d. $\frac{1}{2}$

7. Find the sum of 5.67 and 2.3.
   a. 7.97
   b. 7.7
   c. 8.97
   d. 8.7

8. Round 5.99739 to the nearest hundredth place.
   a. 5.997
   b. 5.9974
   c. 6
   d. 5.9

9. Which of the following fractions is equivalent to 0.75?
   a. $\frac{1}{75}$

   b. $\frac{3}{25}$

   c. $\frac{75}{2}$

   d. $\frac{3}{4}$

10. Multiply the following: $7 \times \frac{2}{11}$.
    a. $\frac{9}{11}$

    b. $\frac{14}{11}$

    c. $\frac{2}{77}$

    d. $\frac{1}{9}$

11. Katie has 64 boxes of cookies, and each box contains 10 cookies. Let x represent the total number of cookies. Which of the following equations represents the total number of cookies?
    a. $64 = 10 \times x$
    b. $64 \times 10 = x$
    c. $64 + 10 = x$
    d. $\frac{64}{10} = x$

12. Consider the equation $4(5 \times \blacksquare) + 40 = 100$. What does $\blacksquare$ represent?
    a. 1
    b. 2
    c. 3
    d. 4

13. Let y equal the total number of lemonade drinks sold last Saturday. This Sunday they plan on selling 8 more than double the amount sold last Saturday. Which of the following expressions represents the amount they plan on selling this week?
    a. $2y + 8$
    b. $2 + y + 8$
    c. $2y - 8$
    d. $8y + 2$

14. Factor the following completely: $14x + 18$.
   a. $14(x + 4)$
   b. $2(7x + 18)$
   c. $2(7x + 9)$
   d. $7(2x + 9)$

15. Evaluate the following expression for $x = -2$: $-5x - 4$.
   a. -14
   b. -6
   c. -4
   d. 6

16. What is the point shown below on the coordinate grid?

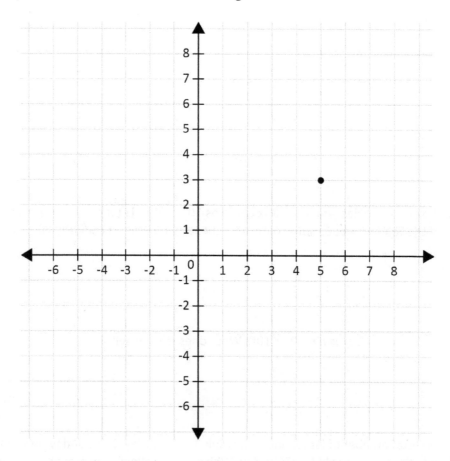

   a. (5,3)
   b. (3,5)
   c. (5,4)
   d. (5,5)

17. What kind of polygon has four straight sides and four right angles?
   a. Hexagon
   b. Quadrilateral
   c. Pentagon
   d. Octagon

108

18. Given that the following triangles are congruent, what is the measure of angle B?

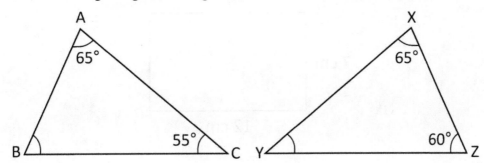

a. 90°
b. 65°
c. 60°
d. 55°

19. What quadrant does the point (-4, -4) lie in on the coordinate plane?
    a. Quadrant I
    b. Quadrant II
    c. Quadrant III
    d. Quadrant IV

20. How many lines of symmetry does a square have?
    a. 1
    b. 2
    c. 3
    d. 4

21. Matthew is 6.25 feet tall. How many inches tall is Matthew? Use the conversion that 1 foot is equal to 12 inches.
    a. 75
    b. 72.25
    c. 72
    d. 75.25

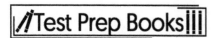

22. What is the area of the following rectangle?

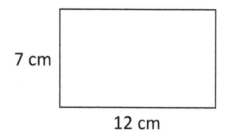

7 cm

12 cm

a. 19 cm
b. 84 cm
c. 84 cm^2
d. 19 cm^2

23. What is the perimeter of the following figure?

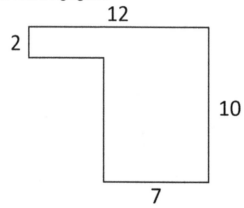

12

2

10

7

a. 31 units
b. 26 units
c. 42 units
d. 44 units

24. Find the area of the following triangle, given that the area of a triangle is $\frac{1}{2} \times$ base $\times$ height.

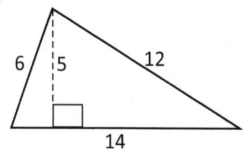

6   5   12

14

a. 32
b. 19
c. 30
d. 35

110

25. What is the perimeter of the following rectangle, given that $P = 2L + 2W$.

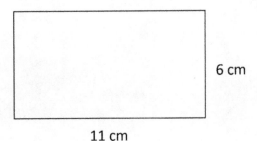

6 cm

11 cm

    a. 66 cm^2
    b. 17 cm
    c. 132 cm^2
    d. 34 cm

26. What is the mode of the following data set: {13, 14, 15, 13, 19, 20, 18, 14, 13}.
    a. 13
    b. 14
    c. 15.4
    d. 15

27. Find the mean of the following data set: {13, 14, 15, 13, 19, 20, 18, 14, 13}. Round your answer to the nearest tenth.
    a. 13.0
    b. 17.4
    c. 15.4
    d. 15.1

28. What is the probability of rolling a 3 on a six-sided die?
    a. $\frac{1}{2}$

    b. $\frac{1}{3}$

    c. $\frac{1}{6}$

    d. 1

29. In an elementary school classroom there are 6 left-handed students and 19 right-handed students. What is the probability that a student is left-handed if they are randomly selected from the entire class?
    a. $\frac{19}{25}$

    b. $\frac{6}{25}$

    c. $\frac{6}{19}$

    d. $\frac{19}{25}$

30. Find the range of the following data set: {15, 19, 13, 20, 25, 11, 24}.
    a. 9
    b. 13
    c. 10
    d. 14

Answer Explanations #1

Verbal Reasoning

1. C: An orchard is most like a grove. Both are areas like plantations that grow different kinds of fruit. Peach is a type of fruit that may be grown in an orchard. However, *peach* is not a synonym for orchard. Many citrus fruits are grown in groves. But either word can be used to describe many fruit-bearing trees in one area. Choice *A, farm,* may have an orchard or grove on the property. However, they are not the same thing, and many farms do not grow fruit trees.

2. D: *Permit* can be a verb or a noun. As a verb, it means to allow or give permission for something. As a noun, it refers to a document or something that has been authorized like a parking permit or driving permit. This would allow the authorized person to park or drive under the rules of the document.

3. B: To demonstrate something means to show it. A demonstration is a show-and-tell type of example. It is usually visual.

4. C: To abandon something is most like leaving it. Finding or replacing something is unrelated to abandoning it and *destroy* is a more active and destructive word than *abandon.*

5. A: A textile is another word for a fabric. The most confusing choice in this case is Choice *B, knit.* This is because some textiles are knit, but *textile* and *knit* are not synonyms. Plenty of textiles are not knit.

6. D: Offspring are the kids of parents. This word is common when talking about the animal kingdom, though it can be used with humans as well. *Offspring* does have the word *spring* in it. But it has nothing to do with *bounce,* Choice *A.* Choice *B, parent,* may be tricky because parents have offspring, but they are not synonyms.

7. A: If someone is inspired, they are motivated to do something. Someone who is an inspiration motivates others to follow their lead.

8. B: A woman is a lady. You must read carefully and remember the difference between *woman* and *women. Woman* refers to one person who is female. *Women* is the plural form and refers to more than one, or a group of ladies. A woman can be a mother, but not necessarily. *Woman* and *mother* are not synonyms.

9. A: Something that is consistent is steady, predictable, reliable, or constant. The tricky one here is that the word *consistency* comes from the word *consistent. Consistency* may describe a texture or something that is sticky, Choices *C* and *D. Consistent* also comes from the word *consist.* Consist means to contain, Choice *B.*

10. D: A principle is a guiding idea or belief. Someone with good moral character is described as having strong principles. You must be careful not to get confused with the homonyms *principle* and *principal,* Choice *A.* These two words have different meanings. A principal is the leader of a school. The word principal also refers to the main idea or most important thing.

11. D: A symbol is an object, picture, or sign that is used to represent something. For example, a pink ribbon is a symbol for breast cancer awareness. A flag can be a symbol for a country. The tricky part of

113

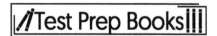

this question was also knowing the meaning of *emblem*. An *emblem* is a design that represents a group or concept, much like a symbol. Emblems often appear on flags or a coat of arms.

12. B: The word *oppressed* means being exploited or helpless, Choice *B*. Choice *A*, acclaimed, means being praised. To be beloved, Choice *C*, means to be cherished and adored. To be pressured, Choice *D*, means to be pushed into doing something, in some contexts.

13. A: The word *triumph* most closely means victory, Choice *A*. *Burial*, Choice *B*, is the act of burying someone or something. *Animosity*, Choice *C*, means strong dislike or hatred, and is very different from the word *triumph*. Choice *D*, *banter*, is the act of teasing.

14. B: *Bland* is an adjective that can mean lacking in strong, defining characteristics, and as a result uninteresting. *Complex, novel*, and *superior* are all adjectives that themselves refer to strong or defining characteristics—by describing something as *complex, novel,* or *superior*, one is describing something as being, in one way or another, interesting. *Dull*, on the other hand, is an adjective that can be defined as lacking interest or excitement, and it is therefore synonymous with the word *bland*.

15. C: *Spectator* is a noun that means a person who looks on, or watches. *Assistant, guardian*, and *participant* are all nouns describing people involved in a certain process or action—the act of assisting, guarding, or participating—rather than someone who is just watching something occur. *Observer* is a noun meaning an individual who observes, and the verb phrases *watches* or *looks on* and *observes* are synonyms. Therefore, *observer* is a synonymous term with *spectator*.

16. A: *Pamphlet* is a noun that refers to any small booklet that contains information or arguments about a single subject. The noun *letter* can refer to any written communication, but a letter generally refers to a private communication, whereas a *pamphlet* is usually used to spread information publicly. While a *newspaper* and a *pamphlet* both represent public means of written communication, a *pamphlet* is generally smaller than a newspaper, and is usually more focused on a single topic. A *tome*, which is a noun referring to a large, scholarly book, is much more massive in physical size and scope than a *pamphlet*. A *brochure*, which is a noun defined as a small book containing information about a product or service, is functionally the same as a *pamphlet*, and the two words are synonymous.

17. C: *Enchant* is a verb that can be defined as either to subject to magical influence or to fill one with delight. The verb *complicate*, which can be defined as to make difficult, has no connection to the idea of magic and is clearly unrelated to the concept of delight. *Inform* is a verb that simply means to give or impart knowledge and *suffice* is a verb that simply means to be adequate or enough. Therefore, neither are related to the ideas of delight or magical influence. *Mesmerize* is a verb that means either to hypnotize or to fascinate, and therefore is closely synonymous with *enchant*.

18. C: Jackson wanted to relieve his *parched* throat. *Parched* is the correct answer because it means *thirsty*. Choice *A*, *humid*, means moist, and usually refers to the weather. Choice *B*, *scorched*, means blackened or baked, and doesn't fit in this context. While Jackson's throat could have been dusty, Choice *D*, from playing baseball, one usually doesn't need to relieve a dusty throat, but instead clean it.

19. C: Usually when someone is afraid or nervous, their hands start to shake. Choice *A*, *dancing*, does not make sense in the context of the sentence. Choice *B*, *glowing*, is incorrect; hands usually do not glow when one is afraid of something. Choice *D*, *throbbing*, is closer than *A* or *B*, but Choice *C*, *shaking*, is a better answer than *throbbing*.

114

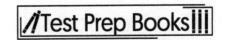

20. A: Choice *B* is incorrect; runners who begin a race usually don't skip toward the finish line. Choice *C* does not fit within the context of the sentence, as normally runners would be *sprinting* and not *rejoicing* toward a finish line. Choice *D*, *herded*, means to gather around something; usually *herded* is used for animals and not for runners.

21. D: When people go to the bank with a check, they usually don't celebrate it, Choice *A*, but do something more practical with it, like deposit it. Choice *B*, *neutralize*, means to counteract something, and is incorrect in this sentence. Choice *C, eliminate*, means to get rid of something, and is also incorrect here.

22. B: The word *inspired* means encouraged or stimulated. Sales are usually seen as a positive experience, so the sale *inspired* the dad to buy more avocados. The rest of the words (*intimidated*, *dismayed*, and *berated*) have negative connotations and therefore do not fit within the context of the sentence.

23. C: Choice *A*, *acclaim*, is an expression of approval, and is not the right fit here. Choice *B*, *astound*, means to amaze. Usually we don't hear of people "amazing" other people's parties. This is not the best choice. Choice *D*, *amend*, means to improve or correct. Again, this is not the best choice for the context; the speaker is wondering what gift to bring Lindsay and is not thinking about ways to correct the party.

24. A: Choice *B*, *offended*, is the wrong choice here. You can offend a person because they have emotions, but you cannot offend a fire alarm. Choice *C*, *unplugged*, is also incorrect. You cannot unplug a fire alarm by burning a casserole. Choice *D*, *disbanded*, is the opposite of *activated* and is incorrect in this context.

25. D: Choice *A*, *refreshing*, is not an adjective used to describe a dentist's office, especially when the patient is about to take care of a cavity. Choice *B*, *creative*, also does not fit within the context of the sentence. Choice *C*, *rapturous*, means ecstatic or happy, and is the opposite sentiment of what we are looking for.

26. B: *Obedient* means well-behaved. The dog hasn't learned to heed commands yet, so he is not obedient. *Peaceful* and *reserved* are related to good behavior, but *obedient* is a better choice to complete the sentence. *Impudent* means bold which does not fit with the rest of the sentence.

27. D: Choices *A* and *C*, *exploded* and *thundered*, are too extreme for the context. *Deteriorated*, Choice *B*, means to have crumbled or disintegrated, which is not something an eel's body is likely to do on its own. Choice *D* is the best answer for this sentence, as eels and similar creatures like snakes are known to slither.

28. A: *Directed*, Choice *B*, means to supervise or conduct, and does not make sense in the context of the sentence. Choice *C*, *mourned*, means to grieve over, and is also incorrect. Choice *D*, *endorsed*, means to approve or support something. Pay attention to words like *even though* that suggest a contrast of surprising facts.

29. D: The word *unlike* tells us that Gabriel would do the opposite of what Leo would do at the time. Choices *A* and *B* talk about different times, in the morning and at lunch, so they are not the best answer choices here. Choice *C* is exactly the same as what Leo would do, so Choice *D* is the correct choice.

30. D: Choices *A, B,* and *C* all reference activities that don't have anything to do with writing a paper. If her paper was about any one of these things, like going to the gym or teaching someone to read, then

115

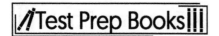

perhaps these would be decent answers. However, we are not given enough information to know what the topic of the paper is. Therefore, Choice *D* is the correct answer.

31. A: Becoming healthier is a direct effect of consuming fruits and vegetables, so Choice *A* is the best answer choice here. Becoming healthier might lead to Choices *B*, *C*, and *D*, but these are not the best answers for this question.

32. A: Since Thomas put on a safety harness prior to beginning whatever he did, it is only logical that the action he went on to do required the use of a harness in one way or another. Out of the answer choices, only *climb the rock wall* describes an action that generally requires a safety harness. The other answer choices are all regular life events that do not place the subject in harm's way and therefore need no special safety equipment to be performed.

33. C: The preposition *despite* indicates that the course of action Diego took was contrary to how the others in the gym class expected him to behave. Additionally, if Diego was picked last, it makes sense that the general consensus in the class was that Diego would not be good at dodgeball. Therefore, the correct answer choice is *eliminating all of the members of the other team*, as no other answer choice contradicts his classmates' opinions of him.

34. D: Since the observation of how small the inside of a lunar module was caused Jason to understand whatever he did, it makes logical sense that what he understood has to be related to the size of the lunar module. The only answer choice that then makes sense is *only a few astronauts could travel to the Moon on any single mission*, as no other answer choice would be dependent on the size of the lunar module.

Quantitative Reasoning

1. B: A prime number is a number whose only factors are itself and 1, but only numbers greater than 1 can be considered prime.

2. A: Order of operations follows PEMDAS: Parentheses, Exponents, Multiplication and Division from left to right, and Addition and Subtraction from left to right.

3. B: A rectangle is a specific type of parallelogram. It has 4 right angles. A square is a rhombus that has 4 right angles. Therefore, a square is always a rectangle because it has two sets of parallel lines and 4 right angles.

4. A: A common denominator must be found. The least common denominator is 15 because it has both 5 and 3 as factors. The fractions must be rewritten using 15 as the denominator.

5. B: The perimeter of a rectangle is the sum of all four sides. Therefore, the answer is:

$$P = 14 + 8\frac{1}{2} + 14 + 8\frac{1}{2}$$

6. C: Variants of "gram" (including kilograms) and variants of "meter" (including kilometers, centimeters, and millimeters) belong to the metric system. The other units listed above are not part of the metric system.

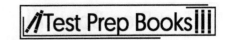

7. C: A compass is a tool that can be used to draw a circle. The compass would be drawn by using the length of the radius, which is half of the diameter.

8. D: The expanded or decomposed form represents the sum of each place value of a number. The numbers are added back together to find the standard form of the number.

9. C: The method used to convert a fraction to a decimal is to divide the numerator by the denominator.

10. D: Three girls for every two boys can be expressed as a ratio: $3:2$. This can be visualized as splitting the school into five groups: three girl groups and two boy groups. The number of students that are in each group can be found by dividing the total number of students by five:

$$\frac{650 \text{ students}}{5 \text{ groups}} = \frac{130 \text{ students}}{\text{group}}$$

To find the total number of girls, multiply the number of students per group (130) by the number of girl groups in the school (3). This equals 390, Choice *D*.

11. C: Phrases such as *divided by*, *quotient of*, or *half of* can all be used to indicate the use of the division symbol in a mathematical expression. More than typically indicates the addition symbol. The multiplication symbol is represented by the phrase product of. Results in is another way to say equal to and is shown by the equal sign.

12. A: The sequence presented is a geometric sequence where each step is multiplied by 3 to get the next subsequent step. $27 \times 3 = 81$, so the correct answer is 81.

13. B: The correct formula for calculating the area of a triangle is $A = \frac{1}{2} \times b \times h$, where A is equal to area, b is equal to base, and h is equal to height. Therefore, the two measurements needed to calculate the area of a triangle are base and height.

14. C: A line does connect two points, but it extends indefinitely in both directions. If the line does end at the two points, then it is a line segment. A line also has no thickness.

15. D: An angle measuring less than 90 degrees is called an acute angle. An angle measuring more than 90 degrees is an obtuse angle. A right angle is an angle that measures 90 degrees. A complementary angle is one of two angles which when added together equal 90 degrees.

16. D: The most appropriate unit to use when measuring the size of a book is inches. This is based on the knowledge of the approximate size of most books and knowing the approximate size of the unit of measurement. Both yards and feet are too large for most books, while millimeters are too small.

17. B: The US customary units of measurement for volume of liquids from largest to smallest are gallon, quart, pint, cup, and fluid ounces.

18. A: Morgan will need to do 22 more minutes of exercise to reach his goal of 3 hours for the week. The information given in hours must be converted to minutes, and then the following equation can be used to find the solution.

$$\left(3 \text{ hours} \times \frac{60 \text{ minutes}}{1 \text{ hour}}\right) - 35 \text{ minutes} - 22 \text{ minutes} - 41 \text{ minutes} - \left(1 \text{ hour} \times \frac{60 \text{ minutes}}{1 \text{ hour}}\right)$$

19. C: The median in a data set is the data point found in the middle of the set when arranged in numerical order from least to greatest. The mean is the average of a data set. The mode is the value that occurs the most in a data set. Range refers to the spread of values in a data set.

20. C: The mode of a data set is 46 because it appears most often. In this data set, there are three 46s which is more than any other value. 18 and 25 both appear only twice in the sample. 33 is the median of the data set.

21. A: The correlation between the two variables in this scatter plot is positive because the line of best fit that can be drawn would have a positive slope. If the correlation was negative, the line of best fit would have a negative slope. Independent refers to the variables on the x-axis and does not address correlation. If the data points were not in a linear formation, and no line of best fit could be drawn, there would be no correlation.

22. D: In this bar graph, 5 children prefer brownies and cake. The children columns for brownies and cake have heights of 3 and 2, respectively. Added together that makes a total of 5 children.

23. D: A cube is a three-dimensional solid shape. Two-dimensional shapes are flat like circles, triangles, hexagons, squares, and other similar shapes.

24. A: Trevor bought 2 boxes of pens. If he bought 3 notebooks, 2 packages of paper, and 1 pencil sharpener, then he spent $8.25, $3, and $3 on those items respectively. The total of those items then is $14.25. The difference between the total of those items and the total spent of $18.25 is $4. Therefore, he bought 2 boxes of pens at $2 apiece for $4.

25. C: The correct order of operations is PEMDAS, or Parentheses, Exponents, Multiply and Divide, and finally, Add and Subtract. According to PEMDAS, the parentheses calculation should come first, followed by multiplication and division, and then addition and subtraction. There are no exponents. Working through PEMDAS, the parentheses should be calculated first, making 2(4) equals 8. Then the equation is $125 \div 5 + 17 - 3 \times 8$. Again, working through PEMDAS, the next thing to do is to start at the beginning of the equation and complete any multiplication or division: $125 \div 5 = 25$. Now we have $25 + 17 - 3 \times 8$. There is still multiplication: $3 \times 8 = 24$. Now our equation is $25 + 17 - 24$. The last step of PEMDAS is addition and subtraction. Working in order, $25 + 17 = 42$ and $42 - 24 = 18$. So, the solution to the equation is 18. Choice *A* goes through the equation in order rather than following PEMDAS. Choice *B* goes through the equation completing the addition and subtraction first, and Choice *D* mistakes the subtraction for addition.

26. D: Of the 300 students, some bring their lunches, and some go home to eat. Subtracting those students, there are 219 students left who buy their lunches at school. Choice *A* counts all 300 students as needing lunch each day, but many students either bring their lunches or go home for lunch. Choice *B* calculates the number of students needing milk rather than those needing to buy lunches. Choice C subtracts the number of students who trade food every day, which is an irrelevant number for this problem.

27. D: Two dozen means each player has to make 24 cookies or brownies; 13 players times 24 equals 312 cookies and brownies for the bake sale. Choice *A* multiplies by 2 rather than by two dozen. Choice *B* multiplies by one dozen rather than two, and Choice *C* multiplies by two dozen cookies AND two dozen brownies, which would be a lot of treats.

28. A: A gallon of milk rounds up to $4 per gallon, so 2 gallons would be $8. The oranges are $6 per dozen, but her mother is only buying half a dozen, which would be $3. Rounding the apples up to $2 per pound means that 2 pounds would be approximately $4. The cost of the cereal rounds down to $4, and the cost of the bread rounds up to $3. If we add the numbers together, we get $8 + $3 + $4 + $4 + $3, which equals $22. The answer for Choice *B* forgets that Mom bought 2 gallons of milk, and Choice *C* counted a full dozen of oranges rather than half a dozen. Choice *D* rounded the cereal up rather than down to the nearest dollar.

29. B: The anime trading cards plus the box of sidewalk chalk totals $9.94. Choice *A*, the trading cards plus two candy bars, adds up to $8.87. Choice *C*, the baseball plus two candy bars, is too expensive at $11.17. Choice *D*, the sidewalk chalk plus the baseball, is too much at $12.24.

30. B: The rule that is applied here is to add 14 to every "In" number. The first "In" number is 2, and the "Out" number is 16. Going through the other numbers, you can see that this same rule is applied to every number. Choice *A* works on the first set of numbers but not the others. Choice *C* works on the third set of numbers, but again, not on all of them, and although some of the numbers are prime, Choice *D*, many of them are not.

31. D: The rule for this machine is plus 8. The first number on the "In" side is 3. If we add 8, we get 11. The second "In" number is 5. $5 + 8 = 13$, so $x = 13$. We can work backward to solve for the "In" numbers. To solve for *y*, take the "Out" number and subtract 8, so $y = 10$. $25 - 8 = 17$, so $z = 17$. You can check your work by putting the numbers for *y* and *z* "In" to the machine: $10 + 8 = 18$, and $17 + 8 = 25$. Choice *A* found a solution for the first set of numbers, adding 8, but that does not work for the rest of the numbers. Choice *B* found a rule that applies to the last set of numbers and applied that to the missing numbers, but the plus 9 rule does not work for all of the number pairs. Choice *D* applied the rule to the first set of numbers but then used the results of the rule ($10 - 2 = 8$) as the answer for all three missing numbers.

32. A: Collinear points are points that are all on the same line. Beth, Charlotte, and Daniel all live on the straight line that is May Street. Albert and Joseph also live in collinear points, but Daniel's house is not collinear with theirs, Choice *B*. The same is true of Beth, Charlotte, and Amy, Choice *C*. Albert, Amy, and Daniel, Choice *D*, all live on different streets and therefore on three different lines.

33. C: A line has no ending points, as shown by the arrows at each end. A line segment has ending points on both ends, which is what Jackson and Micaela, Choice *A*, picked. Toby, Choice *B*, picked the rays, which are lines with one end point. Marigold, Choice *D*, also picked a ray.

34. B: Marietta wants a hat shaped like a cone. A cone is a 3-dimensional figure that looks like a circle with a triangle on top of it. A sphere, Choice *A*, is a shape such as a ball. Choices *C* and *D* are both 2-dimensional, flat shapes.

35. C: Area is measured by multiplying the length times the width: $20 \times 15 = 300$ sq. ft. Choice *A* is the area for the whole backyard rather than just the area of the garden space, and Choice *B* adds the measurements for the whole backyard instead of multiplying. Choice *D* uses the correct measurements but adds them instead of multiplying them.

36. A: To find the perimeter of a space, add the length of each side: $18 + 18 + 18 + 18 = 72$ ft. Choice *B* multiplied the length times the width, which would give the area of the garden rather than the

119

perimeter. Choice *C* added the length and width of two sides but did not account for fencing on all four sides of the space. Choice *D* added three sides instead of all four.

37. A: The graph shows that Jill completed 9 problems, which is the most of the four friends. Alex, Choice *D*, completed the next highest number of problems, followed by Jayden, Choice *C*. Kai, Choice *B*, had the lowest number at 3.

38. C: The Eagles and the Tigers had the two highest scores (98 and 94), so they will compete in the championship game. Choice *A* shows the two teams with the lowest scores. Although Choice *B* does show the Eagles, who had the highest score, the Chargers had the lowest score and will not be in the game. Choice *D* shows the two teams that scored in the middle of the four teams.

Reading Comprehension

1. D: The passage does not proceed in chronological order since it begins by pointing out Christopher Columbus's explorations in America, so Choice *A* does not work. Although the author compares and contrasts Erikson with Columbus, this is not the main way the information is presented; therefore, Choice B does not work. Choice C is also incorrect because there is no mention of or reference to cause and effect in the passage. However, the passage does offer a conclusion (Leif Erikson deserves more credit) and premises (first European to set foot in the New World and first to contact the natives) to substantiate Erikson's historical importance. Thus, Choice *D* is correct.

2. C: Choice *A* is wrong because it describes facts: Leif Erikson was the son of Erik the Red and historians debate Leif's date of birth. These are not opinions. Choice *B* is wrong; Erikson calling the land Vinland is a verifiable fact, as is Choice *D*, because he did contact the natives almost 500 years before Columbus. Choice *C* is the correct answer because it is the author's opinion that Erikson deserves more credit. Another person could argue that Columbus or another explorer deserves more credit, which makes it an opinion rather than a historical fact.

3. B: Choice *A* is wrong because the author aims to go beyond describing Erikson as merely a legendary Viking. Choice *C* is wrong because the author does not focus on Erikson's motivations, let alone name the spreading of Christianity as his primary objective. Although it's true that Erikson contacted the natives 500 years before Columbus, Choice *D* is wrong because it isn't the author's main conclusion, it is simply a fact used to support the main conclusion. Choice *B* is correct because it accurately identifies the author's statement that Erikson deserves more credit than he has received for being the first European to explore the New World.

4. B: Although the author is telling the readers of Leif Erikson's unheralded accomplishments, the word alert, Choice *C*, carries a sense of urgency or warning that is not found in this passage. Rather, the author would want the reader to be informed about it, which is more substantial and academic, Choice *B*.

5. D: Choice *A* is wrong because the author never addresses the Vikings' state of mind or emotions. Choice *B* is wrong because the author does not elaborate on Erikson's exile and whether he would have become an explorer if not for his banishment. Choice *C* is wrong because there is not enough information to support this premise. It is unclear whether Erikson informed the King of Norway of his findings. Although it is true that the king did not send a follow-up expedition, he could have simply chosen not to expend the resources after receiving Erikson's news. It is not possible to logically infer

120

whether Erikson told him. Choice *D* is correct because the uncertainty about Leif Erikson's birth year is an example of how historians have trouble pinning down important details in Viking history.

6. B: The author is opposed to tobacco. The author cites disease and deaths associated with smoking, and points to the monetary expense and aesthetic costs. Choice *A* is incorrect because alternatives to smoking are not addressed in the passage. Choice *C* is incorrect because it does not summarize the passage but rather is just a detail. Choice *D* is incorrect because, while these statistics are a premise in the argument, they do not represent a summary of the piece. Choice *B* is the correct answer because it states the three critiques offered against tobacco and expresses the author's conclusion.

7. C: We are looking for something the author would agree with, so it should be anti-smoking or an argument in favor of quitting smoking. Choice *A* is incorrect because the author does not speak against means of cessation. Choice *B* is incorrect because the author does not reference other substances but does speak of how addictive nicotine, a drug in tobacco, is. Choice *D* is incorrect because the author would not encourage reducing taxes to encourage a reduction of smoking costs, thereby helping smokers to continue the habit. Choice *C* is correct because the author is attempting to persuade smokers to quit smoking.

8. D: Here, we are looking for the author's opinion rather than a fact or statistic. Choice *A* is incorrect because quoting statistics from the CDC is stating facts, not opinions. Choice *B* is incorrect because it expresses the fact that cigarettes sometimes cost more than a few gallons of gas. It would be an opinion if the author said that cigarettes were not affordable. Choice *C* is incorrect because yellow stains are a known possible adverse effect of smoking. Choice *D* is correct as an opinion because smell is subjective. Some people might like the smell of smoke rather than considering it "a pervasive nastiness," so this is the expression of an opinion.

9. C: The author of this passage is clearly attempting to warn readers away from smoking. Each paragraph presents evidence of this, and the author directly tells the reader that "smoking is not worth the risks." Choice *A* is incorrect because the essay does not tell a story. Choice *B* is incorrect because the author is not providing a description of the act of smoking based on their own experiences. Choice *D* is incorrect because the essay clearly takes sides on the issue of smoking.

10. B: In the third paragraph, the passage states, "According to the Centers for Disease Control and Prevention (CDC), tobacco products cause nearly six million deaths per year. This number is projected to rise to over eight million deaths by 2030." If the number of deaths is currently less than six million and will rise to over eight million, that suggests that deaths from tobacco use will increase by over two million per year within the next decade. Choices *A*, *C*, and *D* are incorrect because they were not mentioned in the passage.

11. C: The primary topic of this passage is the use of serious themes in children's literature. The passage does not state that it is only to be enjoyed by children. The passage does say that children's literature holds a special place in many people's hearts; it does not say that it is universally loved by everyone. Happy endings are mentioned, but only in passing to prove a larger point.

12. D: The word *gruesome* means horrible and grim. In the passage, this word is used to describe stories that contain violence and death. The words numb, peculiar, and comfortable would not be as fitting to describe such stories.

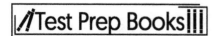

13. B: The original stories were darker and more grim than recent adaptations. The passage does not discuss the stories being translated from other languages or formats. While the themes from the original stories were more mature, there is no suggestion that they were intended for adults.

14. B: This statement is an example of figurative language called personification, where a thing or an animal has human characteristics. In this example, the stories speak to the children. The passage discusses how children interpret stories, so the correct answer is Choice *B*.

15. B: This passage primarily gives information about children's literature. It is not attempting to convince the reader of anything specific, as in Choice *A*, nor is it directly describing the author's experiences, Choice *C*. While the passage is about narratives, in the form of children's literature, it is not itself a narrative because it does not tell a story, making Choice *D* incorrect.

16. B: Choice *B* is correct because the passage is generally addressing the reader with words like *we* and *you*. Choice *A* is incorrect because first person would feature the use of *I* and *me*. Choice *C* is incorrect because third person would feature the use of *he, she,* and *they*. Choice *D* is incorrect because fourth person is not a recognized perspective.

17. A: Choice *A* is correct because none of the other inventors obtained patents for their telephone designs. Although they may have contributed to the telephone first, it is not officially recognized as being their invention. Choice *B* is incorrect because there is nothing to suggest that Bell participated in sabotage. Choice *C* is incorrect because there is nothing in the passage that says Bell paid a large amount of money for the patent. Choice *D* is incorrect because readers have no way of judging how much work each inventor put into the telephone.

18. B: Choice *B* is correct because the passage states that "the cellular telephone or cellphone was developed in the 1980s". Choice *A* is incorrect because smartphones came out in the 2010s. Choice *C* is incorrect because rotary telephones were invented in the 1970s. Although touch-tone telephones did exist, they are not mentioned at all in this passage, making Choice D incorrect.

19. B: Choice *B* is the correct answer because *riveted* means to be incredibly interested or focused on something. *Captivated* means to be intensely focused on something. These two meanings are very similar. Choice *A* is incorrect because *uninterested* means that a person is not interested in something. This is the opposite of *riveted*. Choice *C* is incorrect because *sympathetic* means to have pity for someone. This definition is unrelated to the context of the passage. Choice *D* is incorrect because *overjoyed* means to be incredibly happy about something. The word *riveted* has nothing to do with happiness.

20. C: Choice *C* is the correct answer because the television has experienced similar developments to the telephone. Both have gotten slimmer and lighter. Both are more readily available for the average person. Choice *A* is incorrect because the blender has not been revolutionized multiple times like the phone or television. Choice *B* is incorrect because the radio is a device that has not changed drastically over the decades. Choice *D* is incorrect because the microwave has remained the same in both concept and function.

21. B: Choice *B* is correct because the intended purpose of this passage is to educate readers about different species of penguins. It does so by providing facts about a few different species. Choice *A* is incorrect because there is no persuasion taking place. Conservation is never mentioned. Choice *C* is incorrect because the different species are not being presented as superior or inferior to one another.

122

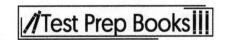

There are only facts being given. Choice *D* is incorrect because there is no questioning about why penguins live in different parts of the world.

22. D: Choice *D* is correct because Choices *A*, *B*, and *C* are not included in the paragraph about macaroni penguins. Each paragraph in the passage discusses the geographical location, diet, and lifespan of the penguin being featured. The paragraph on African penguins notes their predators, but macaroni penguin predators aren't mentioned. The scientific name of only one penguin species is mentioned, and it was the little blue fairy species. The conservation status was not listed for any penguin species.

23. C: Choice *C* is correct because the emperor penguin is the largest penguin species, while the little blue fairy species is the smallest. This is their biggest difference. Choice *A* is incorrect because there is no mention of the little blue fairy penguins' colony size, so we cannot compare the two. Choice *B* is incorrect because there is no mention of the emperor penguins' feather colors, so we cannot compare the two. Choice *D* is incorrect because the two species share a similar diet of fish.

24. B: Choice *B* is correct because *hostile* means confrontational. *Aggressive* means ready to attack. These are very similar definitions. Choice *A* is incorrect because *friendly* means kind. This is the opposite of being ready to attack someone. Choice *C* is incorrect because *fast* means to move with great speed. This has nothing to do with being confrontational. Choice *D* is incorrect because *fearful* means to be afraid. If someone is willing to attack someone else, then they are not afraid.

25. D: Choice *D* is correct because emperor penguins are the largest species of penguins. Macaroni penguins are not named after the dish, they're named after an 18th century fashion term known as *macaroni*. Choice *B* is incorrect because little blue fairy penguins only have a lifespan of 6.5 years, which is the shortest out of the mentioned species. Choice *C* is incorrect because African penguins are known for having pink skin above their eyes, while macaroni penguins are known for their bright yellow feathers.

Mathematics Achievement

1. B: 80 is a multiple of 8 because it is equal to 8 times 10. 32 is a multiple of 8 because it is equal to 8 times 4. 48 is a multiple of 8 because it is equal to 8 times 6. 2 is not a multiple of 8. It is actually a factor of 8.

2. D: To find the value of the sum, line up the numbers and then add each column individually working from right to left. $3 + 2 = 5$. $3 + 9 = 12$. Therefore, carry the 1 to the next column and leave the 2 in that place value. $1 + 2 + 5 = 8$. Putting these values together, the answer is 825.

3. B: Order of operations must be followed. First, perform the multiplication and division from left to right. This leaves the expression $2 + 24 - 2$. Then, perform the addition and subtraction from left to right. The answer is 24.

4. C: To perform long division, first divide 5 into 6. The answer is 1. Then multiply 1 times 5 to get 5. Write this under the 6 and then subtract to obtain $6 - 5 = 1$. Next, bring down the 0 and divide 10 by 5. The answer is 2. 5 times 2 is 10, so subtracting 10 from 10 results in 0. Finally, bring down the 3. 3 is not divisible by 5, so this is the remainder.

5. A: The distributive property allows one to take the value in front of the parentheses and distribute it to each value in the parentheses through multiplication. Therefore, the distributive property results in $5(9) - 5(4) = 45 - 20$.

6. C: The answer can easily be seen by changing each fraction to its corresponding decimal form. $\frac{1}{4}$ is equivalent to 0.25, $\frac{2}{3}$ is equivalent to $0.\overline{6}$, $\frac{3}{8}$ is equivalent to 0.375, and $\frac{1}{2}$ is equivalent to 0.5. The fractions given in the problem are $\frac{1}{3} = 0.\overline{3}$ and $\frac{2}{5} = 0.4$. Therefore, the correct answer is $\frac{3}{8} = 0.375$.

7. A: To add decimals, place the decimals on top of each other making sure to line up the decimal points. Then, add column by column starting from the right. 2.3 is equivalent to 2.30. Therefore, 5.67 + 2.3 = 7.97.

8. C: The number in the hundredth place is the second nine from the left of the decimal point. The digit to its right is a 7, so we must round up. Therefore, the 9 rounds to 10, and a 1 gets added to the 9 to its left. That 9 becomes a 10, so a 1 is added to the 5. The rest of the place values become 0. The answer is 6.

9. D: To find the fraction form of 0.75, write 75 over 100. We use 100 since the 5 is in the hundredth place. Then, reduce the fraction by dividing both the numerator and denominator by 25. The answer is $\frac{75}{100} = \frac{3}{4}$.

10. B: To multiply a whole number times a fraction, write the whole number over a denominator of 1 and then multiply the numerators together and the denominators together. The result is $7 \times \frac{2}{11} = \frac{7}{1} \times \frac{2}{11} = \frac{14}{11}$.

11. B: If each box contains 10 cookies, then the number of boxes must be multiplied times 10 to obtain the total number of cookies. The correct answer is $64 \times 10 = x$.

12. C: To find the missing value, we can work backwards. First, subtract 40 from both sides to obtain $4(5 \times \blacksquare) = 60$. Then, divide both sides by 4 to obtain $(5 \times \blacksquare) = 15$. Then, divide both sides by 5 to obtain $\blacksquare = 3$.

13. A: If y represents the total amount of drinks sold last week, then $2y$ is double the amount. 8 more than double the amount is equal to $2y + 8$.

14. C: This expression has a common factor of 2 because a 2 can be divided out of both 14 and 18. Taking a 2 out of each term results in $2(7x + 9)$.

15. D: Substitute -2 into the equation for x to obtain $-5(-2) - 4 = 10 - 4 = 6$.

16. A: The x-coordinate can be found by counting the number of units to the right from the y-axis. The point is 5 units to the right of the y-axis. The y-coordinate can be found by counting the number of units up from the x-axis. The point is 3 units up from the x-axis. The point is (5,3).

17. B: A quadrilateral has 4 sides and 4 right angles. A hexagon has 6 sides, a pentagon has 5 sides, and an octagon has 8 sides.

18. C: If two triangles are congruent, they have the same shape and size. Angles A and X are the same, angles B and Z are the same, and angles C and Y are the same. Therefore, because angle Z is 60°, angle B is also 60°.

19. C: In the first quadrant, both coordinates are positive. In the second quadrant, the *x*-coordinate is negative, and the *y*-coordinate is positive. In the third coordinate, both coordinates are negative. Finally, in the fourth quadrant, the *x*-coordinate is positive, and the *y*-coordinate is negative. Therefore, because both coordinates are negative in (-4, -4), the answer is Quadrant III.

20. D: There are 4 lines of symmetry in a square. A line of symmetry is a line in which you can fold the object over and the sides align perfectly. The lines of symmetry for a square are horizontal, vertical, and both diagonals.

21. A: Because 1 foot is equal to 12 inches, multiply 6.25 times 12. 6.25 times 12 is equal to 75. Therefore, there are 75 inches in 6.25 feet, and Matthew is 75 inches tall.

22. C: The area of a rectangle is length times width. $12 \times 7 = 84$. The units are square centimeters since area is measured in square units. The correct answer is 84 cm².

23. D: The perimeter of a figure is the sum of all the side lengths. There are two missing side lengths. The horizontal missing side length can be found by subtracting the length of 12 minus the length of 7 to obtain 5 units. The vertical side length can be found by subtracting the length of 10 minus the length of 2 to obtain 8 units. Therefore, the perimeter is 2+12+10+7+8+5=44 units.

24. D: In this figure, the height is 5 units, and the base is 14 units. The area of the triangle is $\frac{1}{2} \times 5 \times 14 = 35$ square units.

25. D: The rectangle has length equal to 11 cm and width equal to 6 cm. Therefore, the perimeter is $P = 2(11) + 2(6) = 22 + 12 = 34$ centimeters.

26. A: The mode is the number that appears most often in the data set. The number 13 appears 3 times, which is the largest number of times any one value appears. Therefore, 13 is the mode.

27. C: To find the mean, find the sum of all the numbers. Then, divide by the total number of values in the data set. The sum of all of the numbers is 139, and there are 9 data values. $\frac{139}{9} \approx 15.4$ rounded to one decimal place (the nearest tenth).

28. C: There are six sides on the die, and there is only one option for rolling a three. The probability of rolling a three is the total number of ways a certain result can occur divided by the total number of possibilities. Therefore, the correct probability is $\frac{1}{6}$.

29. B: There are $6 + 19 = 25$ total students in the class, and 6 of them are left-handed. The probability of a student being left-handed is the number of left-handed students divided by the total number of students, which is $\frac{6}{25}$.

30. D: The range of a data set is equal to the difference between the maximum and minimum values. The maximum value is 25, and the minimum value is 11. $25 - 11 = 14$, so the range is 14.

Practice Test #2

Verbal Reasoning

Synonyms

1. APPROXIMATE
    a. Define
    b. Estimate
    c. Populate
    d. Subject

2. JUBILATION
    a. Happiness
    b. Memorial
    c. Pollution
    d. Transformation

3. THWART
    a. Ignore
    b. Invest
    c. Patronize
    d. Prevent

4. NONCHALANT
    a. Busy
    b. Intense
    c. Problematic
    d. Unconcerned

5. TREMOR
    a. Ache
    b. Chill
    c. Shake
    d. Sickness

6. PROTRUDE
    a. Bulge
    b. Dissect
    c. Insert
    d. Suspect

7. BASK
    a. Handle
    b. Lounge
    c. Spill
    d. Toil

8. VOW
   a. Adage
   b. Oath
   c. Maim
   d. Vex

9. VIVID
   a. Generic
   b. Intense
   c. Maddening
   d. Suave

10. PEDESTRIAN
    a. Conductor
    b. Driver
    c. Pilot
    d. Walker

11. AROMA
    a. Distant
    b. Distinct
    c. Horror
    d. Odor

12. LEGENDARY
    a. Cynical
    b. Judicial
    c. Mythical
    d. Typical

13. DEMONSTRATE
    a. Attack
    b. Lie
    c. Show
    d. Reply

14. RUIN
    a. Destroy
    b. Idolize
    c. Transform
    d. Reconstruct

15. MANUFACTURE
    a. Disrupt
    b. Produce
    c. Recognize
    d. Trigger

16. HOIST
    a. Attach
    b. Hamper
    c. Lift
    d. Volunteer

17. ILLEGIBLE
    a. Disqualified
    b. Poetic
    c. Scrawny
    d. Unreadable

Sentence Completion A

18. In order to attack the castle from afar without risking the lives of his men, the medieval king decided to attack with _____.
    a. catapults
    b. cavalry
    c. infantry
    d. tanks

19. After his team lost the game on a controversial call at home plate, the baseball manager voiced his frustration with the _____.
    a. announcer
    b. executive
    c. teacher
    d. umpire

20. For years, travelers and explorers have formulated theories about the so-called Bermuda Triangle, an area of the Caribbean Ocean infamous for many plane crashes and _____.
    a. beaches
    b. dolphins
    c. shipwrecks
    d. tornadoes

21. Biologists studying _____ creatures such as the mighty T-rex and the megalodon shark must base their theories on evidence like fossil remains since such creatures have long been extinct.
    a. bizarre
    b. imaginary
    c. miniscule
    d. prehistoric

22. Marty regretted not bringing a tent with him to go stargazing when it began to rain, and he was forced to quickly throw together a(n) _____ structure.
    a. airtight
    b. insulated
    c. makeshift
    d. premade

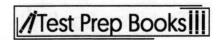

23. Watching his children struggle with online schooling made Damien _____ about his childhood, a time when things were simpler, and it was easier to just be a kid.
    a. concerned
    b. mournful
    c. nostalgic
    d. resentful

24. Halfway through her trip to the front door, Hailey realized how _____ it was to carry all her groceries in one go, and she regretted her decision to do so.
    a. cumbersome
    b. efficient
    c. rewarding
    d. simple

25. It was only after several months of fruitless planting and maintenance that the monks discovered the soil around their temple was entirely _____.
    a. barren
    b. dormant
    c. obedient
    d. primitive

26. All the candidates in the race for city council were desperately seeking the _____ of the current mayor, a well-liked figure whom most citizens respected and listened to.
    a. endorsement
    b. jealousy
    c. removal
    d. sabotage

27. After hours of wandering through the desert, the lost travelers finally got glimpse of a(n) _____ and were relieved that they had finally found water.
    a. courier
    b. oasis
    c. warden
    d. zenith

28. Although she was initially resistant, Amy soon discovered that she enjoyed babysitting. In particular, she enjoyed how she felt when she got to care for and _____ little kids.
    a. belittle
    b. irritate
    c. nurture
    d. vindicate

Sentence Completion B

29. Except for a single student who said they liked to relax once they got home, everyone in Ms. Mclaughlin's class agreed that they preferred to _____
    a. meditate on their day.
    b. start their homework immediately.
    c. play video games with their friends.
    d. chill and talk to their parents about their days.

30. Since the athlete had only recently recovered from a serious injury, he carefully spent the first few minutes of his first match back _____
    a. screaming at the match officials.
    b. regaining his bearings and his confidence.
    c. going all out, throwing his body on the line.
    d. attempting to sabotage his fellow teammates.

31. After the massive tornado rolled through the town, the local schoolteacher was upheld as a hero for _____
    a. giving his students A pluses on all their exams.
    b. safely escorting all the children to a tornado shelter.
    c. sleeping in late and forgetting to show up to work on time.
    d. continuing to teach class as the tornado approached the school.

32. The blockbuster movie was so intense that Richard found himself _____
    a. sneaking looks at his phone.
    b. falling asleep halfway through.
    c. laughing at the ridiculousness of the plot.
    d. gripping the arms of the chair throughout the entire movie.

33. Although her mother disagrees, Stacy thinks arcade games are obsolete when compared to modern video games because _____
    a. going to the arcade with your friends is more fun than playing over a screen.
    b. you can win real prizes at an arcade, which isn't true with most video games.
    c. arcade games look much less interesting and artistically beautiful than modern video games.
    d. there's more variability with the controls and design of arcade games than modern video game consoles.

34. Knowing that the restaurant was at maximum capacity and that all tables were reserved for the rest of the night, Katie made sure to tell anyone looking to dine that _____
    a. they should return another night.
    b. there was space at the counter to sit.
    c. there was going to be a wait for a table.
    d. she just needed to clear off a table for them.

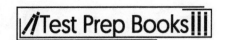

Quantitative Reasoning

1. The basketball team's bake sale was a huge success. The team managed to raise $465. The coach said that after everyone gets a new uniform, the remaining money can be used to buy new basketballs. New uniforms cost $25 each, and there are 13 players on the team. New basketballs cost $10 each. How many basketballs will the team be able to buy?
   a. 46
   b. 5
   c. 14
   d. 140

2. Paul's family is taking a trip next summer. They are going to visit several national parks around the country. His dad says they will drive approximately 1800 miles during their month-long vacation. Paul's dad also said they will need a lot of gas for the car. If the family's car gets approximately 24 miles per gallon, which equation calculates how many gallons of gas they will use throughout the trip?
   a. $1800 \div 24$
   b. $1800 + 24$
   c. $1800 - 24$
   d. 1800×24

3. The animal shelter is trying to estimate how many new toys they need to buy next year. They want to round the number of dogs and cats to the nearest ten and get three toys for each animal. If they have 48 dogs and 27 cats, approximately how many toys will they need?
   a. 225
   b. 210
   c. 240
   d. 180

4. Jacinda is going to her first professional car racing event. She is very excited! Her mom told her that there will be 43 cars racing and that they will each go around the track 288 times! How many total combined laps will the cars race by the end of the event?
   a. 288
   b. 12,000
   c. 11,520
   d. 12,384

5. Using the divisibility rules, the number 2,567,940 is evenly divisible by which of the following numbers?
   a. 2, 3, and 4
   b. 5, 6, and 7
   c. 6, 7, and 8
   d. 2, 3, and 9

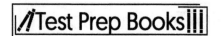

6. Susan's teacher has asked her to list all the prime numbers up to 50. She did it, but she thinks she forgot some. So far, she has 2, 3, 5, 7, 11, 13, 19, 29, 31, 43, and 47. Which ones are missing?
    a.   17, 24, 37, and 42
    b.   17, 23, 37, and 41
    c.   16, 23, 37, and 41
    d.   17, 23, 33, 37, and 41

7. The party supply store is having a sale on balloons. They have 25 red ones, 38 blue ones, 19 green ones, 29 yellow ones, and 34 purple ones. What percentage of the balloons are yellow?
    a.   0.20%
    b.   5%
    c.   17%
    d.   20%

8. Mrs. Hansen's class is celebrating Rainbow Day. Each student got to dress up in any color of the rainbow they wanted. There are 34 students in the class. Of those students, 10 wore blue, 12 wore red, 8 wore green, and 4 wore yellow. What fraction represents the number of students who wore red?
    a. $\frac{5}{17}$
    b. $\frac{6}{17}$
    c. $\frac{8}{34}$
    d. $\frac{4}{34}$

9. The fifth-grade class is going on a picnic, and everyone needs to bring some food to share with the class. Of the students, $\frac{1}{3}$ are bringing sandwiches, $\frac{1}{5}$ are bringing potato chips, $\frac{1}{10}$ are bringing cookies, $\frac{1}{6}$ are bringing brownies, and 6 are bringing drinks. What fraction of the class is bringing dessert?
    a. $\frac{1}{10}$
    b. $\frac{1}{6}$
    c. $\frac{2}{16}$
    d. $\frac{4}{15}$

10. Mr. Jones has to write 90 questions for his students' math tests. If he writes $\frac{1}{6}$ of the questions per day, how many questions will he have finished by the end of the third day?
    a.   15
    b.   6
    c.   45
    d.   90

11. Toby's fifth-grade class is learning how to find equivalent forms of fractions. His teacher, Ms. Robinson, wrote the fraction $\frac{12}{200}$ on the board and asked the class to list three equivalent fractions. Which of the following would NOT be a correct answer?

    a. $\frac{12}{50}$

    b. $\frac{6}{100}$

    c. $\frac{24}{400}$

    d. $\frac{3}{50}$

12. Andre could really use some help with his homework today. He has three fractions that he is supposed to convert to percentages, and he does not remember how to do it! Which of the following shows the correct steps to change a fraction to a percentage?

    a. Divide the denominator by the numerator; then multiply by 100.
    b. Divide the numerator by the denominator; then multiply by 10.
    c. Divide the numerator by the denominator; then move the decimal one place to the right.
    d. Divide the numerator by the denominator; then multiply by 100.

13. Mrs. Abrams's class is having a lot of trouble coming in from the playground on time! Of her 28 students, 5 took too long taking their coats off and getting to their desks, 4 stopped at the water fountain on the way back to the classroom, and 2 went to use the restroom. What fraction of the students were late because they went to get water?

    a. $\frac{2}{28}$

    b. $\frac{1}{7}$

    c. $\frac{4}{14}$

    d. $\frac{11}{28}$

14. Kenya wants to use a number line to figure out which of her friends has a birthday closest to her own. Their birthdays are June 23, October 10, February 12, May 9, and July 31, and Kenya's birthday is September 28. Using the number line below, which birthday is closest to Kenya's?

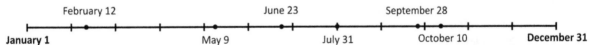

    a. June 23
    b. October 10
    c. February 12
    d. July 31

15. Mrs. Owens needs to figure out exactly how many miles she drives on each trip to work. She drives 120 total miles each week and makes 10 trips per week. Which equation shows the correct simplified algebraic expression to solve the problem?
   a. $120(10) = x$
   b. $10x = 120$
   c. $x + x + x + x + x + x + x + x + x + x = 120$
   d. 12

16. Chase's mother asked him to go to the store and buy a few things. The groceries cost $26, and Chase got $14 back in change. How much money did Chase's mother give him to go to the store?
   a. $14
   b. $26
   c. $12
   d. $40

17. Frank, Josie, and Larry are going to drive to the beach for the day. They decided to share the driving. The beach is 62 miles away from Frank's house, and Josie and Larry's house is on the way. Frank drove 5 miles to Josie and Larry's house, and then the three of them split the remaining driving equally. How many miles did they each drive?
   a. 19
   b. 20.67
   c. Frank = 24; Josie = 19; Larry = 19
   d. Frank = 15.67; Josie = 20.67; Larry = 20.67

18. Joshua had 90 minutes to complete a project for his boss at work. After he had been working for x minutes, his boss came in and told him that he only had 25 minutes left. How long had Joshua been working on the project when his boss came in?
   a. 115 minutes
   b. 65 minutes
   c. 75 minutes
   d. 60 minutes

19. Mandy has two boards that are both 14 feet long. She has cut the boards to make 3 shelves of the same size from each board. How long was each shelf (in feet), and how much wood does she have left over?
   a. 4 feet; 4 feet left over
   b. 3 feet; 1 foot left over
   c. 5 feet; 2 feet left over
   d. 6 feet; no wood left over

20. Johnathan was hanging a poster up in his room. He put a thumbtack in the bottom right corner, and when he let go of the poster to get another tack, it swung around the axis of the tack that was holding it in the wall. What type of transformation was this?
   a. Rotation
   b. Dilation
   c. Translation
   d. Reflection

21. Angel and her friend were sitting outside studying for a test. They had six papers on the table. A breeze came and blew one of Angel's papers, making it slide in a straight line a little way along the table. What type of geometric transformation is this?
   a. Reflection
   b. Rotation
   c. Dilation
   d. Translation

22. George and Charles are supposed to meet Edward and Trevor in the park, but they are having trouble finding them. Trevor said they would be at coordinates (4, −5). In which quadrant of the park should George and Charles be looking for them?
   a. Quadrant I
   b. Quadrant II
   c. Quadrant III
   d. Quadrant IV

23. Tobias is looking for the ice cream stand in his town. He knows the coordinates are (3, 5). Which point on the graph shows the location of the ice cream stand?

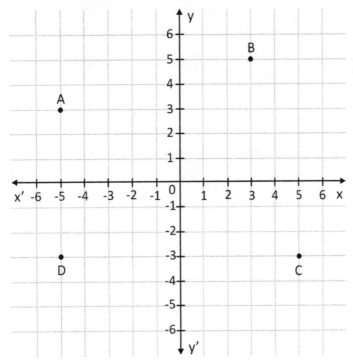

   a. A
   b. B
   c. C
   d. D

135

24. The town of Orchard Park is planning to put in a new park near the edge of town. The town planners have published a drawing of the plans for the park for all of the citizens to see.

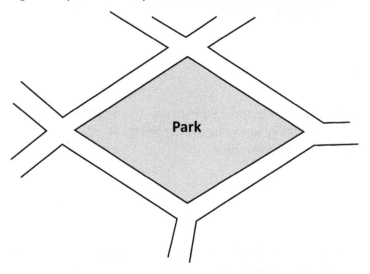

Liam and his friends are trying to decide what shape the park looks like. Liam thinks it's a square. Olivia is pretty sure it's a rhombus, but Emma thinks it's more like a rectangle. Noah says it is definitely a trapezoid. Who is right?

    a. Liam
    b. Olivia
    c. Emma
    d. Noah

25. A triangle has one angle that is 60 degrees and another angle that is 28 degrees. What is the measurement of the third angle?

    a. 2 degrees
    b. 272 degrees
    c. 92 degrees
    d. 90 degrees

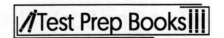

26. Isabella just started a new job as a delivery driver. She wants to determine how many miles she drives each day on her route. Look at the figure of Isabella's route and calculate how many miles she drives if she starts and ends at the same point.

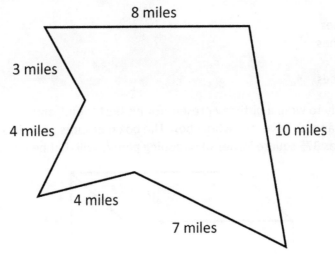

8 miles

3 miles

4 miles

10 miles

4 miles

7 miles

a. 32
b. 33
c. 72
d. 36

27. Benjamin is planning on selling a piece of land that he owns, but it has a very unusual shape. He needs to calculate the area of the property for prospective buyers. Use the measurements shown on the drawing of the property to calculate its area.

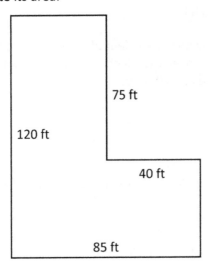

75 ft

120 ft

40 ft

85 ft

a. 10,200 square feet
b. 3000 square feet
c. 320 square feet
d. 7,200 square feet

137

28. Skyler wants to send a package of goodies to her brother who is in the navy. In order to calculate the shipping cost, she needs to know the volume of the box she is using. The box's measurements are 18 inches long, 14 inches wide, and 6 inches high. The box's empty weight is 0.4 pounds. What is the volume of the box?
   a. 1512 cubic inches
   b. 60.48 cubic inches
   c. 38 cubic inches
   d. 38.04 cubic inches

29. Lucas is getting ready to wrap a birthday present for his best friend, and he needs to make sure he has enough wrapping paper to cover the whole box. The box measures 12 inches long, 8 inches wide, and 4 inches high. He has 375 square inches of wrapping paper. Will that be enough?

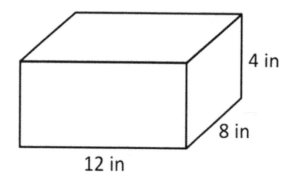

   a. Yes. He needs 176 square inches.
   b. Yes. He needs 352 square inches.
   c. No. He needs 384 square inches.
   d. No. He needs 768 square inches.

30. Micah needs to figure out exactly how many feet of pipe he needs to finish working on the drain system for his yard. He knows he still needs 150 inches to finish the job, but the pipe is only sold by the foot. How many feet of pipe does he need to buy?
   a. 18
   b. 12.5
   c. 13
   d. 150

31. Henry's house is 3 kilometers from Mia's house. How far is that distance is meters?
   a. 30,000
   b. 30
   c. 300
   d. 3,000

138

32. Evelyn has a long piece of rope. She gave 3 meters 50 centimeters to Allison to make a jump rope. She gave Luke 2 meters 26 centimeters, and she gave Evan a piece that was 6 meters 7 centimeters long. She kept 10 meters 17 centimeters for herself. How many meters long was the rope to start with?

    a. 2,200
    b. 21
    c. 22
    d. 11

33. Anthony, Emily, Christopher, and Ryan went to pick apples. Together they picked a total of 300 apples. Anthony and Emily both picked 75 apples each, Christopher picked 120 apples, and Ryan picked 30 apples. Which circle graph shows the percentage of the total apples that each person picked?

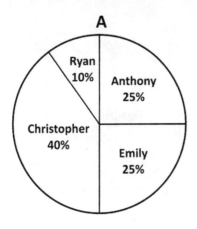

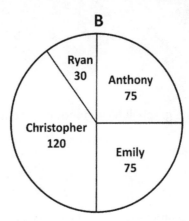

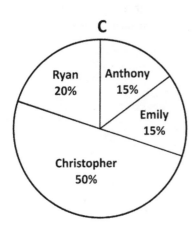

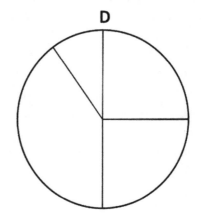

    a. Graph A
    b. Graph B
    c. Graph C
    d. Graph D

34. The city of Fairbanks, Alaska, has one of the most extreme temperature ranges in the United States.

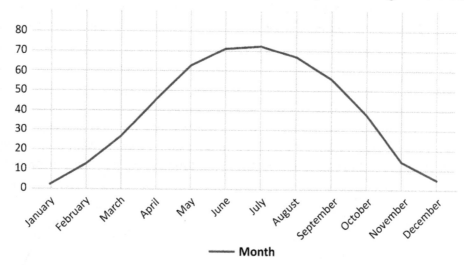

According to the graph, which month has the lowest average temperature?
   a.   January
   b.   December
   c.   June
   d.   July

35. Nicholas is planning a visit to Fairbanks, Alaska. He does not like very warm weather or very cold weather. His sister loves it when the temperature is single digits, but Nicholas's favorite temperature is approximately 55 degrees. Which month would be the best time for him to visit Alaska?

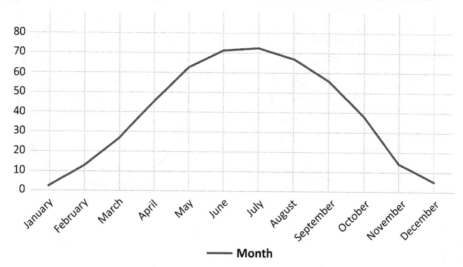

   a.   June
   b.   July
   c.   December
   d.   September

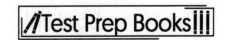

36. Sally's mom measured the heights of Sally and her siblings. Sally is 57 inches tall. Her little brother, Joey, is 54 inches tall, and the twins, Mark and Allison, are 61 and 55 inches tall. Susanna is 59 inches tall. What is the mean of their heights?
   a. 286 inches
   b. 71.5 inches
   c. 56.75 inches
   d. 57.2 inches

37. Ten weeping willow trees were planted in the city park five years ago. Yesterday, the city workers went out to measure how tall the trees had grown. The heights of the trees (in feet) were 10, 12, 8, 9, 9, 15, 14, 7, 13, and 11 feet. What is the range of the trees' heights?
   a. 9
   b. 10.8
   c. 8
   d. 15

38. Mrs. Sousa has just finished grading the tests for her English class. She wants to find out the mode of all the grades. The students' grades were 85, 87, 92, 95, 71, 78, 87, 65, 98, 92, 90, 78, 87, 81, and 69. What is the mode?
   a. 98
   b. 65
   c. 83.67
   d. 87

Reading Comprehension

Questions 1 – 5 are based on the following passage.

Lunar New Year is a holiday celebrated by many different cultures, namely those found in East and Southeast Asian countries. It is often called the Chinese New Year because it originated in China. However, it is celebrated all around the world. The holiday celebrates the beginning of the lunar calendar and the arrival of spring. The second new moon after the winter solstice marks the beginning of the celebration. This typically takes place between January and February. The celebration spans multiple days and officially ends once the full moon arrives.

During the Lunar New Year, people take time to honor their household, family, and ancestors. The holiday is often called the Spring Festival and is accompanied by a multitude of traditions. Many people partake in feasts with their loved ones. The dishes that are eaten often hold cultural significance. For example, serving a whole fish is believed to bring good luck to those at the feast. Households are cleaned thoroughly and decorated with paper banners and lanterns. These decorations are usually red which is a color that represents good energy. Adults will often give children red envelopes containing money to celebrate the holiday. This gift is a symbol of wishing safety and success for the person who receives it.

The Lunar New Year in China ends with the Lantern Festival. This festival is very culturally significant, and people look forward to it all year. People come together to dance, eat special treats, and play games. Lanterns of all different sizes and styles are displayed across the festival. The biggest attractions for the festival are the lion and dragon dances. Before the lion dance, two dancers will put on a vivid and unique lion costume. The costume may be a vibrant yellow,

Practice Test #2

pink, red, or orange. With the sound of drums and gongs in the background, the lions will run around the festival. This is meant to bring good luck to all the festivalgoers who come across the lion. The dragon dance is done by a team of highly skilled dancers, sometimes up to twelve. With poles attached to a gigantic dragon puppet, the dancers perform moves that make the dragon look alive. This dance is also meant to impart good luck and wisdom to those watching.

1. What is the main purpose of this passage?
   a. To prove that the Lunar New Year is unlike any other holiday
   b. To educate readers about the Lunar New Year
   c. To compare the Lunar New Year with other holidays
   d. To convince readers to celebrate the Lunar New Year

2. What does the word *vivid* in paragraph three most nearly mean?
   a. Realistic
   b. Ugly
   c. Bright
   d. Basic

3. What do people believe that eating a whole fish during the Lunar New Year will give them?
   a. Good luck
   b. Happiness
   c. A new job
   d. Perfect test scores

4. What do the adults give to children during this holiday?
   a. New clothing
   b. New school supplies
   c. Blue envelopes of money
   d. Red envelopes of money

5. Where is the Lunar New Year celebrated?
   a. South America
   b. All over the world but mostly in Asian countries
   c. Only China
   d. All over the world but mostly in African countries

Questions 6 – 10 are based on the following passage.

Pip and Squeak were deer mice who lived in a cozy burrow near a river. They were small and round with soft brown fur. They could run quickly and spent their days foraging for nuts, flowers, and insects in the grassy field near their home. Pip was brave and always willing to take on a challenge. Squeak preferred to remain quiet and cautious. Despite their differences, Pip and Squeak were the best of friends. One day they became bored with their daily routine and decided to go on an adventure.

Pip came up with the idea that the two mice would venture down to the riverbank and catch a glimpse of creatures they had never seen before. Frogs, fish, beavers, and dragonflies! Pip and Squeak couldn't wait. They packed all the supplies they needed and headed out after sunrise.

142

Pip preferred to race along the trail, humming his favorite songs. Squeak wanted to enjoy the breeze and went along in quiet silence. As they neared their destination, Squeak was imagining all the creatures they would soon see when he heard something peculiar.

"Pip, did you hear that?" he called out.

Suddenly a snake popped out of the tall grass! The snake loomed over the two mice and hissed down at them with a menacing look in its eyes. The threat was clear; Pip and Squeak were about to become dinner! Right as the snake lunged, they bolted through the grass and raced toward the riverbank. The snake trailed close behind.

Pip and Squeak zig-zagged, trying to lose the snake. After gaining a bit of distance from the snake, they burst out of the grass onto the muddy bank of the river. What now?! Pip and Squeak had never swum before. They looked to their right and left when they saw a beaver waving frantically to them. They raced over to the beaver and saw that she was outside of a dam. Perfect!

"Hurry! Into the lodge!" she whispered.

The two mice scurried into the dam, hiding among the branches. The beaver remained outside, continuing to add branches to her home as if nothing had happened. Looking through a small opening in the branches, the mice watched as the snake slithered past the dam, paying no mind to the beaver, who was much larger and stronger. They were safe!

After the coast was clear, the mice came out of hiding and approached the beaver. They showered her with thanks and promised to pay her back for her kindness. They left the dam to collect glimmering river stones, fragrant flowers, and plump berries. Before carefully heading back to their burrow, the two mice presented the beaver with all of their gifts and promised to visit again in the future. What an adventure!

6. What is the conflict in this story?
   a. The personality differences between the two mice
   b. The snake chasing the mice
   c. The mice not being able to swim
   d. The beaver helping the two mice

7. What does the word *menacing* in this passage most nearly mean?
   a. Friendly
   b. Annoyed
   c. Threatening
   d. Approachable

8. Why was Squeak most likely the one that heard the snake coming?
   a. Squeak was being quiet, while Pip was humming loudly.
   b. Pip was too busy looking at the map to hear the snake.
   c. The snake was closer to Squeak than Pip.
   d. Squeak has better hearing than Pip.

9. Why did the snake not attack the beaver?
   a. The snake and the beaver were friends.
   b. The snake did not notice the beaver because she was small.
   c. The beaver threatened the snake.
   d. The beaver was too large for the snake to successfully defeat.

10. What does the word *peculiar* in this passage most nearly mean?
   a. Loud
   b. Unusual
   c. Normal
   d. Quiet

Questions 11 – 15 are based on the following passage.

Everyone should support their local zoo. However, before visiting the zoo, it is important to make sure that it is Association of Zoos & Aquariums (AZA) accredited. Their job is to make sure that the zoo adheres to certain standards to keep the animals happy and healthy. This means that the animals have enough space, the proper nutrition, and access to veterinarian care. These zoos are positive forces for enriching the lives of both animals and visitors.

An accredited zoo should not have animals purely for entertainment purposes. However, there are a number of reasons why an animal may be at a zoo instead of in its natural habitat. Some animals are endangered and need the safe environment of the zoo to survive and repopulate. Pandas are one example of an animal that often needs the intervention of wildlife professionals. This is due to the destruction of their environment and poachers that wish to harm the pandas. Zoos provide a safe place for the pandas to live. Animals may also need to be in a zoo because they would not cope well with the dangers found in the wild. For example, some animals are illegally bred in captivity for entertainment or to become pets. These animals have never experienced the wild and would not fare well among predators. Zoos host many of these animals and take care of them so that they can live the best lives possible. By visiting the zoo and supporting their mission, you can help these animals!

Zoos are also an incredible educational tool. Zoo visitors are given the opportunity to participate in programs and activities that let them learn about the different animals and perhaps even interact with them. Another important part of zoo education is learning about habitat protection and conservation. While the zookeepers are taking good care of the animals in captivity, there are still millions of animals in the wild that need our help. The best way that we can help wild animals is by protecting their homes, and a visit to the zoo can teach you how to do that. Visiting the zoo might even inspire some people to volunteer and help the animals directly. It's a win-win for you and the animals!

11. What is the purpose of this passage?
   a. To tell the life story of the panda at the zoo
   b. To answer the reader's question about why animals live at the zoo
   c. To explain why zoos are bad
   d. To convince readers to support their local zoo

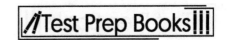

12. What does the word *enriching* in this passage most nearly mean?
    a. Teaching
    b. Observing
    c. Improving
    d. Worsening

13. According to the passage, which of the following is NOT a reason that an AZA-accredited zoo would have an animal in captivity?
    a. The animal is endangered due to poaching.
    b. The animal has faced habitat loss.
    c. The animal is entertaining for visitors at the zoo.
    d. The animal was bred in captivity and cannot survive in the wild.

14. How can visitors best help wild animals that are not at the zoo?
    a. By learning about habitat conservation
    b. By feeding the animals at the zoo
    c. By eating only organic food
    d. By owning a pet at home

15. Which of the following is a cause-and-effect relationship?
    a. Zoos take in animals → Exotic animals are bred in captivity
    b. Environmental destruction → Zoos take in animals
    c. Zoo animals become happier → Donations pay for new animal exhibits
    d. Visitors wear comfortable shoes to the zoo → Zoo sees increased profits for the year

Questions 16 – 20 are based on the following passage.

Roald Dahl was a prolific British author who wrote many books for children during his lifetime. Some titles written by Dahl include *James and the Giant Peach* and *Charlie and the Chocolate Factory*. These are famous stories that have become successful movies as well. Dahl's stories are celebrated all around the world for their creativity, with over 250 million copies sold. They are known for being whimsical and unique.

Dahl was born in the country of Wales in 1916. He was raised by his mother and attended boarding school so that he could obtain the best possible education. Just like many authors, Dahl's life events contributed greatly to his writing. It was during his time at boarding school that he often received boxes of chocolates, which inspired *Charlie and the Chocolate Factory*. Dahl had encounters with other famous authors in his youth, such as Beatrix Potter, who wrote *The Tale of Peter Rabbit*. Dahl himself was never considered to be an extraordinary writer while growing up.

After his education was complete, Dahl worked for an oil company before eventually becoming a wartime fighter pilot. He was highly successful in the military and even managed to survive a crash in 1940. After his recovery he went back to serving his country until the war was over. It was after the war that Dahl began writing for Britain to tell his story of being in the military. He also worked as a spy during this time! As his talent for writing became more widely known, he shifted towards writing fictional short stories for adults.

Dahl eventually got married and had a family of five children. This is when he became inspired to write children's stories. What began as bedtime stories for his own children soon became novels that millions of children around the world could enjoy. His stories are fun to read and include a friendly giant, a young girl with psychic powers, and a waterfall made of chocolate. He used experiences from his childhood and from meeting other famous writers to weave these enthralling tales that captured the hearts of his readers.

16. What does the word *enthralling* in this passage most nearly mean?
   a. Hilarious
   b. Boring
   c. Fascinating
   d. Scientific

17. Which of the following statements is most likely true based on this passage?
   a. Dahl was an amazing writer since childhood.
   b. Dahl was not happy that his stories became popular.
   c. Dahl does not include his life experience in his writing.
   d. Dahl's children helped inspire his stories.

18. What is the purpose of this passage's sequence of events?
   a. To explain Dahl's works in the order that they were written
   b. To detail Dahl's life from his birth to his death
   c. To show Dahl's progression from writer to pilot
   d. The sequence of events is random and has no exact purpose

19. What does the word *prolific* in this passage most nearly mean?
   a. Forgettable
   b. Highly productive
   c. Unsuccessful
   d. Victorious

20. Based on the information provided in this passage, what word best describes Dahl's books?
   a. Saddening
   b. Basic
   c. Uninspired
   d. Magical

Questions 21 – 25 are based on the following passage.

Marissa fidgeted with the corner of her exam. She had studied all night—why was she feeling nervous now? It was the end of the year and this exam was the last one before she would be heading to high school. She had completed her English, science, and history exams. She just had to submit this math exam, and she was officially on summer break!

Marissa had always been an exemplary student. She received straight A's and played for the school's soccer team. She was never shy and always raised her hand to answer questions during class. However, something about tests made Marissa's heart beat faster, and she found it hard to focus. This time was no exception.

She looked down at the paper, and the numbers became a jumble. How was she going to check her answers now?! She tried to remember what her counselor had told her. She had to center herself. She took a deep breath and blocked out all the noise in the classroom. She could do this. She looked over her test answers two times and made a few small corrections. The bell rang and she walked to the teacher's desk to turn in her exam. Her heart skipped a beat as she placed the paper down. She was done!

"Great job, Marissa! I saw you start to get nervous near the end, but you did it!" her teacher said.

"Thanks, Ms. Jones, I think I'm just happy to be done," Marissa replied while laughing.

Marissa left school that day and waited nervously for her results to be posted online. After dinner, she logged on to her account and saw the grade. She had gotten a B! It wasn't the perfect grade she had hoped for, which disappointed her slightly, but Marissa was proud of herself for trying her best and overcoming her fear. Now she knew that she could do even better next time!

21. What word best describes the tone of this passage?
    a. Tragic
    b. Anxious
    c. Sentimental
    d. Arrogant

22. Which of the following statements can we assume as being true based on this passage?
    a. Marissa rushed through the exam because of her excitement for summer break.
    b. Marissa does not usually care about her grades but wants to do well on this one exam.
    c. Marissa is jealous of her peers who all performed well on the exam.
    d. Marissa is normally a confident student but experiences test-taking anxiety.

23. What is the best description of Marissa's feelings regarding her exam grade?
    a. Sad and dejected
    b. Thrilled and excited to try again
    c. Mildly disappointed but hopeful
    d. Angry but unsurprised

24. What can we assume from the second paragraph?
    a. Marissa is too scared to tell anyone about her fear.
    b. Marissa has never experienced fear while taking tests until this exact moment.
    c. Marissa has received extra time on her exam due to her fear.
    d. Marissa has talked with her counselor for help with her fear.

25. What does the word *exemplary* in this passage most nearly mean?
    a. Excellent
    b. Disappointing
    c. Troublesome
    d. Disinterested

Mathematics Achievement

1. Which of the following equations highlights the associative property of multiplication?
    a. $(6 \times 4) \times 2 = (6 \times 4) \times 4$
    b. $(6 \times 4) \times 2 = 6 \times (4 \times 2)$
    c. $(6 \times 4) \times 2 = 4 \times 6 \times 2$
    d. $(6 \times 4) \times 2 = 48$

2. Which of the following is a factor of 27?
    a. 54
    b. 2
    c. 9
    d. 13

3. Find the value of $16 \times 4 - 8 \div 2$.
    a. 28
    b. 62
    c. 60
    d. 56

4. Round 1,458,983,239 to the nearest ten million.
    a. 1,460,000,000
    b. 1,459,000,000
    c. 1,450,000,000
    d. 1,500,000,000

5. Multiply the following: $239 \times 10,000,000,000$.
    a. 2,390,000,000
    b. 2,390,000,000,000
    c. 23,900,000,000
    d. 239,000,000,000

6. A fish can swim at speeds of 31.5 meters per second. How far could it travel in 30 seconds at this same speed?
    a. 61.5 meters
    b. 945 meters
    c. 930 meters
    d. 94.5 meters

7. Subtract $121.2 - 39.1$.
    a. 160.1
    b. 82.1
    c. 83.1
    d. 92.1

148

8. Which of the following is NOT equal to $\frac{2}{3}$?

    a. 0.6666666667

    b. $0.\overline{6}$

    c. $\frac{6}{9}$

    d. $\frac{3}{4.5}$

9. Write 0.05% as a decimal.

    a. 0.005

    b. 0.5

    c. 0.0005

    d. 0.00005

10. Find 8% of 60.

    a. 4.8

    b. 48

    c. 0.48

    d. 8

11. There are 150 packs of pencils, and 30 students share them equally. How many packs of pencils does each student have?

    a. 3

    b. 5

    c. 120

    d. 30

12. 18 bananas were in a basket. Some of the bananas were removed, and now there are 5 bananas left. How many bananas were taken out of the basket?

    a. 13

    b. 23

    c. 15

    d. 5

13. What is the next number in the sequence: 5, 1.5, -2, -5.5,...

    a. -3.5

    b. -8

    c. -9

    d. -8.5

14. The nth term of a sequence is $2n + 1$. Find the 8th term of the sequence.

    a. 16

    b. 17

    c. 19

    d. 11

15. Which of the following is equivalent to: $2(x + 2)$?
    a. $x + 2$
    b. $x + 4$
    c. $2x + 2$
    d. $2x + 4$

16. The following triangles are similar. What is the length of the missing side?

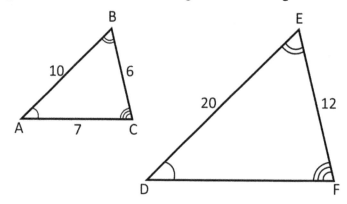

    a. 18
    b. 14
    c. 20
    d. 16

17. Which of the following geometric transformations involves resizing the shape?
    a. Rotation
    b. Reflection
    c. Translation
    d. Dilation

18. Which of the following properly describes a pentagon?
    a. A five-sided polygon
    b. A polygon with four interior angles
    c. A four-sided polygon
    d. A two-dimensional shape with four right angles

19. How many line segments are in a trapezoid?
    a. 2
    b. 3
    c. 4
    d. 5

20. Which of the following three-dimensional shapes has a cross-section that is a circle?
    a. Cone
    b. Cube
    c. Triangular Prism
    d. Rectangular Prism

21. Calculate the area of a square with a side equal to 18 inches.
    a. 324 square inches
    b. 324 inches
    c. 72 square inches
    d. 36 inches

22. 1 millimeter is equal to 0.001 meters. How many meters is 68,456 millimeters?
    a. 6.8456 meters
    b. 68.456 meters
    c. 684.56 meters
    d. 68,456,000 meters

23. What is the volume of the following three-dimensional solid?

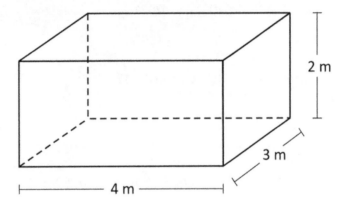

    a. 9 cubic meters
    b. 12 cubic meters
    c. 24 cubic meters
    d. 12 square meters

24. How many inches are in 9 yards?
    a. 27 inches
    b. 324 inches
    c. 3 inches
    d. 54 inches

25. The formula for converting degrees Celsius to degrees Fahrenheit is $F = \frac{9}{5}C + 32$ where F is degrees Fahrenheit, and C is degrees Celsius. How many degrees Fahrenheit is 25 degrees Celsius?
    a. 87
    b. 71
    c. 64
    d. 77

26. The following chart represents the profit of a company each year in millions of dollars.

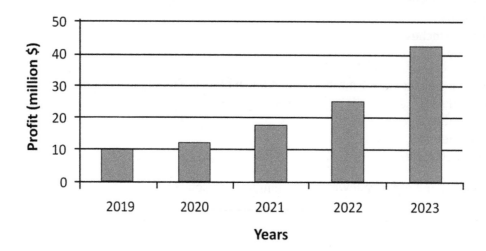

How much more did the company make in 2022 than in 2021?
   a. 25 million dollars
   b. 7 million dollars
   c. 18 million dollars
   d. 3 million dollars

27. Find the median of the following dollar amounts: $8, $10, $15, $7, $9, $11, $16, $20.
   a. 10
   b. 10.5
   c. 11
   d. 10.75

28. A bag has 6 red apples, 5 green apples, and 4 oranges. If a piece of fruit is randomly selected from the bag, what is the probability that it is a green apple?
   a. $\frac{1}{3}$
   b. $\frac{5}{11}$
   c. $\frac{2}{5}$
   d. $\frac{1}{5}$

29. Which is the largest for the following data set: {5, 6, 8, 9, 5, 6, 7, 6, 8}.
   a. Mean
   b. Median
   c. Mode
   d. Minimum

30. The following pie chart shows the percentages of students and their favorite hobbies. If 200 students were polled, how many of the students said reading books was their favorite hobby?

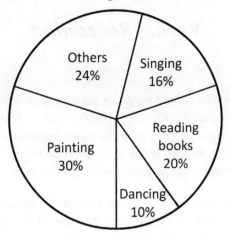

a. 20
b. 40
c. 100
d. 120

Answer Explanations #2

Verbal Reasoning

Synonyms

1. B: *Approximate,* as a verb, means to come near to or nearly meet. *Define* is a verb that means to determine the meaning or boundary of, so it's more specific than an approximation. *Populate* means to settle in or fill an area, which has nothing to do with the word *approximate*. *Subject,* as a verb, means to control someone or something, or to expose them to certain conditions. *Estimate* means to approximately calculate and it's directly synonymous with *approximate*.

2. A: *Jubilation* is a noun meaning a feeling of or expression of joy. Accordingly, *happiness* is a directly synonymous term. *Memorial, pollution,* and *transformation* are all nouns that express concepts that are not necessarily—or at all—related to the concept of joy or happiness.

3. D: *Thwart* is a verb meaning to oppose successfully and prevent from fulfilling an intended purpose. *Invest* is a verb that means to support a cause, which is nearly the opposite meaning of *thwart*. *Patronize* means to talk down to someone and has nothing to do with thwart. *Ignore* is defined as to refrain from noticing, so it is not similar to *thwart*, either. *Prevent*, a verb meaning to keep from happening, is synonymous with *thwart*.

4. D: *Nonchalant* is an adjective that can be best defined as coolly unconcerned or indifferent and is therefore directly synonymous with the term *unconcerned. Busy, intense,* and *problematic* are all adjectives that describe stress-provoking moods or atmospheres, making them nearly opposite in meaning to *nonchalant*.

5. C: *Tremor* is a noun that can be defined as an involuntary quivering motion. *Shake*, as a noun, refers to the act of trembling or shivering, both of which are synonymous with quivering. *Ache, chill,* and *sickness* are related to the word tremor because of the connection to cold air and physical illness, but they are not synonymous terms.

6. A: *Protrude* is a verb that means to project or thrust forward. *Suspect* is a verb that means to believe to be guilty and is not a physical action verb like *protrude. Dissect* and *insert* are both physical action verbs, but have distinct meanings, with *dissect* meaning to cut open and *insert* meaning to place in. *Bulge* is a verb meaning to swell or bend outward and is therefore synonymous with the verb *protrude*.

7. B: *Bask* is a verb that means to lie in or enjoy a pleasant warmth. *Handle* and *toil* are both verbs that imply some degree of work and responsibility and are therefore not synonymous with the idea of basking. *Spill* is a verb that means to escape from a container, usually by accident, and is also therefore not synonymous with the relaxation implied by the word *bask. Lounge,* which is a verb meaning to rest or pass time lazily, is synonymous to *bask*.

8. B: *Vow* is a noun referring to a solemn promise or commitment. *Maim* and *vex* are both verbs that involve the infliction of some harm or perceived harm against an individual, and therefore are not related to the idea of a pledge. *Adage* is a noun meaning a traditional and meaningful saying or expression, it does not have the same personal connotation as a *vow*. An *oath*, however, is a personal promise or commitment, and is therefore synonymous with *vow*.

154

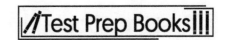

9. B: *Vivid* is an adjective that means visually striking, and it's also used to describe something that is intense. Therefore, *intense* is a synonymous term with *vivid*. *Suave* is an adjective that is used to describe people and their behaviors and is therefore not synonymous with *vivid*, which is used to describe the sensory experience of something. *Maddening* is an adjective that means annoying or infuriating. *Generic* refers to members of a whole group of similar things, which has nothing to do with *vivid*.

10. D: *Pedestrian* is a noun that means a person who goes or travels on foot. *Conductor, driver,* and *pilot* are all nouns that describe individuals operating or controlling a form of transportation, and by their nature are not *pedestrians*. Therefore, the synonymous term is *walker*, which similarly can be defined as a person that walks.

11. D: *Aroma* is a noun that means an odor or fragrance, especially an agreeable or pleasant one. *Odor*, then, is the synonymous term. *Distant* and *distinct* are both adjectives that refer to an object's positioning in relation to some other object or concept. *Horror*, like *aroma*, is a noun describing a sensory experience, but *horror* is associated with terror and fear rather than pleasantness.

12. C: *Legendary* is an adjective meaning of or relating to a legend and is specifically associated with stories that are nonhistorical or fantastical in one way or another. *Typical* is an adjective that can be defined as conforming to a particular type and is used synonymously with terms like normal and average. Therefore, *typical* and *legendary* have nearly opposite meanings. *Cynical* and *judicial* are both adjectives that can be used to describe a person's mindset or beliefs and are not specifically related to the concept of legend in any way. *Mythical* is an adjective meaning pertaining to or involving a myth. Since myth and legend are essentially synonymous terms, *mythical* is accordingly synonymous with *legendary*.

13. C: *Demonstrate* is a verb meaning to make evident or to exhibit. *Attack* is a verb that can refer to actions ranging from physical violence to verbal abuse. In any case, it is not synonymous with *demonstrate*. *Lie* is a verb that means to speak falsely and is therefore somewhat opposite to the concept of making something evident. *Reply* is a verb meaning to answer a response, but the term does not imply if such a response is making anything evident. The verb *show,* on the other hand, can be defined as to exhibit or display and is accordingly synonymous with *demonstrate.*

14. A: *Ruin* is a verb meaning to bring or reduce to a diminished or decayed state. *Idolize* is a verb meaning to worship as a god and so is somewhat contradictory to the idea of ruining something. *Transform* and *reconstruct* both refer to the alteration of something but in neither term is there the idea that the thing being altered is being made worse or being diminished. *Destroy* is a verb meaning, among other things, to reduce to a useless form and to render ineffective. Therefore, *destroy* is the synonymous term.

15. B: *Manufacture* is a verb meaning to make by hand or machinery and is usually associated with the making of something on a large scale. *Disrupt* is a verb that means to cause disorder or even to destroy and so is somewhat contrary to the meaning of *manufacture*. *Recognize* is a verb that involves the memory of another person and is therefore more personal than the concept of manufacturing something. *Trigger* is a verb that means to cause or initiate something but does not refer to a specific process of creating something in the way *manufacture* does. *Produce* is a verb that specifically refers to the process of creating or bringing something about. *Produce* is therefore synonymous with *manufacture*.

16. C: *Hoist* is a verb that means to raise or haul something up. *Attach* is a verb that means to join or to fasten and does not refer to the raising up of something. *Hamper* and *volunteer* are both verbs that refer to the effect one's actions may have or intend to have on another and similarly are not synonymous with *hoist.* The correct choice, therefore, is *lift.* Lift can be defined quite similarly to *hoist* as to raise or bring to a higher level.

17. D: *Illegible* is an adjective meaning not legible, or impossible to read or decipher. The adjective *unreadable*, therefore, is directly synonymous with illegible. *Scrawny* is an adjective meaning thin or lean, while *poetic* is a somewhat opposing adjective to *illegible*, meaning possessing the qualities or being related to poetry. *Disqualified* is a verb that means to deprive of qualification and, while it is not itself synonymous with illegible, it does have a synonym that sounds quite similar: *ineligible.*

Sentence Completion A

18. A: The phrase *without risking the lives of his men* disqualifies *cavalry* and *infantry*, both of which would involve putting soldiers' lives directly at risk. The adjective *medieval* disqualifies *tanks*, which are a much more modern invention. The adverb *afar* indicates that the king wants to attack from a distance, and catapults are devices designed to hurl objects from afar. Therefore, *catapults* is the correct answer.

19. D: The mention of *baseball* indicates that the missing term is related in some way to the game of baseball, and so *executive* and *teacher* do not logically make sense. Since the manager's frustration is directly aimed at the result of the game itself, *announcer* also does not logically make sense, since an *announcer* would have no effect on the outcome of a game. Therefore, the correct answer is *umpire*, an official tasked with ruling on plays that occur during a game.

20. C: Since the Bermuda Triangle is said to be a part of the Atlantic Ocean, *tornadoes* do not logically make sense as an answer, as tornadoes can only occur on land. Furthermore, the adjective *infamous* implies that the missing term is something bad or negative. Neither *beaches* nor *dolphins* are generally considered to be bad or negative things in and of themselves, so they do not make logical sense as answers. *Shipwrecks*, meaning the remains of crashed or otherwise destroyed ships, is therefore the correct term.

21. D: The terms *imaginary* and *miniscule* do not logically make sense to associate with either a T-rex or a megalodon shark, as both were real and quite massive creatures. Although both creatures may in some contexts certainly be classified as *bizarre*, the phrase *since such creatures have long been extinct* indicates that the common factor that links these two animals is not how bizarre they are, but rather that they existed long before humans were around to investigate them. Therefore, the correct answer is *prehistoric.*

22. C: Since the sentence implies that Marty lacked the time and resources to properly protect himself from the rain, the only answer that logically makes sense is *makeshift.* All the other answer choices would imply higher levels of craftsmanship than the sentence implies Marty has.

23. C: It is clear Damien has positive associations with his childhood in relation to how he feels about his own children's experiences. Therefore, the only answer choice that logically makes sense is *nostalgic*, which is defined as experiencing a sentimental yearning for a past happiness. All the other answer choices imply Damien has negative associations with his childhood, which does not logically make sense given the rest of the sentence.

24. A: If Hailey regrets her decision to carry all her groceries in one go, she must not be enjoying the experience of doing so. The only term that consequently makes sense is *cumbersome*, which can be defined as specifically unwieldy or also just generally troublesome. The other answer choices all imply a positive experience, which does not logically make sense.

25. A: The sentence implies that, despite the monk's best efforts, they were unable to cultivate any plants in the soil around their temple. Soil from which crops and plants cannot grow and be cultivated is generally defined to be *barren*. Although the other terms may make sense as a descriptor of soil under some other circumstances, the specific reference to the inability to successfully cultivate crops indicates the only logical answer is *barren*.

26. A: Since the sentence implies that the mayor is a popular figure and that the candidates were seeking something from him, the only logical conclusion is that the candidates were seeking to gain something positive from the mayor. Therefore, only *endorsement* makes logical sense, as all of the other answer choices would seem to pit the candidates against the mayor in one way or another.

27. B: The mention of water, and especially of water being found in the desert, is an indication that *oasis* is the logical answer here. *Oasis* can be defined as a small fertile area in a desert region, usually having a water source. Additionally, the other terms do not logically make sense because none of them imply the presence of water.

28. C: Based on the phrasing of the sentence, the missing term is going to have to be to some degree synonymous with the idea of caring for little kids. Therefore, *nurture* must be the correct answer. It alone refers to the idea of supporting and protecting something, whereas all the other answer choices have more negative associations.

Sentence Completion B

29. B: The proposition *except* indicates that the one student who said they like to relax once they get home is the sole member of the classroom who enjoys relaxing. Therefore, the correct answer choice has to involve an action that is not relaxing or generally considered to be relaxing. The only answer choice that fits that description is *start their homework immediately*, as the other three actions may be considered relaxing or potentially relaxing to one degree or another.

30. B: The adverb *carefully* indicates that the action the player took was cautious and thought out, and the adverb *since* further indicates that he acted carefully due to his recent injury. The only answer choice that would make sense as an example of a cautious action after a recent injury would be *regaining his bearings and his confidence*. All the other answer choices indicate behaviors that are careless and thoughtless.

31. B: The order of events provided in the sentence indicates that the schoolteacher was upheld as a hero after the tornado came through the town. Consequently, it makes logical sense that the teacher's heroism was somehow related to the tornado. The only answer choice that accurately describes heroic actions in the face of a natural disaster like a tornado is *safely escorting all the children to a tornado shelter*. All of the other answer choices either do not specifically mentioned the tornado or are non-heroic actions to take under such circumstances.

32. D: The adjective *intense* indicates that Richard's reaction should be a logical reaction to the experience of something intense. The only answer choice that describes a logical reaction to an intense

157

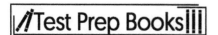

experience is *gripping the arms of the chair throughout the entire movie.* All the other answer choices describe reactions more consistent with boredom or outright dislike.

33. C: The adjective *obsolete*, meaning no longer in general use or outdated, serves in this sentence as a descriptor of how Stacy feels about arcade games, particularly when compared to modern video games. Due to this, the only logical answer choice is *arcade games look much less interesting and artistically beautiful than modern video games,* since only that option lists a flaw about arcade games. In all of the other answer choices, arcade games are described positively, especially in comparison to modern video games.

34. A: The phrase *maximum capacity* indicates that there would be absolutely no table for another party to sit at. Additionally, the phrase *reserved for the rest of the night* indicates that all those tables will remain full for the rest of the night. Therefore, there is logically going to be no way to seat any more parties in the restaurant that night, no matter the conditions. Therefore, the correct answer choice is *they should return another night.*

Quantitative Reasoning

1. C: The team will spend $325 on the new uniforms ($25 times 13 players). There will be $140 left over. The basketballs cost $10 each. $140 divided by $10 means that the team can get 14 new basketballs. Choice *A* forgot to buy the uniforms first and instead spent all the money on basketballs. Choice *B* counts the same price of $25 for the basketballs and the uniforms. Choice *D* is the amount of money left over rather than the number of basketballs the team can buy.

2. A: The way to solve this problem is to divide the number of miles the family will drive by the number of miles per gallon that the car can travel: $1800 \div 24 = 75$. So, the car will go through 75 gallons of gas during the trip. Choices *B*, *C*, and *D* use incorrect operations (adding, subtracting, and multiplying).

3. C: Both the number of dogs and the number of cats need to be rounded up, meaning that they have 50 dogs and 30 cats. Adding those together equals 80 animals. Then, multiply the number of animals times 3 toys for each, which means they will need approximately 240 toys. Choice *A* is the exact total rather than an estimation. Choice *B* rounds the number of dogs up to 50 but rounds the number of cats down to 20 rather than up to 30. Choice *D* rounds the numbers of dogs and cats down rather than up.

4. D: To solve this problem, multiply the number of cars times the number of laps they will each run: $43 \times 288 = 12,384$ laps. Choice *A* is just the total laps; it does not count that each car will race all those laps. Choice *B* uses rounding to estimate the total rather than calculating the exact number of laps raced. Similarly, Choice *C* rounds the number of cars and multiplies that by the number of laps.

5. A: According to the divisibility rules, a number is divisible by 2 if it is an even number, by 3 if the sum of the digits is divisible by 3, and by 4 if the last two digits are divisible by 4. So, 2,567,940 is divisible by 2, 3, and 4. The number is also divisible by 5 (it ends in 0) and by 6 (it is both an even number and divisible by 3), but not by 7, Choice *B*. It is also not divisible by 8, Choice *C*, or by 9, Choice *D*.

6. B: Prime numbers are divisible only by themselves and 1. The prime numbers up to 50 are 2, 3, 5, 7, 11, 13, 17, 19, 23, 29, 31, 37, 41, 43, and 47. Susan forgot numbers 17, 23, 37, and 41. Choice *A* has two even numbers, 24 and 42, which are also divisible by 2 and therefore not prime. Similarly, Choice *C* includes 16, which is not prime, and Choice *D* includes 33, which is divisible by 3 and 11 and therefore is not a prime number.

7. D: The first step is to find out how many balloons the store has in total: $25 + 38 + 19 + 29 + 34 = 145$. Then, divide the number of yellow balloons by the total number of balloons: $29 \div 145 = 0.20$. Move the decimal two places to the right to get the percentage. Choice *A* forgot to move the decimal. Choice *B* divided the number of total balloons by the number of yellow balloons instead of the other way around, and Choice *C* calculated the percentage of red balloons rather than the yellow ones.

8. B: The number of students who wore red was 12 out of 34 students, which creates the fraction $\frac{12}{34}$. That can be reduced to $\frac{6}{17}$ students. Choice *A* is the number of students who wore blue, Choice *B* is the unreduced fraction of students who wore green, and Choice *D* is the unreduced fraction of students who wore yellow.

9. D: $\frac{1}{10}$ of the class is bringing cookies, and $\frac{1}{6}$ is bringing brownies: $\frac{1}{10} + \frac{1}{6}$. Because these fractions have different denominators, they must be converted before adding. The common denominator is 30, so the equation becomes $\frac{3}{30} + \frac{5}{30} = \frac{8}{30}$. Then, reduce to the lowest form, $\frac{4}{15}$. Choice *A* is the number who are bringing cookies, and Choice *B* is the number who are bringing brownies. Because both are desserts, they must be added together to solve the problem. Choice *D* adds the fractions by adding the top and bottom numbers rather than finding a common denominator.

10. C: $\frac{1}{6}$ of 90 questions is 15 questions per day (90 divided by 6). By the end of the third day, Mr. Jones will have written 15×3 questions, or 45 questions. Choice *A* is the number of questions he writes each day, and Choice *B* is the total number of days it will take him to write all the questions. Choice *D* is the total number of questions he has to write.

11. A: $\frac{12}{50}$ reduces the denominator by 4 but does not also reduce the numerator by the same amount. Choices *B* and *D* both reduce the fraction, whereas Choice *C* multiplies the numerator and denominator by 2, which also creates an equivalent fraction.

12. D: To change a fraction to a decimal, first divide the numerator by the denominator, and then move the decimal point two places to the right (or multiply by 100, which would do the same thing). Choice *A* mixes up the numerator and denominator. Choice *B* multiplies by 10 rather than 100, and Choice *D* moves the decimal by one place rather than two.

13. B: To find the fraction, write the number of students who went for water over the total students: $\frac{4}{28}$. Then, reduce that to its lowest form by dividing the numerator and denominator by 4: $\frac{1}{7}$. Choice *A* is almost correct, but it instead counts the students who were late because of using the restroom, and it does not reduce the fraction. Choice *C* reduces the denominator but not the numerator, and Choice *D* counts all the students who were late instead of only those getting water.

14. B: The number line shows the birthdays in the correct order, and looking at the line, we can see that the closest birthday to Kenya's (September 28) is the one on October 10. The other birthdays are further from September 28 on the number line, so the other choices are incorrect.

15. B: The missing number, x, is the number of miles Mrs. Owens drives on each trip. The number of trips times the number of miles each trip equals the total miles she drives each week. Choice *A* multiplies the total miles times the number of trips rather than finding out how many miles each trip is.

Choice *C* is not a simplified algebraic expression. Choice *D* solves the equation rather than identifying which equation is correct.

16. D: The unknown number for this equation is how much money Chase started with. To solve this problem, set up the equation as x minus the cost of the groceries equals the change Chase got back, or $x - 26 = 14$. Choices *A* and *B* are factors already given in the problem rather than the solution to the missing number. Choice *C* subtracts 14 from 26 rather than adding 14 to 26.

17. C: To solve this problem, first subtract the 5 miles that Frank drove from the total. Then, divide the remaining miles by 3. The equation looks like this: $\frac{62-5}{3}$. First, solve the top of the equation by completing the subtraction: $62 - 5 = 57$. Then, divide $57 \div 3 = 19$. This means that Josie and Larry each drove 19 miles and Frank drove 24 miles (19 + the first 5 miles he drove to their house). Choice *A* does not include the extra 5 miles Frank drove to pick up Josie and Larry. Choice *B* has them all driving the same number of miles from the start rather than Frank driving the first 5 miles alone. Choice *D* subtracts the first 5 miles before dividing but then subtracts it again from Frank's total.

18. B: The equation to solve this problem is $x + 25 = 90$, where x is how long Joshua had been working and 25 minutes is how long he had left. To solve the problem, subtract 25 from both sides of the equation: $x = 90 - 25$. Choice *A* adds 25 minutes to the equation rather than subtracting it. Choices *C* and D are just errors in subtraction.

19. A: The first step is to find out how long each shelf was. We know she made 3 shelves of equal length (x) from each board, so: $3x = 14$. Divide 14 by 3 to get $x = 4$ with a remainder of 2 feet. That's for one board. If she did that for two boards, she made 6 shelves of 4 feet each and had 4 feet of wood left over.

20. A: When the poster fell, it rotated around a single point, the thumbtack. *Dilation*, Choice *B*, is when the shape stretches or shrinks. *Translation*, Choice *C*, is when the shape slides or moves, and Choice *D*, *reflection*, is when the shape flips to create a mirror image.

21. D: Translation is when a shape—in this case, the rectangle paper—slides or moves. Choice *A* is when a shape flips, creating a mirror image. Choice *B* refers to a shape rotating or turning around a single point, and Choice *C* is when a shape stretches or shrinks.

22. D: Point (4, −5) refers to (x, y), where the first point is on the x-axis, and the second point is on the y-axis. In this case, point (4, −5) would be in Quadrant IV. Choice *A* requires two positive coordinates. Choice *B* needs a negative coordinate followed by a positive coordinate, and Choice *C* needs two negative coordinates.

23. B: The ice cream stand is located at (3, 5), which means the point is at 3 on the x-axis and 5 on the y-axis, in Quadrant I. Choice *A* is (−5, 3). Choice *C* is (5, −3), and Choice *D* is (−5, −3).

24. B: Olivia is correct because a rhombus is a four-sided figure where the opposite sides are parallel. Liam's guess of a square, Choice *A*, is a four-sided figure, but a square has four equal and parallel sides with four right angles. Similarly, Emma's choice of a rectangle, Choice *C*, has four sides and four right angles, but only the opposite sides are congruent. In a trapezoid, Choice *D*, only one set of the lines is parallel, and there are no right angles.

25. C: The angles of a triangle add up to 180 degrees. If a triangle has one angle that's 60 degrees and one that's 28 degrees, subtract those figures from 180 degrees: $180 - 60 - 28 = 92$. Choice *A* adds the

160

angles to 90 degrees rather than 180 degrees. Choice *B* uses 360 degrees, and Choice *D* mistakenly assumes that the question is referring specifically to a right triangle.

26. D: To calculate the distance Isabella drives, add the number of miles shown on each section of the route: $8 + 10 + 7 + 4 + 4 + 3 = 36$ mi. Choices *A* and *B* both add the number of miles but forget to include the miles back to the starting point (either 3 or 4, depending on the direction around the route). Choice *C* adds the miles around the route twice.

27. D: To calculate area, multiply the length times the width of the shape. However, this shape has a piece missing from the corner, so simply using the length times width will not give a correct calculation. You must also subtract the area of the missing piece. The area of the full shape is 120 feet times 85 feet, which equals 10,200 feet. The area of the missing corner is 40 feet times 75 feet, or 3000 feet. So, the area of the property is $10,200 - 3000 = 7200$ sq. ft. Choice *A* includes the area of the missing piece. Choice *B* is the area of the missing piece. Choice *C* is the perimeter of the shape rather than the area.

28. A: The formula for calculating volume is length times width times height: $18 \times 14 \times 6 = 1512$ cu. in. Choice *B* included the extra information of the box's weight, which is not part of the formula. Choice *C* added the figures instead of multiplying them, and Choice *D* added in the weight figure as well.

29. B: To calculate the surface area of a figure, calculate the area of each side and add them together. The two ends are both $12 \times 4 = 48$ sq. in. The two sides are $8 \times 4 = 32$ sq. in., and the top and bottom are each $12 \times 8 = 96$ sq. in. Then, add the totals for all six sides: $48 + 48 + 32 + 32 + 96 + 96 = 352$ sq. in. of surface area. Choice *A* calculates the surface area of the sides but only adds three sides rather than six. Choice *C* is the volume of the box rather than the surface area, and Choice *D* calculates the volume twice.

30. C: There are 12 inches in one foot, so to convert from inches to feet, divide the number of inches by 12. In this case, 150 inches divided by 12 equals 12.5 feet. However, the question notes that pipe is only sold by the foot, so we need to round up to 13 feet, so the answer must be Choice *C*, 13 feet.

31. D: One kilometer equals 1000 meters, so 3 kilometers equals 3000 meters. Choice *A* is the distance in decimeters, Choice *B* is dekameters, and Choice *C* is hectometers.

32. C: To solve this equation, add the number of meters first: $3 + 2 + 6 + 10 = 21$ m. Then, add the number of centimeters: $50 + 26 + 7 + 17 = 100$ cm. Because 100 cm $= 1$ m, add that to the sum of the meters: 21 m $+ 1$ m $= 22$ m. All of the numbers can be converted to centimeters and added, such as in Choice *A*. However, the total must be converted back to meters to answer the question. Choice *B* added the meters but did not include the centimeters, and Choice *D* forgot to include the centimeters and the length of rope that Evelyn kept for herself.

33. A: To solve this problem, figure out the percentage for each person by dividing the number of apples they picked by the total number of apples and multiplying by 100. For example, the equation to find Anthony's and Emily's share is $75 \div 300 = 0.25 \times 100 = 25\%$. Anthony and Emily each picked 25%, or $\frac{1}{4}$ of the total. Christopher picked 40%, and Ryan picked 10%. Choose the pie graph that reflects those percentages. Choice *B* shows the correct graph, but it is labeled by number rather than by percentages. Choice *C* shows incorrect percentages, even though it does show Christopher as picking the most apples, and Choice *D* is missing all the labels.

34. A: The lowest temperature in Fairbanks, 2 degrees, occurs in January. Choice *B*, December, is close but is the second lowest. Choices *C* and *D* show the two warmest months.

35. D: According to the graph, the average temperature in September is 56 degrees, which is almost perfect for Nicholas. June and July, Choices *A* and *B*, are both in the 70s, which would be too warm, and December, Choice *C*, is too cold for Nicholas, although it sounds like his sister would love it!

36. D: The mean is the average of a set of numbers. To find the mean, add the numbers and divide by how many numbers there are: $57 + 54 + 61 + 55 + 59 = 286 \div 5 = 57.2$. Choice *A* adds the numbers but does not divide by the total number of figures. Choice *B* divides the total by 4 instead of 5. Choice *C* is incorrect because it is the mean of only the first four numbers, forgetting Susanna's height.

37. C: Range is the difference between the highest and lowest numbers. In this case, the highest number (the tallest tree) is 15, and the lowest number is 7: $15 - 7 = 8$. Choice *A* is the mode, which is the number that appears most often. Choice *B* is the mean, and Choice *D* is the highest number.

38. D: The mode is the value that occurs the most in a set of data. In this case, the score that was given the most was 87. Choice *A* shows the highest score, and Choice *B* shows the lowest score. Choice *D* is the average, or mean, of all the scores.

Reading Comprehension

1. B: Choice *B* is the answer that best describes the main purpose of this passage. This passage provides information about the Lunar New Year holiday. It educates the reader about traditional practices and beliefs about the holiday. Choices *A* and *C* are incorrect because the passage never mentions another holiday. Choice *D* is incorrect because the passage never claims that readers should participate in any of the practices mentioned.

2. C: Choice *C* is the answer that best defines what *vivid* means in this passage. When describing the costume, the passage says that it comes in many different vibrant colors. This is the context clue that shows us that *vivid* can also mean *bright* in this scenario. Choice *A* is incorrect because the costume is described as colorful which is not realistic to an actual lion. Choice *B* is incorrect because the lion costume is never described as being unsightly. Choice *D* is incorrect because the passage says that the lion costume is *unique*, which is the opposite of *basic*.

3. A: Choice *A* is the correct answer because people believe that eating whole fish will give them good luck. In the second paragraph, the feast is described in detail. The important line for this question reads as, "For example, serving a whole fish is believed to bring good luck to those at the feast." This sentence directly gives us the answer. Choices *B*, *C*, and *D* are eliminated because of this direct quote.

4. D: Adults give children red envelopes of money during this holiday. This information is found near the end of the second paragraph. The second-to-last line describes the red envelopes that adults give to children while the line directly after it explains why the gift is significant. Note that the envelope is specifically described as being red. Choices *A*, *B*, and *C* are never mentioned and are incorrect.

5. B: Choice *B* is the correct answer regarding the location that the Lunar New Year is celebrated. This is discussed in the first paragraph. The passage says that the Lunar New Year is "celebrated all over the world" in the third line. In the first line it says, "East and Southeast Asian countries" are where the holiday is most popular. This shows us that the holiday is celebrated mostly in those countries but also in

countries all around the world. This aligns with Choice *B*. Choice *A* is incorrect because South America is never mentioned as a significant continent for this holiday. Choice *C* is incorrect because the passage specifically says that it is celebrated in other nations. Choice *D* is incorrect because the passage never mentions Africa as being a significant continent for the holiday.

6. B: Choice *B* is the answer choice that best explains the conflict in this story. Conflict in a story is when a problem arises between two or more opposing forces. For the two mice in this story, the problem that arises is the snake trying to attack them. Choice *A* is incorrect because the personality differences between the two mice never cause a problem. Choice *C* is incorrect because the mice not being able to swim does not involve an opposing force. Choice *D* is incorrect because the beaver helping the mice is a positive thing.

7. C: The word *menacing* means suggesting danger. *Threatening* means to have dangerous intentions for another. These two words have similar definitions and are synonymous. Choice *A* is incorrect because *friendly* is a positive trait, meaning pleasant, which the snake is not. Choice *B* is incorrect because *annoyed* means to be irritated, which does not accurately describe the snake's intentions of harm. Choice *D* is incorrect because the snake is not *approachable*, which means friendly.

8. A: The story describes Squeak as being quiet during the walk to the riverbank. Pip was loudly humming and not paying attention to his surroundings. This is most likely why Squeak was the one to hear the snake first. Choice *B* is incorrect because there was no mention of a map in this story. Choice *C* is incorrect because the location of the snake relative to the two mice was never mentioned. Choice *D* is incorrect because it was never mentioned that Pip has worse hearing.

9. D: The story says that the snake was, "paying no mind to the beaver, who was much larger and stronger," which is the context clue we need to determine why they did not fight. The snake knew that it could not defeat the beaver. Choice *A* is incorrect because the beaver and the snake were never said to be friends. Choice *B* is incorrect because in the sentence previously mentioned, it is said that the snake noticed the large beaver and ignored her. Choice *C* is incorrect because the beaver and the snake never had an interaction together.

10. B: *Peculiar* means odd or strange. *Unusual* means uncommon or abnormal. These two words are similar in meaning and can be considered synonyms. Choice *A* is incorrect because *loud* means that something makes noise at a high volume. This is unrelated to the word *peculiar*. Choice *C* is incorrect because *normal* is the opposite of what *peculiar* means. Choice *D* means something is producing sound at a low volume and is incorrect since this has no correlation to the word *peculiar*.

11. D: Choice *D* is the answer choice that best explains the purpose of this passage. The major context clue is the repeated encouragement for readers to visit their local zoo. The first sentence in the passage is an example of this. Choice *A* is incorrect because the passage does not go into depth about the life of pandas at the zoo. Choice *B* is incorrect because there are no reader questions that are directly addressed. All the information provided is generally educational. Choice *C* is incorrect because this passage shows zoos in a positive light.

12. C: Choice *C*, improving, is the answer choice that best matches the meaning of *enriching*. *Enriching* means to improve or enhance something. The key context phrase in this sentence is *positive forces*, which points towards *enriching* being a positive word. Choice *A* is incorrect because the word *teaching* does not make sense in this sentence. A zoo would not be teaching the lives of the visitors. Choice *B* is incorrect because the word *observing* does not make sense in this sentence. A zoo would not be

observing the lives of the visitors. Choice *D* is incorrect because *enriching* is a positive word, and *worsening* is the opposite of this.

13. C: In the second paragraph, the passage explains multiple reasons why an animal would be kept at a zoo. Choices *A*, *B*, and *D* are all mentioned in this paragraph as good reasons for an animal's captivity. Choice *C* is not one of the reasons provided, and the paragraph states that entertainment is never a good reason for captivity.

14. A: Choice *A* is the best answer for how people can help wild animals. Learning about habitat conservation and following the advice on how you can help is the best way for zoo visitors to help wild animals. Choice *B* is incorrect because although feeding zoo animals helps them, it does not help animals in the wild. Choice *C* is incorrect because the passage never mentions that eating organic is the best method for helping wild animals. Choice *D* is incorrect because the passage never mentions that owning a pet will help wild animals.

15. B: Choice *B* is the correct answer because it accurately identifies a cause-and-effect relationship. The first part is the cause, which is the destruction of the environment that the animals live in. The effect is that the zoos are required to take these animals in so that they can survive. This is a cause-and-effect relationship. Choice *A* is incorrect because it has the effect coming first and the cause coming second. Choice *C* is incorrect because the cause and effect are switched, similar to Choice *A*. Choice *D* is incorrect because there is no clear correlation between visitors wearing comfortable shoes to the zoo and zoo profits increasing.

16. C: *Enthralling* means that something captures your interest. The last sentence of the last paragraph gives this context clue. *Fascinating* means nearly the same thing and is a good substitute word. Choice *A* is incorrect because *hilarious* is never a word mentioned as a feature of Dahl's stories. Choice *B* is incorrect because *boring* is the opposite of *enthralling*. Choice *D* is incorrect because there is nothing in this passage to suggest that Dahl's stories are *scientific*.

17. D: Choice *D* is the answer choice that we can determine is most likely true based on the passage. In the last paragraph, the connection between Dahl's stories and his children is made clear. He first told his stories to his children and then they later became popular. It is a safe assumption that his children inspired his writing because of this. Choice *A* is incorrect because paragraph two states that he was never considered an extraordinary writer as a child. Choice *B* is incorrect because there is no indication that Dahl did not want his stories to become popular. Choice *C* is incorrect because it is mentioned in paragraph two that the chocolates he received as a young boy inspired his story *Charlie and the Chocolate Factory*.

18. B: Choice *B* is the correct answer because that is the intended effect of the passage's sequence of events. The passage begins with Dahl's childhood and continues to discuss events in Dahl's life in the order that they happened. Choice *A* is incorrect because the passage does not list Dahl's works in the order that they were written. Choice *C* is incorrect because the passage details that Dahl was a pilot before he was a renowned writer. Choice *D* is incorrect because the sequence is intentional.

19. B: Choice *B* is the correct answer because *prolific* means that an author produces many notable works. This is true of Dahl. The context clue that tells us this is when the sentence says that Dahl "wrote many books" during his lifetime. Choice *A* is incorrect because Dahl is not forgettable, based on his many famous works that are now novels. Choice *C* is incorrect for nearly the same reason; Dahl has

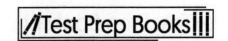

many successful novels. Choice *D* is incorrect because Dahl is never mentioned as competing in anything so that he could be considered *victorious*.

20. D: Choice *D* is the correct answer because *magical* is the best word to describe Dahl's books. The context clues that lead us to this word are the adjectives used in the first paragraph. This includes *whimsical* and *unique*. The last paragraph also describes some of the features of his novels, such as a girl with psychic powers. This is best described as *magical*. Choice *A* is incorrect because Dahl's novels are never described as being sad. Choice *B* is incorrect because Dahl's works are described as *unique*, which is the opposite of *basic*. Choice *C* is incorrect for the same reason as Choice *B*.

21. B: Choice *B* is the correct answer because Marissa displays signs of anxiety throughout the passage. She is worried about her exam. This is what gives the passage an *anxious* tone. Choice *A* is incorrect because there is no tragedy in the passage. The outcome is overall positive. Choice *C* is incorrect because Marissa does not display any signs of feeling nostalgic or reflective. Choice *D* is incorrect because Marissa is not arrogant. She is unsure of her ability to take the exam.

22. D: Choice *D* is the correct answer because it accurately describes Marissa. In the second paragraph we learn that she always raises her hand and gets good grades. This shows that she is a confident student. It is also accurate to say that she has test-taking anxiety based on this passage. Choice *A* is incorrect because Marissa checked over her test multiple times (mentioned in the third paragraph). She did not rush through it. Choice *B* is incorrect because Marissa is known for her good grades, so it is safe to say that she cares about her studies. Choice *C* is incorrect because the passage never mentioned that Marissa is jealous of her peers.

23. C: Choice *C* is the correct answer because it accurately describes Marissa's reaction to her final grade. In the last paragraph it is mentioned that Marissa was disappointed that she did not receive a perfect score. However, in the next sentence it also says that Marissa is proud of herself, and she believes she can do better next time. This is how we know that Marissa is hopeful. Choice *A* is incorrect because although Marissa may be a bit sad about her grade, her overall tone at the end is hopeful for her future. This means that she is not dejected. Choice *B* is incorrect because it is mentioned that Marissa is disappointed and not thrilled overall. Choice *D* is incorrect because there is nothing that indicates that Marissa is angry.

24. D: Choice *D* is the correct answer because it is the best assumption that we can make from the information provided in the second paragraph. Marissa has received advice from her counselor about centering herself and taking deep breaths during the exam. We can deduce from this information that Marissa has talked to her counselor about her anxiety before. Choice *A* is incorrect because Marissa has talked to her counselor before, based on the information just discussed. Choice *B* is incorrect because there is no information that leads us to believe that this is Marissa's first time experiencing test-taking anxiety. This is especially true based on the assumption that she has talked to her counselor about it in the past. Choice *C* is incorrect because the second paragraph never mentioned that Marissa received extra time on her exam.

25. A: Choice *A* is the correct answer because *exemplary* means that someone is the best model for what they are doing. In this case, Marissa is the best model of a student or in other words she is an *excellent* student. Choice *B* is incorrect because Marissa always gets grades, so she is not *disappointing*. Choice *C* is incorrect because the passage never mentions that Marissa gets in trouble for anything. Choice *D* is incorrect because Marissa seems to care about her grades a lot, so she cannot be described as *disinterested*.

Mathematics Achievement

1. B: The associative property of multiplication states that the way in which the numbers are grouped within multiplication does not change the answer. Changing the order of the numbers within a multiplication problem is actually the commutative property. The only option that uses the associative property is $(6 \times 4) \times 2 = 6 \times (4 \times 2)$.

2. C: A factor of a number is a number that can be divided into the given value without a remainder. $27 \div 9 = 3$, so, 9 is a factor of 27. 54 is a multiple of 27, and 2 and 13 are neither factors nor multiples.

3. C: Order of operations must be followed. Therefore, perform the multiplication and division first from left to right to obtain $64 - 4$. Then, perform the subtraction to obtain a result of 60.

4. A: The value in the ten million place is 5. The value to its right is an 8, which is larger than 5. Therefore, we round the 5 up to a 6 and the rest of the values to the right become zeros. The correct answer is 1,460,000,000.

5. B: To multiply by a multiple of 10, count the number of zeros in the multiple of ten. In this case, there are 10 zeros in 10,000,000,000. Then, attach them to the right of 239. The correct answer is 2,390,000,000,000.

6. B: To find the total distance traveled, multiply the speed times the length of time: $31.5 \times 30 = 945$. The fish can travel 945 meters in 30 seconds.

7. B: To subtract decimals, line them up vertically and make sure each corresponding place value is in the correct space. Then, subtract each column from right to left. First, subtract the values in the tenth place: $2 - 1 = 1$. Then, move on to the other side of the decimal. We cannot subtract $1 - 9$, so a 1 must be borrowed from the 2 in the tens place. $11 - 9 = 2$. Next, we have a $1 - 3$. Again, we must borrow from the next place value, which is a 1. Therefore, we are left with $11 - 3$. Putting this together, we obtain the answer of 82.1. We can check our answer by addition: $82.1 + 39.1 = 121.2$.

8. A: The option 0.6666666667 is not equal to $\frac{2}{3}$. $\frac{2}{3}$ is a repeating decimal $(0.\overline{6})$, so 0.6666666667 is an approximation because it is rounded. The other two options are equal to $\frac{2}{3}$ when simplified.

9. C: To write a percent as a decimal, move the decimal place two digits to the left. In this case, two zeros must be added. The correct answer is 0.0005.

10. A: To find 8% of 60, multiply 8% times 60. 8% is converted to a decimal as 0.08. Therefore, multiply 0.08×60. To multiply a whole number times a decimal, remove the decimals and multiply the whole numbers $8 \times 60 = 480$. Then, count the number of decimals in the original problem. In this case there are 2. Then, move the decimal to the left two places. The answer is 4.8.

11. B: An algebraic equation to represent this scenario is $\frac{150}{30} = p$, where p represents the number of packs of pencils per each student. Therefore, divide 150 by 30 to obtain $p = 5$. Therefore, each student receives 5 packs of pencils.

12. A: Let x be the amount of bananas taken out of the basket. This problem can be translated into the following algebraic equation: $18 - x = 5$. Subtract 18 from both sides and then divide each side by -1 to obtain $x = 13$. There were 13 bananas taken from the basket.

166

13. C: Each term in the sequence can be found by subtracting 3.5 from the previous term. For example, $5 - 3.5 = 1.5$. Therefore, the next term in the sequence is $-5.5 - 3.5 = -9$.

14. B: To find the 8th term, plug 8 in for *n* in the given formula. $2(8) + 1 = 17$. The 8th term is 17.

15. D: The distributive property states that the 2 can be multiplied times each term inside the parentheses to remove the parentheses. Therefore, $2(x + 2) = 2 \times x + 2 \times 2 = 2x + 4$.

16. B: Similar triangles have the same shape but not the same size. The sides are proportional. It can be seen in the figure that the side lengths of the second triangle are double the side lengths of the first triangle. Therefore, the side length that is missing is double the side length of 7, so it is 14.

17. D: Dilation involves changing the size of the figure. It involves either making the shape larger or smaller.

18. A: A pentagon is a five-sided polygon that contains five inside angles and five sides that are straight.

19. C: A trapezoid is a four-sided quadrilateral. It has four line segments because of its four sides.

20. A: A cone is a three-dimensional shape that is made up of a circular base. Each horizontal cross section is a circle.

21. A: The area of a square is equal to the side length squared. In this example, each side length is 18 inches, so the area is $18^2 = 18 \times 18 = 324$. The units are square inches because area is a measure of square units.

22. B: To convert millimeters to meters, multiply the amount in millimeters times 0.001. This is equivalent to moving the decimal place three digits to the left. The correct answer is 68.456 meters.

23. C: The volume of a rectangular solid is equal to the length times width times height. The length is 4 m, the width is 3 m, and the height is 2 m. Therefore, the volume is $4 \times 3 \times 2 = 24$. The units are cubic meters since volume is a measure of cubic units. The correct answer is 24 cubic meters.

24. B: There are 3 feet in one yard, so 9 yards is equal to $9 \times 3 = 27$ feet. There are 12 inches in one foot, so there are $12 \times 27 = 324$ inches.

25. D: Plug 25 into the formula for *C*. Therefore, $F = \frac{9}{5}(25) + 32 = 45 + 32 = 77$ degrees Fahrenheit.

26. B: Calculate the difference between the two amounts. In 2022 the profit was about $25 million, and in 2021 the profit was about $18 million. $25 - 18 = 7$, or $7 million.

27. B: To find the median, first place the dollar amounts in numerical order: $7, $8, $9, $10, $11, $15, $16, $20. Because there is an even number of dollar amounts, the mean of the two middle values ($10 and $11) is the median. The mean of $10 and $11 is $\frac{10+11}{2} = \frac{21}{2} = 10.5$.

28. A: There are $6 + 5 + 4 = 15$ total pieces of fruit in the bag. Out of the 15 pieces of fruit, 5 are green apples. Therefore, the probability of selecting a green apple is $\frac{5}{15} = \frac{1}{3}$.

29. A: Putting the data values in numerical order, we obtain {5, 5, 6, 6, 6, 7, 8, 8, 9}. Therefore, the minimum value is 5. The mode is 6 because it appears the greatest number of times. The median is 6

because there are an odd number of values, and it is the middle value. Finally, the mean is the sum of the values divided by the quantity, which is $\frac{60}{9} \approx 6.7$. Therefore, the largest value is the mean.

30. B: The pie chart shows that 20% of the students stated their favorite hobby was reading. 20% of 200 is equal to $0.2(200) = 40$ students.

Practice Test #3

Verbal Reasoning

Synonyms

1. BANQUET
    a. Announcement
    b. Castle
    c. Feast
    d. Rug

2. INDUSTRIOUS
    a. Adventurous
    b. Hardworking
    c. Resistant
    d. Smart

3. BURROW
    a. Bird
    b. Hole
    c. Nest
    d. Habitat

4. VACANT
    a. Empty
    b. Implied
    c. Missing
    d. Unsure

5. DISCLOSE
    a. Confess
    b. Hide
    c. Overlook
    d. Resemble

6. SEEP
    a. Collect
    b. Emerge
    c. Leak
    d. Rest

7. VETO
    a. Elect
    b. Ponder
    c. Reject
    d. Wane

169

8. RIDICULE
   a. Esteem
   b. Evacuate
   c. Highlight
   d. Mock

9. BEWILDERED
   a. Crazed
   b. Puzzled
   c. Quiet
   d. Unrefined

10. CARCASS
   a. Dire
   b. Remains
   c. Satchel
   d. Symptom

11. OUTSKIRTS
   a. Boundary
   b. Oasis
   c. Metropolitan
   d. Reservoir

12. SELDOM
   a. Conventional
   b. Egotistical
   c. Rarely
   d. Sleepy

13. THRIFTY
   a. Economical
   b. Pleasant
   c. Practical
   d. Sneaky

14. JAGGED
   a. Exposed
   b. Revealed
   c. Shocked
   d. Uneven

15. PECULIAR
   a. Gentle
   b. Inquisitive
   c. Observant
   d. Unique

16. FLIMSY
    a. Amusing
    b. Convenient
    c. Rowdy
    d. Thin

17. COAX
    a. Despise
    b. Harm
    c. Persuade
    d. Trouble

Sentence Completion A

18. As someone terrified of flying, Shaun always made sure to bring a _____ with him whenever he had to fly just in case he ever had to jump out of a crashing plane.
    a. blanket
    b. parachute
    c. scythe
    d. windbreaker

19. After missing the hare with his first arrow, the huntsman reached into his _____ to quickly get another one.
    a. glossary
    b. quiver
    c. scroll
    d. vehicle

20. It wasn't until Jasmine saw nature documentaries showing the hunting tactics of lions that she truly understood how _____ they could be when seeking out a meal.
    a. introspective
    b. optimistic
    c. pretentious
    d. ravenous

21. Although she doesn't tell anyone, Miranda loves to _____, and constantly finds herself "tuning in" to other people's conversations when she is out and about.
    a. eavesdrop
    b. illustrate
    c. meditate
    d. mitigate

22. When Elijah first got his cat, Max, he didn't yet know that cats are naturally much more _____ animals than dogs, and so he didn't understand why all Max wanted to do all day was nap.
    a. intense
    b. optimistic
    c. sedentary
    d. subservient

171

23. Michael's grandmom told all of her friends how tech _____ her grandson was after he fixed her tablet, even though all Michael had really done was just turn it off and back on again.
    a. deficient
    b. inferior
    c. neutral
    d. savvy

24. The city council members were deeply impressed with the young student's _____, and they were surprised that she could speak so thoughtfully and passionately on behalf of her teachers and her school.
    a. eloquence
    b. facade
    c. nausea
    d. protocol

25. After the student slipped and fell in the hallway, the school nurse recommended that the student take it easy and use the next class period to _____.
    a. diagnose
    b. exercise
    c. rest
    d. study

26. It was only once the little boy witnessed the animal jump from the lily pad into the water that he realized it was a(n) _____ and could live both in the water and on the land.
    a. amphibian
    b. dinosaur
    c. mammal
    d. marsupial

27. Sarah's mother made sure to emphasize to her that going to get fast food after school was only going to be a(n) _____, and that she shouldn't expect to be getting it all the time now.
    a. anomaly
    b. standard
    c. experience
    d. tradition

28. Despite the majority of the committee agreeing in favor of the proposal, another vote was held, as the decision had to be _____ in order for the proposal to pass.
    a. agreeable
    b. possible
    c. psychological
    d. unanimous

Sentence Completion B

29. While her teacher ran back to their office to grab a fresh copy of the math test, Lizzy figured it would be sensible to use that time to _____
   a. rehearse her times tables once more.
   b. guess what was going to be served for lunch.
   c. move things about in the classroom to frustrate her teacher.
   d. figure out where she and her friends were going to hang out after school.

30. The first sign that Marcus had noticed that his cat Fiona was in a grumpy mood was that she _____
   a. woke him trying to cuddle into bed with him.
   b. seemed much more energetic and playful than usual.
   c. started meowing at the same time she did every morning to get fed.
   d. began hissing and batting her paw at Marcus when he tried to approach her.

31. Although Maria originally thought she understood the gist of the book's plot from a summary she read, it was only once her teacher called on her that she was embarrassed to realize that she _____
   a. could remember even more than she thought.
   b. knew the material even better than her teacher did.
   c. had looked up a summary for a different book entirely.
   d. was the only one in her class who had actually read the book.

32. Due to his parent's brisk stride, the small toddler found it difficult to _____
   a. sit up straight.
   b. eat dinner with them.
   c. contribute to their conversation.
   d. keep up while walking.

33. The protest in the public park escalated much faster than anyone expected, and before anyone knew it, the _____
   a. park was entirely empty.
   b. protestors agreed to stop protesting.
   c. protest became a massive game of tag.
   d. crowd became too big for the confines of the park.

34. When prescribing the new medication, Dr. Lewis made sure to tell Ms. Jackson that drowsiness was a side effect, and therefore she should expect to _____
   a. lose her appetite almost entirely.
   b. feel much more creative and inspired.
   c. become tired and sleepy much more easily.
   d. find herself becoming more irritable than normal.

Quantitative Reasoning

1. Mrs. Simpson instructed her class to divide themselves into three groups. All of the groups must include a composite number of students (or NOT a prime number of students), and each group should be of similar size. If there are 34 students in the class, how many students should be in each group?
   a. 12, 12, and 10
   b. 11, 11, and 12
   c. 10, 11, and 12
   d. 9, 10, and 13

2. Michael is a delivery driver for ChocoCakes. He has several large orders to deliver today, and he wants to make sure he loads his truck with enough ChocoCakes for all his customers. Check his orders and decide how many ChocoCakes he needs for the day's deliveries:

      374 to Alpha Market
      681 to Qwick Stop
      422 to Mr. Spock's Shop
      136 to Shop-a-While
      97 to Arianna's Grocery
      233 to Roadside Deli

   a. 1833
   b. 1933
   c. 1943
   d. 1900

3. Brianna drives the library's very popular Bookmobile. She goes to MLK Elementary School on Mondays and Wednesdays and ABC-XYZ Day Camp on Mondays, Wednesdays, and Fridays. She goes to the middle school every Thursday, and the high school has her come by every Tuesday and Friday. She also makes weekly stops at Cute Kids Daycare, Sunrise Elementary, and Forest Middle School and twice weekly stops at Riverside High School and Elm Park Boys and Girls Club. How many stops does Brianna make each week?
   a. 9
   b. 8
   c. 17
   d. 15

4. David, Aidan, Marian, and Ellen are working on their math homework. One of the problems is to write 93,567 in expanded form. David wrote $90000 + 3000 + 500 + 60 + 7$. Aidan wrote $(9 \times 10,000) + (3 \times 1000) + (5 \times 100) + (6 \times 10) + (7 \times 1)$. Marian wrote $93,000 + 500 + 67$. Ellen wrote $(93 \times 1000) + (56 \times 10) + (7 \times 1)$. Who got the problem correct?
   a. David
   b. David and Aidan
   c. Marian and Ellen
   d. Ellen

5. The Bears and the Jaguars were playing a football game. Bears players Smith, Jones, and Sampson each scored 6 points. Jaguars players Thomas, Lindenfeld, and Davidson also scored 6 points each, and Davidson also scored 2 extra points. The Jaguars' kicker made two 3-point field goals. How many points did each team score?

    a. Bears 26; Jaguars 18
    b. Bears 18; Jaguars 18
    c. Bears 18; Jaguars 26
    d. Bears 18; Jaguars 20

6. James, Beth, and Anna worked together doing lawn care work over the summer. They made $355 in June, $420 in July, and $296 in August. How much will each of them get if they share all the money equally?

    a. $1071
    b. $357
    c. $355, $420, $296
    d. $320

7. James is doing some calculations for his boss at the XYZ Box Factory. The boss has given him a list of numbers that he needs to put in order so he can find the least and greatest numbers. When the numbers are in the correct order, what are the least and greatest numbers?

$$
\begin{array}{c}
0.4534 \\
1.6954 \\
1.2348 \\
2.6359 \\
0.4578 \\
1.3342 \\
2.6351
\end{array}
$$

    a. 0.4578; 2.6351
    b. 0.4534; 2.6359
    c. 1.2348; 1.3342
    d. 0.4534; 2.6351

8. Claire, Kenneth, Nora, and Max are playing with their race cars and race car track. Claire has 44 inches of track, Kenneth has 26 inches, Nora has 97 inches, and Max has 107 inches. If they put all their tracks together, how long with their racetrack be?

    a. 274 inches
    b. 179 inches
    c. 300 inches
    d. 167 inches

9. Jonathan is catering a wedding, and he wants to make sure he has enough sweet tea to serve to all of the guests. Each guest should get at least 12 ounces of tea with their meal. If he has 2309.28 ounces of tea, how many guests can he serve?

    a. 191
    b. 1924.40
    c. 192
    d. 19244

Practice Test #3

10. The Seattle area is due to get a lot of rainfall over the next five days: $\frac{2}{10}$ inches, 3.49 inches, $\frac{5}{8}$ inches, 1.93 inches, and $\frac{15}{20}$ inches. How much total rain will the city get?
    a. 11.62 inches
    b. 5.42 inches
    c. 1.575 inches
    d. 6.995 inches

11. Jose and his four friends are comparing the grades they got on the last science test. Jose got $\frac{90}{100}$, Timothy got 0.625, Andrew got 0.87, Mary Jane got $\frac{42}{50}$, and Arya got $\frac{24}{25}$. Who got the highest grade on the test?
    a. Arya
    b. Jose
    c. Andrew
    d. Mary Jane

12. Mr. Williams's class is going to have a pizza party! Mr. Williams needs to know how many pizzas to order so he can figure out how much the party will cost. He asked the class how many slices each student wanted. Four students said they could eat 3 slices. Ten students said they wanted 2 slices each, and eight students wanted 1 slice each. Three students are not going to have any pizza. If each pizza has 8 slices and costs $13.67, how many pizzas does Mr. Williams need to order, and how much will it cost?
    a. 5 pizzas; $68.35
    b. 40 pizzas; $546.80
    c. 6 pizzas; $82.02
    d. 5.375 pizzas; $73.48

13. Kevin and his sister have a combined age of 16. If Kevin is 7 years old, how old is his sister?
    a. 9
    b. 16
    c. 8
    d. 7

14. There were 21 pies for sale at Delicious Desserts bakery this morning. If there were 3 bakers working, and they all made the same amount of pies, how many pies did each person bake?
    a. 3
    b. 21
    c. 7
    d. 63

15. Stanley's math teacher wrote an equation on the board and told the class to work in groups to figure out how to group like terms, but NOT to finish solving the equation. The equation was $z - 4 = 10 + 2z$. What is the correct equation when the like terms are grouped?
    a. $-14 = z$
    b. $-4 = 10 + 2z - z$
    c. $z - 4 - 10 = 2z$
    d. $-4 - 10 = 2z - z$

176

16. Melissa is 12 years old, which is 2 years older than her little sister, Betsy. Their cousin James is twice Betsy's age. How old is James?
   a. 20
   b. 24
   c. 22
   d. 28

17. Mackenzie found 14 shells when her family went to the beach on vacation. After adding those to her collection at home, she now has 56 shells. How many shells did she have before she went on vacation?
   a. 70
   b. 14
   c. 42
   d. 56

18. A number decreased by 81 is 147. What is the original number?
   a. 81
   b. 147
   c. 228
   d. 66

19. Travis's mother bought Halloween candy for him to share with his whole fifth-grade class. If there are 72 pieces of candy and every student got 3 pieces, how many students are in Travis's class?
   a. 216
   b. 24
   c. 69
   d. $3x$

20. Which type of triangle has three angles that all measure 60 degrees?
   a. Acute and equilateral
   b. Right and scalene
   c. Obtuse and equilateral
   d. Acute and isosceles

21. The preschool classroom has lots of toys for the children to play with. While Amelia's mom was picking up her little brother, Amelia was looking at the toys and deciding which 3-dimensional shape they represented. The ball was easy, and so were the blocks, but she had some trouble with a strange toy that had triangular ends and three, flat parallelogram sides. What is this shape?
   a. Square prism
   b. Square pyramid
   c. Triangular pyramid
   d. Triangular prism

22. Oliver is helping his mother put away groceries. He is practicing his geometry while he helps, identifying the shape of each item. So far, he has put away a box of tissues, a can of soup, some cookies, a ball for his little sister, and a bag of potato chips. Which item is the cylinder?
   a. Tissue box
   b. Chips
   c. Soup
   d. Ball

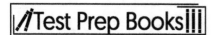

23. Ms. O'Brien's class is learning about symmetry. She explained that many of the letters in the alphabet are symmetrical, especially when they are written in capital letters. The students are guessing words that have all symmetrical letters. Which of the following guesses is correct?
   a. HAM
   b. TOP
   c. BALL
   d. TOYS

24. Elijah is looking at his dad's delivery route through a neighborhood. He notices that it looks like two triangles. His dad asks him if the triangles are similar or not. How long do the two missing sides, segment AC and segment DE, have to be to make these two triangles similar?

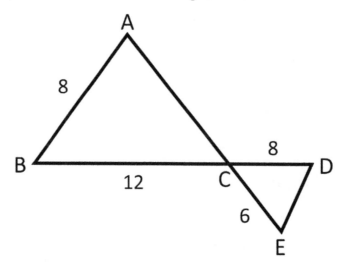

   a. Segment AC = 4; segment DE = 16
   b. Segment AC = 12; segment DE = 4
   c. Segment AC = 16; segment DE = 6
   d. Segment AC = 16; segment DE = 4

25. Diana has to choose two congruent triangles for her math homework question. Which pair should she choose?

a.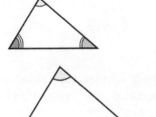

b.

c.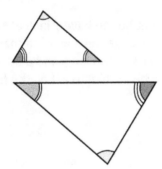

d.

26. Theo has to change the oil in four cars in his shop. He bought six gallons of oil (and there are four quarts in a gallon). Two of the cars take 5 quarts of oil each. One car takes 6 quarts of oil, and one only needed 4 quarts. How many quarts of oil will Theo have left over when he finishes all the oil changes?
   a. 4
   b. 9
   c. 364
   d. 20

27. Martin has a lot of errands to do today, and he wants to make sure he finishes in time to watch the football game on television later. He has made a list of all his errands and included how much time he thinks each one will take. How long does Martin need to complete all his errands?

   Bank: 15 minutes

   Car wash: $\frac{1}{2}$ hour

   Grocery store: 1 hour and 10 minutes

   Post office: $\frac{1}{3}$ hour

   a. 1 hour, 15 minutes
   b. 2 hours, 15 minutes
   c. 2 hours, 10 minutes
   d. 2 hours, 35 minutes

28. Jasmine needs to be in bed by 10:00 pm. If she needs 15 minutes to get a shower and 10 minutes to brush her teeth and hair, what time does Jasmine need to start getting ready for bed?
a. 9:35 am
b. 10:25 pm
c. 9:45 pm
d. 9:35 pm

29. Anthony needs to collect oranges to take to the farmers' market. He has two crates that can hold 150 oranges each, one crate that can hold 90 oranges, and two small crates that can each hold 15 oranges. How many oranges can Anthony take to the market?
a. 270
b. 420
c. 405
d. 255

30. Andrew wants to get some pet fish. He has learned that he can have 1 inch of fish per gallon of water. The tank he has holds 15 gallons of water. He wants to get an angel fish that is 6 inches long, a beta shark that is 7 inches long, two goldfish that are each 3 inches long, and a dozen neon fish that are each 1 inch long. How much bigger does his tank need to be for him to get all the fish he wants?
a. 31 gallons
b. 5 gallons
c. 16 gallons
d. 1 gallon

31. Zachary knows that water freezes at 32 degrees Fahrenheit and boils at 212 degrees Fahrenheit. But the only thermometer he has displays the temperature in Celsius. What are the freezing and boiling points for water in Celsius?
a. 0 degrees and 212 degrees
b. 32 degrees and 100 degrees
c. 0 degrees and 100 degrees
d. 32 degrees and 212 degrees

32. Once Mrs. Sousa finished grading the papers for her English class, she wanted to know the range of the grades. If the grades were 88, 90, 98, 76, 65, 76, 92, 84, 76, and 86 then what is the range?
a. 65
b. 33
c. 98
d. 76

33. Sarah competes on her school's track team. She has been getting faster and faster at running the 40-yard dash. Her times are 5.59, 5.38, 5.51, 5.47, 5.45, 5.30, 5.47, 5.39, and 5.28 seconds. What is Sarah's median time?
a. 5.47 seconds
b. 5.45 seconds
c. 5.59 seconds
d. 5.28 seconds

34. Danielle has been working hard all summer. She has been mowing lawns, washing cars, and helping do extra chores for the neighbors. She earned a total of $87.50. She wants to see how much of her total money came from each type of job she did. Which type of graph would be best?
   a. Bar
   b. Line
   c. Circle
   d. Mode

35. Marcus is rolling a six-sided die. What is the probability that he will roll a 6 if he rolls the die one time?
   a. $\frac{6}{6}$

   b. $\frac{1}{6}$

   c. $\frac{2}{6}$

   d. $\frac{3}{6}$

36. A deck of cards has 52 cards. There are 13 red hearts, 13 red diamonds, 13 black spades, and 13 black clubs. What is the probability of drawing a red card from the deck?
   a. $\frac{1}{2}$

   b. $\frac{1}{4}$

   c. $\frac{1}{26}$

   d. $\frac{4}{52}$

37. Ashley's teacher has a big jar of colored marbles on her desk. There are 200 marbles in the jar: 26 are red, 48 are blue, 60 are green, 20 are yellow, and 46 are purple. If Ashley chose one marble from the jar, what is the probability that she would choose a purple one?
   a. $\frac{23}{100}$

   b. $\frac{6}{25}$

   c. $\frac{13}{100}$

   d. $\frac{1}{10}$

38. Katherine is trying to figure out how much it might rain in her area this April. She looked up the rainfall amounts for April for the last five years:

    2022: 5 inches

    2021: 6 inches

    2020: 10 inches

    2019: 4 inches

    2018: 1 inch

Which prediction would probably be the most accurate?
    a. 5 inches
    b. 11 inches
    c. 1 inch
    d. 0 inches

Reading Comprehension

Questions 1 – 5 are based on the following passage.

The space race was a part of the Cold War, which took place August 1955 to July 1975. The space race was a competition between the United States and the Soviet Union to develop the best technological advancements for space exploration. Most famously, this included a competition to see who could go to space first and who could land on the moon first.

The reason that the Soviet Union and the United States engaged in this competition is because the country that emerged on top would be considered the most powerful, economically successful, and technologically advanced. This mattered greatly during the Cold War, which was all about political image and propaganda.

The major space race accomplishments began in 1957 with the Soviet Union launching Sputnik, an artificial satellite, into space. This was the first man-made object to be launched into the orbit of the Earth. The US was unhappy with this development and created the National Aeronautics and Space Administration, better known as NASA. It was NASA's job to explore the possibilities of space. Although the US now had a federal agency dedicated to the space race, the Soviet Union continued to dominate. They had two more major accomplishments. In 1959, they launched the Luna 2, a space probe that hit the moon. In 1961, they also launched the Vostok 1, which carried the first person to ever orbit the earth.

The US was not going to be dissuaded from their goals—they began to move forward as quick as lightning. NASA was thriving and had created the Apollo project, which would put a man on the moon. The project was not without faults, though. Three astronauts were killed during a launch simulation in 1967. Finally, in 1969, Apollo 11 launched and successfully landed on the moon. Neil Armstrong became the first man to walk on the moon, and the US had achieved a major victory for the space race.

The Soviet Union struggled to advance. They attempted four lunar launch attempts with every single one failing. The Cold War waned and ultimately the Americans were seen as the space-race winners. The space race left its mark on the American people, who developed an extreme

182

interest in space travel and astronauts. This can be seen in much of the media from that time period. For example, *The Jetsons* was a popular cartoon set in the space-age year of 2062. Flying cars, robots, and other futuristic gadgets were featured in the show, which captivated Americans who had been closely following the real-life technological advancements of the space race. The space race also changed the way that Americans viewed the Soviets. They were seen as enemies who were trying to challenge the US and its power.

Interest in space exploration dwindled after the space race was over. However, the technological advancements and constant media coverage have inspired Americans to advance in other ways. Much of the world's present-day technology was made possible by developments that occurred during the space race. Solar panels, water filtration systems, and firefighting equipment are a few examples of things that were developed from space-race technology. There are numerous medical advancements that have come from the space race, such as the invention of the artificial limb. Even though the US might not be interested in space exploration like we once were, the space race was and continues to be a catalyst for pushing the limits of what humans can do.

1. How many years passed between the Soviet Union's first satellite launch and the United States' moon landing?
    a. 6 years
    b. 10 years
    c. 12 years
    d. This cannot be determined by the information provided in the passage.

2. Which two vocabulary words from this passage are most closely related?
    a. *Dissuaded* and *struggled*
    b. *Dwindled* and *waned*
    c. *Dominate* and *catalyst*
    d. *Futuristic* and *exploration*

3. What is the purpose of the last paragraph in the passage?
    a. To explain how the space race changed the world technologically
    b. To emphasize that the United States won the space race
    c. To detail the second space race that is happening in modern times
    d. To summarize everything that has already been said in the previous paragraphs

4. The phrase "began to move forward as quick as lightning" is an example of what?
    a. Metaphor
    b. Personification
    c. Simile
    d. Irony

5. The second paragraph of this passage mainly answers which question regarding the space race:
    a. Who?
    b. How?
    c. Why?
    d. When?

Questions 6 – 10 are based on the following passage.

There are historically significant locations scattered around the Earth that are known as the Seven Wonders of the Ancient World. These are notable structures that date back to many centuries ago. The Seven Wonders are: the Great Pyramid of Giza, the Hanging Gardens of Babylon, the Statue of Zeus at Olympia, the Temple of Artemis at Ephesus, the Mausoleum at Halicarnassus, the Colossus of Rhodes, and the Lighthouse of Alexandria. All of these structures are historically important and have their own stories.

The Great Pyramid of Giza is one of the most recognizable wonders. It was built from 2584–2561 BC by the Egyptians to serve as the tomb for a pharaoh named Khufu. It is the only one of the Seven Wonders that is still mostly intact and can be visited and seen today. However, it has been badly damaged over the years due to erosion and earthquakes. It is 481 feet tall, and it was the tallest man-made structure for almost 4,000 years!

The Hanging Gardens of Babylon no longer exist but was extremely impressive during its existence. It featured numerous tiered gardens. It is said that the gardens were built by a Babylonian king for his wife because she was homesick for the green hills she grew up with. The Hanging Gardens are only known through classical literature, which means that a lot of facts about them are unknown.

The Statue of Zeus at Olympia was a 41-foot statue that was sculpted in 435 BC in Olympia, Greece. It was created for the Temple of Zeus. Zeus is the god of the sky and thunder in Greek mythology. The statue was composed of ivory and gold, making it very expensive and precious. The end of the statue's existence is largely unknown except that it was destroyed sometime during the 5th century AD.

The Temple of Artemis at Ephesus was built during the 6th century BCE and was located in modern Turkey. The size of the temple was immense and much larger than Greek temples. Ephesus was a Greek colony that especially worshipped Artemis. Artemis is the goddess of hunting and fertility in Greek mythology. Unfortunately, the temple was set on fire and destroyed during the 4th century BCE. It was rebuilt two more times and subsequently both were destroyed.

The Mausoleum at Halicarnassus was built during 350 BC in modern Turkey. It was constructed for a powerful figure named Mausolus. It was an elevated tomb that reached almost 150 feet in height. Each side had detailed sculptures. It was so important that the word mausoleum is used to this day to describe tombs that are above ground. Unfortunately, this specific mausoleum was destroyed by multiple earthquakes from the 12th to 15th century.

The Colossus of Rhodes was a 108-foot-tall statue depicting Helios, the sun god in Greek mythology. It was located in the city of Rhodes in Greece. The city of Rhodes successfully defended against an extensive attack by a Macedonian navy and army. They constructed this sculpture in 280 BC to celebrate. Unfortunately, it was destroyed by a conqueror in the year 653.

The Lighthouse of Alexandria was a lighthouse constructed in 247 BC in Alexandria, Egypt. It was 330 feet tall. It was damaged repeatedly by earthquakes over the years before it collapsed in 956. The lighthouse was continuously repaired and was ultimately replaced by a medieval fort.

184

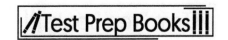

6. What is the purpose of this passage?
    a. To teach readers about the differences between the ancient world and the modern world
    b. To educate readers with general facts about the Seven Wonders of the Ancient World
    c. To detail why the Seven Wonders of the Natural World are better than those of the ancient world
    d. To convince readers to visit the Seven Wonders of the Ancient World

7. What is the purpose of this passage's structure?
    a. To show the order that the Seven Wonders were built
    b. To show the order that the Seven Wonders were destroyed
    c. To compare and contrast the Seven Wonders
    d. To list each of the Seven Wonders and give facts about each one with a separate paragraph

8. What is a common theme between each of the Seven Wonders?
    a. They have all persisted through centuries and still exist today.
    b. Each of the Seven Wonders was built by the same people.
    c. They have all been destroyed or damaged over the years.
    d. There is no common theme between the Seven Wonders.

9. What does the word *immense* in this passage most nearly mean?
    a. Small
    b. Insignificant
    c. Huge
    d. Noticeable

10. Which of the following statements is true based on the information provided in this passage?
    a. Several of the Seven Wonders were dedicated to gods and goddesses.
    b. Only one of the Seven Wonders was located in modern-day Turkey.
    c. Two of the Seven Wonders were destroyed by tornadoes.
    d. None of the Seven Wonders still exist today.

Questions 11 – 15 are based on the following passage.

Henry the Parrot was always made fun of at music school for the strange way he sounded. The other birds sang beautiful songs, while Henry only knew how to honk! The cardinals, sparrows, and finches all had their own special voices. His teachers scolded him for not being able to keep up in class. Henry felt like he didn't fit in with the other birds.

The truth of the matter was that Henry was orphaned as a baby bird when two kind geese came along and saved him. Mama Goose and Papa Goose took care of Henry all throughout his time growing up. However, as an African Grey parrot, Henry adopted the sounds that were most common to him. He didn't know this at the time, but since his family of geese honked, so did Henry!

One day Henry was sitting in his favorite tree when a large colorful bird swooped down to join him. He was in awe of the vibrant blue, yellow, and green feathers that this bird had.

"Hello, my fellow parrot!" said the large bird.

"Fellow parrot? Are you one also?!" Henry said. This was very exciting! He had never met another parrot before.

"My name's Marty. I'm a macaw parrot! I don't see many parrots in these parts, so I thought I would come say hello," Marty told him.

Henry and Marty chatted happily in the tree. They had many common interests. Marty even mentioned that he had gone to the same music school as Henry.

"Oh no! Don't even mention school... I've been having such a hard time keeping up with the other students" Henry lamented.

"I can't imagine that! As a parrot you're sure to have the biggest range and most skill out of any bird there!" Marty exclaimed!

"What do you mean? All I can do is honk," Henry said moodily.

Marty began to explain that parrots can mimic any sound that they hear. In other regions, where parrots are more common, they were renowned for their voices. Everyone loved hearing what the parrots could mimic. Henry simply hadn't learned this skill yet and was used to mimicking his family subconsciously! Upon hearing this, Henry's interest in singing was immediately renewed. He couldn't wait to go back to school and practice copying every song and sound he heard!

"Thank you, Marty, I can't tell you how much it means to me that you came along and helped me understand what I'm capable of! I can't wait to show you what I learn," Henry said happily. He was so happy that he had met Marty. He now felt as if he had a mentor.

The next day, Henry practiced his newfound ability. It wasn't perfect, and he struggled a lot, but just knowing what he could do made him excited for the future. He felt as confident as a lion! Everyone was going to hear him roar! All it took was finding a friend who understood what Henry was capable of, and who encouraged him to keep chasing his dreams. He was different from the other birds, but now he saw it as a unique superpower.

11. Who is the protagonist in this story?
    a. Marty
    b. Henry
    c. The other students
    d. The teachers

12. What word best fits the tone of this story?
    a. Encouraging
    b. Disappointing
    c. Annoying
    d. Romantic

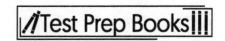

13. What kind of figurative language is "everyone was going to hear him roar"?
    a. Metaphor
    b. Simile
    c. Personification
    d. Oxymoron

14. What is the primary message in this story?
    a. Practice makes perfect.
    b. Life can be hard if you don't make friends.
    c. Your differences may be your biggest strength.
    d. Always stay the course, and you will succeed.

15. What does the word *renowned* in this passage most nearly mean?
    a. Studied
    b. Unknown
    c. Hated
    d. Famous

Questions 16 – 20 are based on the following passage.

Theodore "Teddy" Roosevelt was the 26th president of the United States. He took office in 1901 after the assassination of President William McKinley. The 25th Amendment of the Constitution ensured that since he was vice president to McKinley, he was next in line to take over the presidency. Roosevelt was 42 years old when this happened and was, at that time, the youngest person to have ever become president. Roosevelt remains one of the most famous presidents of all time due to his incredible achievements with the progressive movement.

Roosevelt was born on October 27, 1858, in New York City to a wealthy family. As a child, he struggled with illnesses and weakness. His father encouraged him to take up exercise to improve his health. Through rigorous physical activity, Roosevelt became very fit. He went to Harvard University and participated in the boxing program. After college, Roosevelt went back to New York and became a member of the state assembly for some time. After both his mother and wife passed away unexpectedly, Roosevelt moved out west for a reprieve from his busy life, and he fell in love with the natural world. Roosevelt cared deeply for the landscape, waterways, and animals.

Roosevelt eventually returned to public service and created a group called the Rough Riders, who fought in the Spanish-American War. It was their contributions that directly led to Cuba's independence from Spain. This success shot Roosevelt to fame, and he was elected governor of New York in 1899. Two years later he would be elected vice president under McKinley. It was only six months into the presidency that McKinley was assassinated.

As president, Roosevelt focused on environmental conservation, monopolies (when a company is so powerful that smaller companies can no longer compete), and foreign affairs. He is responsible for creating the United States Forest Service. This led to the creation of 150 national forests and 5 national parks during his presidency alone. The United States is still able to enjoy the great outdoors freely because of Roosevelt's efforts. He was a Nobel Peace Prize winner for his attempts to end the war between Russia and Japan. He is famous for his "speak softly and carry a big stick" policy. This idea meant that when dealing with other countries, it is important

to approach them with diplomatic respect and peace. However, it is equally important to keep the threat of a "big stick" or strong military looming in the background to ensure that the US is not seen as weak. Additionally, he is well-known as a large contributor in the creation of the Panama Canal, which revolutionized trade.

Roosevelt was popular enough to serve a second term. It was successful by all accounts. In 1912, Roosevelt sought to regain the presidency once again. However, he was shot in the chest by a saloonkeeper. Despite the injury, Roosevelt went on to finish his campaign speech. Even with this persistence, Roosevelt lost the presidency to Woodrow Wilson. He spent his remaining years exploring the great outdoors that he loved so much. He passed away in 1919.

16. Which of Roosevelt's presidential terms came about unexpectedly?
    a. First term
    b. Second term
    c. Third term
    d. He always expected that he was to become president.

17. What does the word *persistence* in this passage most nearly mean?
    a. Sadness
    b. Ingenuity
    c. Laziness
    d. Determination

18. Which of the following is something that Roosevelt is famous for?
    a. Being vice president to Woodrow Wilson
    b. Environmental conservation
    c. Saying the phrase, "leave nothing for tomorrow which can be done today"
    d. Creating the Mississippi River

19. The teddy bear was named after Roosevelt after he refused to kill a bear while hunting. What is this an example of?
    a. His perseverance to win the presidency
    b. His foreign policy
    c. His love for the natural world
    d. His dedication to fitness

20. What is the purpose of the second paragraph?
    a. To describe Roosevelt's actions during retirement
    b. To explain Roosevelt's life before the presidency
    c. To provide information about Roosevelt's policies
    d. To go into depth about Roosevelt's contributions during the Spanish-American war

Questions 21 – 25 are based on the following passage.

Two weeks ago, I inherited a very large, very haunted manor from my late grandfather. I had been living in a small apartment in the city, struggling to make ends meet when I received the call.

"He left you Magnolia Manor," the family attorney told me.

188

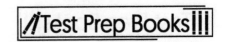

And so here I was, trying to sleep in a creaky old bed on my first night in my new yet very old manor. I couldn't say no to the offer of a free home when I was so low on funds. Sure, the townspeople called the house haunted, but those were just baseless rumors!

My thoughts were swirling, and I couldn't sleep, so I turned on my bedside lamp to read a bit of my novel. As I turned the pages, I saw something move in the corner of my eye. I whipped my head to the side, trying to catch the movement. There was nothing there but shadows. Phew!

A few minutes passed when I heard a crash downstairs. What was that?! I put on my slippers and rushed downstairs to investigate. Nothing seemed amiss. Clearly the rumors of this place being haunted were causing me to imagine things!

"Boo!" something yelled in my ear.

"Ahhh!!!" I screamed, scrambling backwards.

As I turned around, the ghostly form of a young woman stood before me. My eyes widened, and I pointed my finger.

"W-what are you doing here? Who are you?" I stuttered. My heart was pounding, and I felt a bit faint.

"Why, I'm Magnolia! Does Magnolia Manor ring a bell? I owned this manor before your grandfather!"

I took a moment to gather my bearings. I had to be dreaming. I pinched myself, but nothing happened!

"Magnolia? Why are you still here? Aren't you, like, 200 years old?" I asked, my voice shaking with each word.

"Why wouldn't I be here? This is my home! Along with George, Pauline, and Mindy! George is my butler, Pauline is my younger sister, and Mindy is our dear kitty!" she said happily.

I was totally going to faint. This was crazy! One by one, the other three ghosts turned the corner. George and Pauline looked a bit sheepish, like they felt guilty about scaring me. Pauline spoke first.

"Oh, ma'am! There's nothing to be scared of. I know it must be frightening to talk to the dead and all, but we're really quite nice! We kept your grandfather company, and we even have the power to do a few things around the house!"

"Like what?" I asked.

"Well, we keep the manor tidy, and we're quite good at turning the lights on and off! We love to play board games and card games. Really, we're amazing to hang out with!" she proudly exclaimed.

I couldn't believe what I was hearing. How had my grandfather never mentioned this? Not only had I inherited a giant old manor, but it came with a gaggle of ghostly friends! I felt a brush on my ankle. Mindy the cat was purring at my feet.

189

And so, for the rest of that evening, I came to terms with my new life. My ghostly roommates were as amazing company as they claimed to be. It took a few days, but soon enough we were all watching movies and bantering like old friends. They told me stories about their lives from centuries ago. They even told me things I didn't know about my grandfather. Apparently, he was an amazing singer! The manor had grown on me, and I loved all of its unique quirks.

Before I moved to Magnolia Manor, I had been a bit lonely in the big city. I had been apprehensive about being all alone in a big home. I was so happy that things had turned out the way that they did and now I had permanent friends, even if they were a bit transparent!

21. What point of view is this passage written in?
    a. First person
    b. Second person
    c. Third person
    d. Fourth person

22. What is the mood of the first half of this passage?
    a. Optimistic
    b. Morose
    c. Joyful
    d. Eerie

23. What does the word *apprehensive* in this passage most nearly mean?
    a. Excited
    b. Content
    c. Anxious
    d. Angry

24. What will the narrator most likely do in the future based on the events of this passage?
    a. Move out and go back to the city.
    b. Remain in the manor with the ghosts as her friends.
    c. Make the ghosts leave the home.
    d. Demolish the home and build a new one.

25. What is the best summary of this passage?
    a. A woman inherits a spooky manor that is haunted by ghosts. The ghosts turn out to be friendly, and she happily lives with them.
    b. A woman is forced to move into a haunted house where ghosts keep her up at night. She is unhappy with her living situation.
    c. Three ghosts receive an unexpected visit to their home. They play practical jokes on the visitor so that she will leave.
    d. An abandoned manor is restored by a young woman. She later discovers the presence of three unhappy ghosts.

190

Mathematics Achievement

1. Which of the following is equivalent to the value of the digit 3 in the number 792.134?
   a. 3×10
   b. 3×100
   c. $\frac{3}{10}$
   d. $\frac{3}{100}$

2. How would the number 847.89632 be written if rounded to the nearest hundredth?
   a. 847.90
   b. 900
   c. 847.89
   d. 847.896

3. How would $\frac{4}{5}$ be written as a percent?
   a. 40%
   b. 125%
   c. 90%
   d. 80%

4. What are all the factors of 12?
   a. 12, 24, 36
   b. 1, 2, 4, 6, 12
   c. 12, 24, 36, 48
   d. 1, 2, 3, 4, 6, 12

5. A construction company is building a new housing development with the property of each house measuring 30 feet wide. If the length of the street is zoned off at 345 feet, how many houses can be built on the street?
   a. 11 houses
   b. 115 houses
   c. 11.5 houses
   d. 12 houses

6. What number could represent the point marked with a dot on the following number line?

   a. .5
   b. $\frac{1}{4}$
   c. .45
   d. $\frac{2}{5}$

191

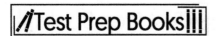

7. Kassidy drove for 3 hours at a speed of 60 miles per hour. Using the distance formula, $d = r \times t$ ($distance = rate \times time$), calculate how far Kassidy traveled.
   a. 20 miles
   b. 180 miles
   c. 65 miles
   d. 120 miles

8. Which of the following figures is NOT a polygon?
   a. Decagon
   b. Cone
   c. Triangle
   d. Rhombus

9. Joan is driving to her aunt's house for Thanksgiving. Her aunt lives 2.5 hours away. Joan stops at a rest stop for 15 minutes along the way. If Joan left at 10:15 a.m., what time will she arrive at her aunt's?
   a. 12 pm
   b. 12:45 pm
   c. 1:00 pm
   d. 1:15 pm

10. What are the coordinates of the point plotted on the grid?

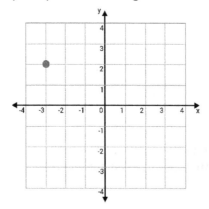

   a. $(-3, 2)$
   b. $(2, -3)$
   c. $(-3, -2)$
   d. $(2, 3)$

11. The perimeter of a 6-sided polygon is 56 cm. The lengths of 3 sides are 9 cm each. The lengths of 2 other sides are 8 cm each. What is the length of the final side?
   a. 11 cm
   b. 12 cm
   c. 13 cm
   d. 10 cm

12. Katie works at a clothing company and sold 192 shirts over the weekend. One-third of the shirts were patterned and the rest were solid. Which mathematical expression would calculate the number of solid shirts Katie sold over the weekend?

a. $192 \times \frac{1}{3}$

b. $192 \div \frac{1}{3}$

c. $192 \times (1 - \frac{1}{3})$

d. $192 \div 3$

13. Evaluate $9 \times 9 \div 9 + 9 - 9 \div 9$.

a. 0
b. 17
c. 81
d. 9

14. Alan currently weighs 200 pounds, but he wants to lose weight to get down to 175 pounds. What is this difference in kilograms? (1 pound is approximately equal to 0.45 kilograms.)

a. 9 kg
b. 11.25 kg
c. 78.75 kg
d. 90 kg

15. Which of the following equations highlights the commutative property of addition?

a. $9 + (4 + 2) = 9 + (4 + 2)$
b. $9 + 4 + 2 = 4 + 9 + 2$
c. $9 + (4 + 2) = (4 + 9) + 2$
d. $9 + 4 + 2 = 15$

16. How many times does the number 3 appear in the prime factorization of 54?

a. 2
b. 4
c. 1
d. 3

17. What is the prime factorization of 80?

a. 2×40
b. $2 \times 2 \times 2 \times 2 \times 5$
c. $2 \times 2 \times 2 \times 2 \times 2 \times 5$
d. 8×10

18. Which of the following is equal to forty million, six hundred twenty-five thousand, nine hundred nine?

a. 400,625,909
b. 4,625,909
c. 40,625,909
d. 40,625,999

193

19. 25% of what number is 150?
    a. 600
    b. 37.5
    c. 50
    d. 500

20. What percent of 800 is 20?
    a. 0.025%
    b. 2.5%
    c. 20%
    d. 0.25%

21. Find the sum: $\frac{1}{6} + \frac{4}{9}$.
    a. $\frac{5}{15}$
    b. $\frac{11}{18}$
    c. $\frac{3}{4}$
    d. $\frac{12}{18}$

22. Find the difference: $\frac{7}{10} - \frac{1}{2}$.
    a. $\frac{6}{8}$
    b. $\frac{3}{4}$
    c. $\frac{2}{12}$
    d. $\frac{1}{5}$

23. Factor the following completely: $18x + 9y$
    a. $18(x + y)$
    b. $9(x + 2y)$
    c. $9(2x + y)$
    d. $9x(2 + y)$

24. Evaluate the expression $5x + 10$ for $x = 3$.
    a. $-\frac{7}{5}$
    b. 15
    c. 25
    d. 18

25. What is the missing term in the following sequence? 2, 6, __, 54, 162.
    a. 18
    b. 12
    c. 27
    d. 3

26. Consider the equation (■ × 4) ÷ 2 = 80. What does ■ represent?
    a. 640
    b. 40
    c. 10
    d. 41

27. Which of the following charts should be used if one wants to highlight the minimum and maximum values in a data set?
    a. Pie chart
    b. Bar chart
    c. Scatter plot
    d. Column chart

28. The following graph shows the number of hot dogs sold per day over the course of a week. How many more hot dogs were sold on Friday than on Tuesday?

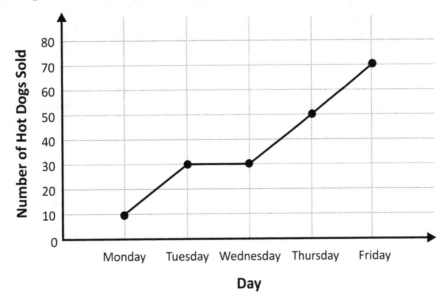

    a. 30
    b. 50
    c. 70
    d. 40

29. Standard deviation measures the amount of variation in a data set. Which of the following data sets have the smallest standard deviation?
    a. {9, 9.1, 9.2, 9.3, 9.4, 9.5}
    b. {9, 10, 11, 12, 13, 14, 15}
    c. {100, 100, 100, 100, 100}
    d. {100, 200, 300, 400, 500, 600}

30. If a coin is flipped 40 times, how many times would you estimate that it would land on heads?
    a. 10
    b. 20
    c. 30
    d. 40

Answer Explanations #3

Verbal Reasoning

Synonyms

1. C: *Banquet* is a noun that can be defined as a lavish meal, usually for ceremonial purposes. *Announcement, castle,* and *tapestry* are all nouns that may be associated with *banquet* due to the connection between ceremonial banquets and medieval kingdoms, but the terms themselves are not directly synonymous. *Feast*, on the other hand, is a noun meaning a rich or abundant meal, and is therefore the synonymous term to *banquet*.

2. B: *Industrious* is an adjective meaning working energetically and devotedly. *Adventurous* is an adjective meaning courageous or bold. While adventurous people may be industrious, the two terms do not have the same meaning. A person who is *resistant* is usually against something or unaccepting of change. This is unrelated to being a devoted worker. A student can be *smart,* displaying above average intelligence, without being *industrious*. *Hardworking,* which is an adjective synonymous with terms like conscientious, dedicated, and diligent, is therefore the synonymous term to *industrious*.

3. B: *Burrow* is a noun that can best be defined as a hole dug by an animal. Therefore, *hole* is the synonymous term. *Bird, nest,* and *habitat* are all nouns that may be associated with the idea of a burrow because of their shared connection to animals and nature, but the terms are not directly synonymous. In particular, *nest* and *burrow* are both nouns that refer to shelters made by animals, but a *burrow* is located in the ground, whereas a *nest* usually refers to the physical structure of a shelter, which may or may not be underground.

4. A: *Vacant* is an adjective meaning unoccupied or deserted. *Implied* is an adjective meaning hidden or unspoken, and something being hidden is clearly not the same as something being deserted. Similarly, *missing* is an adjective that implies something is gone that once was there, whereas in the term *vacant*, all that is implied is that the object itself is unoccupied or deserted. *Unsure* is an adjective that typically refers to a state of mind and not a physical object or place, and therefore is not synonymous with *vacant. Empty,* however, is an adjective that means containing nothing, and is therefore directly synonymous with *vacant*.

5. A: *Disclose* is a verb that means to reveal or make public. *Resemble* is a verb that means to look or seem like, and therefore has nothing to do with the idea of revealing or uncovering something. *Overlook* is a verb that means to disregard or neglect. While the terms *overlook* and *disclose* have similar connotations because they involve some object or fact being unseen, one involves that object or fact being revealed, whereas the other does not. Similarly, the verb *hide* also shares the connotation of something being unseen, but also does not signify that the hidden object has been revealed. *Confess*, a verb meaning to acknowledge or confirm, does, however, have that connotation and is therefore the synonymous term.

6. C: *Seep* is a verb that means to flow or pass through a substance. *Emerge* is a verb that means to arise or come forth, and therefore has a slightly different and more general meaning than *seep. Collect* is another verb that has a more general meaning—to gather or compile—and so it is not synonymous with *seep. Rest* is a verb that can be defined as to recline or relax, and while it's not synonymous with *seep*, the two terms may be confused due to *seep's* visual and phonetic similarity to the term *sleep*, which is

197

synonymous with rest. *Leak* is a verb that can be defined as to let a substance enter or escape, as through a hole or crack, and is therefore synonymous with *seep*, with both terms referring to the passing of one substance through another.

7. C: *Veto* is a verb that means to reject or prohibit, as with a bill or law. *Wane* is a verb that generally means to decrease in strength or power, and therefore is not synonymous with *veto*, which refers to an act of power or some kind or another. *Ponder* is a verb that means to consider something deeply and thoughtfully, and while both *ponder* and *veto* imply a decision is being made, *ponder* does not specify what the outcome of that decision may be. The two terms are therefore not synonymous. *Elect* is a verb that means to select by vote, and more generally, to determine or choose. Although *elect* and *veto* may have similar connotations due to their connection to politics, the two terms actually have fairly opposing meanings, with *elect* meaning to decide for or in favor of, while *veto* means to decide against. *Reject*, a verb meaning to refuse or discard, has a similar meaning to *veto*, in that both verbs refer to the act of rejecting something. The two terms are therefore synonymous.

8. D: *Ridicule* is a verb that means to make fun of or criticize. Both *esteem* and *highlight* are verbs that refer to emphasizing or regarding something in a favorable manner, and therefore have opposing meanings to *ridicule*. *Evacuate*, a verb meaning to leave or remove from an area, has no similarity in meaning to *ridicule*. *Mock,* on the other hand, is directly synonymous with *ridicule*. Both terms are verbs meaning to attack or make fun of.

9. B: *Bewildered* is a verb that can best be defined as entirely confused or puzzled. Therefore, the term *puzzled* is a direct synonym. *Crazed* and *quiet* are adjectives that describe an individual's mental or emotional state, but the terms don't have anything to do with being confused. *Unrefined*, an adjective meaning not purified, or lacking refinement in some way, does not refer a puzzled state of mind.

10. B: *Carcass* is a noun that is defined as the dead body of an animal. The term *dire* is an adjective used to describe desperate or troublesome and is therefore not synonymous with a noun like *carcass*. *Satchel* is a noun referring to any kind of small bag and is not synonymous with or generally associated with the idea of a carcass. *Symptom* is a noun that can generally refer to any phenomenon that serves as evidence for itself or something, and more specifically is usually used to refer to the various bodily functions and signals that serve as evidence of a particular disease or condition. Although *symptom* and *carcass* may be associated due to both terms' connection to disease and death, the two terms are clearly not directly synonymous. *Remains* is a noun that can refer generally to any piece or fragment of something that is left over from another time but is also specifically used to refer to the bodies of humans and animals that have been found after their death. Therefore, *remains* is synonymous with *carcass*.

11. A: *Outskirts* is a noun that refers to the outer or bordering areas of a city or other large settlement of people. *Reservoir* is a noun that refers to any place where a large amount of something is gathered or held and does not refer to any sort of human settlement. Therefore, the two terms are not synonymous. *Metropolis* is a noun that can be defined as any large and busy city. The idea of a *metropolis* is therefore somewhat opposite to the idea of *outskirts*, which must exist away from the city itself. *Boundary* is a noun that generally refers to anything that indicates or defines the limits of something and is therefore synonymous with *outskirts*.

12. C: *Seldom* is an adverb that can be defined as not often or infrequent. Therefore, it is directly synonymous with *rarely*, which similarly can be defined as hardly ever or infrequently. *Conventional*, *egotistical*, and *sleepy* are all adjectives, and therefore cannot be synonymous with an adverb like

198

seldom. Additionally, the term *conventional* refers to something ordinary or commonplace, and therefore would not have the same meaning as seldom.

13. A: *Thrifty* is an adjective that is synonymous with terms like frugal and prudent. *Sneaky* is an adjective that is synonymous with terms like dishonest and devious, and therefore it has much more negative connotations than *thrifty*. *Practical* and *pleasant*, on the other hand, are both adjectives with much more positive connotations, but neither has the exact same meaning as *thrifty*. *Practical* is defined as useful or constructive, while *pleasant* means friendly or polite. *Economical*, on the other hand, is directly synonymous with *thrifty* since the term *economical* is defined as thrifty or frugal management.

14. D: *Jagged* is an adjective that can be defined as having a rough or uneven quality. Therefore, it is directly synonymous with the term *uneven*. The terms *exposed, revealed,* and *shocked* are all adjectives that refer to some form of emotional or mental state, and therefore do not have the same physical quality as the term *jagged*.

15. D: *Peculiar* is an adjective meaning distinctive or specific. *Gentle* is an adjective meaning having a mild disposition, and therefore has no connection to the idea of something being *peculiar*. *Observant* and *inquisitive* are both adjectives that refer to dispositions that are alert and analytical, respectively. Although these terms may be connected to *peculiar* because an individual may be *observant* or *inquisitive* when they witness something *peculiar*, they are not synonymous. *Unique* is an adjective that can be defined as singular or exclusive. *Peculiar* and *unique* are synonymous terms, as both refer to the specific or particular quality of something.

16. D: *Flimsy* is an adjective meaning not strong, as well as light and thin. Therefore, it is directly synonymous with *thin. Amusing* is an adjective synonymous with terms like entertaining or diverting, and therefore has more positive connotations than something being *flimsy*. The adjective *convenient* similarly has positive connotations, with it being synonymous to terms like *favorable* and *good. Rowdy* is an adjective that refers to a noisy or disorderly disposition, and therefore is not commonly associated with the idea of something being weak or light.

17. C: Coax is a verb that means to attempt to influence, usually by flattery. *Despise, harm,* and *trouble* are all verbs that have negative connotations, usually involving the infliction of some discomfort or distress to the receiving party of the action. Therefore, they are not synonymous with *coax*, which has a much gentler connotation. *Persuade* is a verb with a similar connotation to *coax*, with it being defined as to induce to believe. Therefore, *persuade* and *coax* are synonymous.

Sentence Completion A

18. B: If Shaun's specific fear is having to jump out of a crashing plane, the only logical thing for him to bring with him whenever he gets on a plane is a *parachute*, which he could use to safely break his fall and protect himself. All the other answer choices do not logically make sense as things to bring on a plane to alleviate that fear.

19. B: The mention of an *arrow*, as well as the primary subject of the *huntsman*, should serve as indication that the missing term is specifically related to the concept of bows and arrows and hunting. Therefore, the only logical answer is *quiver*, which can be defined as a case for holding and carrying arrows. All the other terms do not logically make sense.

20. D: Since the missing term is a descriptor for a lion hunting, the most logical answer is *ravenous.* All the other terms are adjectives that are mostly or entirely used to describe human beings, and it would

199

be consequently illogical to think of a lion acting *pretentious*, *optimistic,* and *introspective*. However, *ravenous*, an adjective meaning extremely hungry or eager on satisfaction, does logically make sense as a descriptor for a lion hunting.

21. A: The description about Miranda *"tuning in"* to other people's conversations should serve as an indication that the missing term is going to reference such an action. Therefore, the correct answer choice is *eavesdrop*, which can be defined as to listen secretly to a private conversation. All the other answer choices do not logically complete the sentence since those verbs do not reference the act of listening to the conversations of others.

22. C: The sentence makes it clear that Max didn't understand why his cat was napping so much, so the missing term should be a descriptor of cats that is related to their habit of taking frequent naps. Out of all the answer choices, the only term that relates to the concept of cats being nap-loving creatures is *sedentary*, which is defined as tending to rest a great deal and rarely move. Although a cat may be accurately described as *intense, optimistic,* or *subservient* depending on the context and situation, in this specific context only *sedentary* works, as only that term adequately describes why cats take so many naps.

23. D: The usage of *even though* in the final clause of the sentence indicates that Michael's grandmom had described her grandson in a way contrary to what was the truth, or specifically what Michael believed to be the truth. Since the rest of the clause explains the simple and basic steps Michael did to try and fix his grandma's computer, it would make logical sense that Michael's grandma embellished on his accomplishments, especially if she was unable to fix the computer on her own. Therefore, the only answer choice that makes sense is *savvy,* as only that word provides a positive connotation.

24. A: The second clause of the sentence describes the qualities of the young student that the city council members were so impressed with, and it specifically lists her thoughtfulness and passion in speaking on behalf of her teachers and school. It should logically follow that the missing term must be related in some way to the idea of thoughtful and passionate speaking abilities. Consequently, the correct answer choice is *eloquence*, which can be directly defined as the art of using language with fluency and aptness. All the other answer choices do not reflect something about the speaker's thoughtfulness and passion.

25. C: The phrase *take it easy* indicates that the recommendation the school nurse made to the student is one that urges rest of some form or another. *Diagnose, exercise,* and *study* do not make logical sense, as those are all actions that involve active effort. *Rest* is the correct answer choice.

26. A: The description provided of the animal seen by the little boy provides several clues as to the kind of animal the boy realized it was. First, the movement of the animal from the land into the water suggests that the animal must be able to survive on both (as the boy then goes on to point out), which means it cannot be either a *mammal* or a *marsupial*. Additionally, *dinosaur* does not logically make sense, as dinosaurs went extinct long before there were humans around to witness them. Therefore, the correct answer choice is *amphibian*, which is a kind of animal typified by their ability to live both in water and on land. Furthermore, the image of an animal jumping from a lily pad may remind one of a frog, which itself is an *amphibian*, and such a realization would also lead the little boy to conclude the animal he saw was an *amphibian*.

27. A: The final clause of the sentence indicates that their trip to get fast food is something Sarah's mother wants to make sure Sarah knows is not going to happen often. The only logical answer choice,

therefore, is *anomaly*, which can be defined as a deviation from the common rule or norm. *Standard, experience,* and *tradition* all do not logically make sense, as there is nothing about those terms that indicate they happen only rarely or as a deviation from the normal.

28. D: The preposition *despite* at the beginning of the sentence indicates that a majority of the committee in favor of the proposal is not sufficient in order for it pass, and that some additional condition must be met. The only answer choice that would make sense as an additional condition would be *unanimous*, which means of one mind, in complete agreement. The other answer choices do not make sense as an additional condition to be met.

Sentence Completion B

29. A: The adjective *sensible* indicates that Lizzy thinks that what she is intending to do is wise and prudent. Additionally, the mention of the teacher grabbing a math test should indicate that what Lizzy is about to do is in some way related to that test. Therefore, the correct answer is *rehearse her times tables once more*. The other answer choices describe actions that would either not be sensible in general or given the context of that specific moment.

30. D: The adjective *grumpy* indicates that Marcus's cat Fiona acted in some form of ill-tempered manner. Additionally, the phrase *the first sign* indicates that Marcus's cat acted in a way that wasn't typical of how she normally acted. Therefore, the only correct answer choice is *began hissing and batting her paw at Marcus when he tried to approach her*. All the other answer choices list behaviors that are either not signs of grumpiness or are regularly occurring actions for Fiona.

31. C: The conjunction *although* indicates that Maria's original assumption that she understood the book's plot was incorrect. Furthermore, the adjective *embarrassed* indicates that whatever Maria went on to do was something she regretted or felt shame about. The only answer choice that would potentially cause Maria to feel embarrassed while also revealing her mistaken assumption would be that she *had looked up a summary for a different book entirely*. The other answer choices would not logically make sense given the rest of the sentence.

32. D: The phrase *due to* indicates that what the toddler found difficult to do was because of his parent's brisk stride. The only answer choice that makes sense as an action for the toddler to struggle with, therefore, is *keep up while walking*. In all the other answer choices, his parent's brisk walking speed would not hamper the small toddler's ability to complete those actions.

33. D: The verb *escalated* indicates that the change that suddenly occurred involved the intensifying of the protest. The only logical answer choice that makes sense is *crowd became too big for the confines of the park*. In all the other answer choices, the protest itself is resolved or replaced by something else entirely.

34. C: The noun *drowsiness,* meaning the state or condition of being sleepy or sluggish, indicates that the effects Ms. Jackson should expect to see involve her feeling tired or sleepy. Therefore, the correct answer choice is *become tired and sleepy much more easily*. All the other answer choices do not describe effects or feelings commonly associated with the sensation of drowsiness.

Quantitative Reasoning

1. A: Start by dividing the total number of students by the number of groups (34 ÷ 3). This puts 11 students into each group with 1 student left over. However, each group must also include a composite number of students. Composite numbers are numbers that have more than two divisors—in other words, any number that is not a prime number. Because 11 is a prime number, no group can have 11 students. If the students arrange themselves in groups of 10, there would be 4 students left over (3 groups × 10 students = 30 students). If 2 of those students join 2 of the groups, the students would be in groups of 12, 12, and 10 (12 + 12 + 10 = 34), which makes each group of similar size and no group having a prime number of students. Choice *B* includes two groups with a prime number of students, and Choices *C* and *D* do not have the correct total number of students.

2. C: Adding up all of the ChocoCakes means that Michael will deliver 1943 cakes today. He's going to be busy! Choice *B* only carried a 1 from the ones place rather than carrying a 2. Choice *A* carried a 2 rather than a 3 from the tens place to the hundreds place. Choice *D* used rounding rather than adding the exact numbers.

3. D: To solve this problem, add all of Brianna's current stops each week: 2 for MLK; 3 for ABC; 1 for the middle school; 2 for the high school; 1 each for Cute Kids, Sunrise, and Forest Middle; and 2 each for Riverside and Elm Park. 2 + 3 + 1 + 2 + 1 + 1 + 1 + 2 + 2 = 15 stops each week. Choice *A* counted the number of places but did not include places that have multiple stops. Choice *B* only counted the specific days that are listed but did not include the places with weekly stops where no specific day was noted. Choice *C* counted all of the stops but incorrectly added two more.

4. B: David and Aidan are both correct. David used expanded notation, whereas Aidan used expanded factors. David is not the only one who is correct, Choice *A*. Marian and Ellen, Choices *C* and *D*, both only wrote it in partially expanded form.

5. C: The Bears players scored 18 points (3 players with 6 points each). The Jaguars scored 26 points (3 players with 6 points each, plus the 2 extra points and the 6 points made by the kicker). Choice *A* got the total scores reversed. Choice *B* forgot to include Davidson's 2 extra points and the points made by the kicker. Choice *D* got all of Davidson's points but forgot the kicker's points.

6. B: To solve this problem, first add the total money the three kids made over the whole summer ($355 + $420 + $296 = $1071). Then, divide the total by 3: $1071 ÷ 3 = $357 each. Choice *A* adds up the total but doesn't divide it by 3. Choice *C* just lists the money they earned each month but does not calculate even shares for each of them. Choice *D* made an error in the addition step of the problem, which made the division step also incorrect.

7. B: When the numbers are in order, the list looks like this: 0.4534, 0.4578, 1.2348, 1.3342, 1.6954, 2.6351, and 2.6359. That means that 0.4534 is the least and 2.6359 is the greatest. Choice *A* lists the second least number and the second greatest number. Choice *C* shows two of the middle numbers in the ordered list, and Choice *D* has the correct least number but the second greatest number.

8. A: The way to solve this problem is to add each of the four numbers together. Choice *B* adds the numbers incorrectly, Choice *C* adds the numbers correctly but includes Kenneth's track twice, and Choice *D* does not include Max's track.

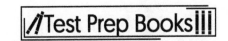

9. C: Divide the total amount of tea by the number of ounces each guest should get: $2309.28 \div 12 = 192.44$. This means Jonathan can serve 192 guests with just a tiny bit of tea left over. Choice *A* rounds the amount of tea down to 2300 before dividing, which gets the answer close but not exactly right. Choice *B* divides by 1.2 instead of 12, and Choice *D* moves the decimal in the dividend before completing the division.

10. D: The first step to solve this problem is to convert the fractions to decimals to make them all easier to add. To do that, divide the numerator by the denominator for each fraction: 0.20, 3.49, 0.625, 1.93, and 0.75. Then list the numbers vertically, lining up the decimals before adding. Choice *A* does not line up the decimals before adding the column of numbers. Choice *B* only adds the numbers that are already in decimal form, and Choice *C* converts and adds only the fractions.

11. A: When all the grades are converted to percentages, Jose scored 90%, Timothy got 62.5%, Andrew earned 87%, Mary Jane scored 84%, and Arya's grade was 96%. So, Arya, the student with $\frac{24}{25}$, or 96%, got the highest score. Choices *B*, *C*, and *D* are the next three highest scores in order.

12. A: The first step is to figure out how many slices the students will eat by multiplying the number of slices by the number of students and then adding them: $12 + 20 + 8 = 40$ slices. If each pizza has 8 slices, 40 divided by 8 equals 5 pizzas. Next, multiply the cost of the pizza by the number of pizzas: $\$13.67 \times 5 = \$68.35$. Choice *B* multiplied the number of slices by the cost of the pizza. Choice *C* included the three students who decided not to eat pizza, and Choice *D* included those three students as well as counting for partial pizzas.

13. A: The equation for this problem is $7 + x = 16$. Subtract 7 from both sides to get $x = 9$. Choice *A* adds 7 to both sides, and Choice *B* just makes an error in subtraction. Choice *D* is Kevin's age, not his sister's.

14. C: The equation here is the number of bakers times an unknown number of pies equals 21, or $3x = 21$. To solve this, divide both sides by 3, so $x = 7$. Each person baked 7 pies. Choice *A* is the number of bakers rather than the number of pies they made, and Choice *B* is the total number of pies rather than how much each person made. Choice *D* multiplies by 3 rather than dividing by 3.

15. D: Because this equation uses addition and subtraction, grouping like terms uses addition and subtraction, too. The idea is to move numbers with a variable (z and $2z$) together on one side of the equal sign and numbers without a variable (10 and 4) on the other side. One way to solve this would be to subtract z from both sides, which leaves $-4 = 10 + 2z - z$. Then, subtract 10 from both sides, leaving $-4 - 10 = 2z - z$. Choice *A* grouped the like terms but also solved the equation, which is not what the teacher asked for here. Choice *B* grouped the variable terms but did not group the integers, and Choice *C* grouped the integers but not the variables.

16. A: Melissa is 12, Betsy's age is $12 - 2$, and James's age is $(12 - 2) \times 2$, so the equation to solve this problem is $(12 - 2) \times 2 = x$. Using PEMDAS for the order of operations, first solve what is inside the parentheses, which will make the new equation $10 \times 2 = x$. James is 20 years old. Choice *B* is twice Melissa's age rather than Betsy's, and Choice *C* adds the sisters' ages together. Choice *D* adds 2 years for Betsy's age rather than subtracting 2 years.

17. C: The number of shells Mackenzie started with is the unknown number, x. That unknown number plus the 14 new shells equals the total number of shells: $x + 14 = 56$. To solve this equation, subtract 14 from both sides, leaving $x = 42$. Choice *A* adds the 14 new shells to the total shells rather than

subtracting them to find the original number. Choice *B* is the number of new shells, and Choice *D* is the total number of shells.

18. C: In this problem, "a number" indicates the missing variable, or x. "Decreased" indicates a subtraction problem. So, $x - 81 = 147$. To solve this, add 81 to both sides of the equation to get $x = 228$. Choices *A* and *B* are numbers in the equation, but they are not solutions for the unknown variable. Choice *D* increases the unknown number by 81 rather than decreasing it.

19. B: The unknown variable here, x, is the number of students in the class, so the equation is 72 pieces of candy divided by 3 pieces per student equals how many students: $72 \div 3 = x$. Choice *A* multiplies the number of pieces of candy by 3, and Choice *C* subtracts 3 from the number of pieces of candy. Choice *D* still includes the variable rather than solving for it.

20. A: An acute triangle is a triangle in which all angles measure less than 90 degrees. Since this triangle has three acute angles that are all equal, it is both acute and equilateral. A right triangle has one angle that is 90 degrees, Choice *B*, and a scalene triangle has no congruent sides. An obtuse triangle, Choice *C*, has one angle greater than 90 degrees, and an isosceles triangle, Choice *D*, has two congruent sides.

21. D: A triangular prism has triangular ends and flat sides. A square prism, Choice *A*, has four sides and squares at the ends. A pyramid, Choices *B* and *C*, has sides that rise to an apex, or a point, rather than having parallelogram sides.

22. C: A cylinder has two circular ends and one curved face, such as a can of soup. The tissue box, Choice *A*, is a polygon, either a cube or cuboid (depending on which type of tissues Oliver's mom likes to buy). The chips, Choice *B*, come in a bag, which is an irregular cuboid due to the closed ends. The ball, Choice *D*, is a sphere.

23. A: Symmetry means that two sides of the figure are mirror images of each other. The word HAM includes three symmetrical letters: H, A, and M. A vertical line can be drawn down the middle of each letter, and the two halves will be identical. Choice *B* has two symmetrical letters, but the letter P is not symmetrical. The letter B in Choice *C* has a horizontal line of symmetry, and the letter A has a vertical line of symmetry; however, the letter L is not symmetrical. In Choice *D*, the letters T, O, and Y are symmetrical, but the letter S is not.

24. D: In order for the two triangles to be similar, the corresponding pairs of angles must be equal, and the corresponding sides have to be proportional. The triangles of $\triangle ABC$ and $\triangle CDE$ have the same angles, and the sides are proportional if segment AC = 16 (twice the length of line segment DC) and segment DE = 4 (half the length of line segment AB). Choice *A* reverses the line segments. Choice *B* shows segment AC as equal to segment CB, and Choice *C* shows segment DE as equal to segment CE, neither of which would create proportional sides between the two triangles.

25. B: Congruent triangles are exactly the same, with the same corresponding angles and the same corresponding sides. Choices *A, C,* and *D* all show similar triangles, meaning that they have the same corresponding angles, but their corresponding sides are of different lengths.

26. A: One gallon has 4 quarts, which means that Theo has 24 quarts of oil to work on the cars. The four cars in the shop need a total of 20 quarts: $24 - 20 = 4$ qt left over. Choice *B* only counts one of the two cars that need 5 quarts. Choice *C* uses ounces rather than quarts, and Choice *D* is the amount Theo will use rather than the amount left over.

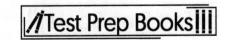

27. B: The easiest way to figure out how much time Martin's errands are going to take him is to add the minutes first and then add the hours. There are two fractions of time, too. An hour is 60 minutes, so $\frac{1}{2}$ hour is 30 minutes, and $\frac{1}{3}$ hour is 20 minutes. Adding all the minutes, $15 + 30 + 10 + 20 = 75$ min, or 1 hour and 15 minutes. Then, add in the hour from the grocery store, and the total time for Martin's chores is 2 hours and 15 minutes. Choice A adds all of the minutes but does not include the hour at the grocery store. Choice C counts $\frac{1}{3}$ hour as 15 minutes instead of 20, and Choice D counts both the car wash and the post office as $\frac{1}{2}$ hour each.

28. D: To solve this problem, subtract the time Jasmine needs from her 10:00 bedtime. To get a shower, she would need to start at 9:45 (15 minutes before 10:00). To brush her teeth and hair, she needs another 10 minutes, which means she needs to start getting ready for bed by 9:35. Choice A mixes up am (morning) and pm (evening). Choice B adds the time rather than subtracting it, making Jasmine late for bed. Choice C only accounts for her shower but not brushing her teeth and hair.

29. B: Adding how much each crate holds, we get 420 oranges. Choice A only counted one of the large crates, and Choice C only counted one of the small crates. Choice D only counted one large and one small crate.

30. C: The fish that Andrew wants total 31 inches, which means that his tank needs to be 16 gallons bigger. Choice A is the total gallons that Andrew needs, which doesn't answer the question. Choice B does not count all 12 of the neons, and Choice D does not count the 12 neons and only counts one goldfish instead of two.

31. C: The Celsius temperatures range from a freezing temperature of 0 degrees to a boiling temperature of 100 degrees. Choices A and B contain a mix of Fahrenheit and Celsius measurements, and Choice D shows the same temperatures for Celsius and Fahrenheit.

32. B: The range is the difference between the highest and lowest numbers in a data set. In this case, the highest number is 98 and the lowest number is 65: $98 - 65 = 33$. Choice A shows the lowest grade, Choice C shows the highest grade, and Choice D shows the mode, or the number that appears most often.

33. B: The median is the middle number. Putting Sarah's scores in order shows that the middle number is 5.45. Choice C shows the highest number, and Choice D shows the lowest number. Choice A shows the mode.

34. C: A circle graph is great for showing percentages of the whole. A bar graph, Choice A, compares different data amounts, which would be great if Danielle wanted to see which job earned her the most money. A line graph, Choice B, is most often used to show changes over time. Choice D is not a type of graph.

35. B: There are numbers 1 through 6 on the die, which means that the chances of rolling any number would be 1 out of 6, which expressed as a fraction is $\frac{1}{6}$. Choice A means that the die has 6s on every side. Choice C or Choice D would be possible if the die had two or three sides, respectively, showing 6.

36. A: Two of the suits are red (hearts and diamonds). This means that 26 of the 52 cards are red, so the chance of drawing a red card from the deck is 26 out of 52, or $\frac{26}{52}$, which when reduced is $\frac{1}{2}$, or 1 out of 2.

Choice B, $\frac{1}{4}$, is the probability of drawing a specific suit (of the four) from the deck. Choice C is the probability of drawing a specific color, such as a red king ($\frac{1}{26}$), and Choice D is the probability of choosing a particular card, such as any king, from the whole deck.

37. A: There are 46 purple marbles out of the 200 total marbles, so the probability of Ashley's choosing a purple marble is 46 out of 200, or $\frac{46}{200}$, which reduces to $\frac{23}{100}$. Choice B is the likelihood of choosing a blue marble. Choice C is for red, and Choice D is for yellow.

38. A: There were two years with exceptionally high and exceptionally low rainfall amounts. The average of the three middle amounts is 5 inches, which would be a reasonable expectation given this data set. Choice B is more than it has ever rained, and Choice C is the lowest recorded rainfall amount, both of which are outside of the more typical amounts in the data set. There is no record that indicates it never rains at all, Choice D.

Reading Comprehension

1. C: Choice C is the correct answer for the number of years between the Sputnik launch and moon landing. The Sputnik launch was in 1957, while the moon landing was in 1969. This is a 12-year difference. The key to this answer is carefully reading to make sure that you are using the correct dates for the specific events that are being asked about.

2. B: Choice B is the correct answer because *dwindled* and *waned* have the most similar meaning. *Dwindled* means to decrease in size or strength. *Waned* means to decrease in vigor or strength. These two meanings are very similar. Choice A is incorrect because *dissuaded* means to be persuaded to not do something, while *struggled* means to engage in conflict. These two words are very different. Choice C is incorrect because *dominate* means to rule or control, while *catalyst* is when something spurs on an event. These two words have different meanings. Choice D is incorrect because *futuristic* means to have a modern design, while *exploration* means to visit an unfamiliar area.

3. A: Choice A is the correct answer because the last paragraph's purpose is to describe how the space race changed the world overall. The last paragraph describes how the world gained an appreciation for developing technology because of the space race. It gives specific examples of technology that came from that time period. It is accurate to say that this paragraph described how the world was changed technologically. Choice B is incorrect because the last paragraph does not stress that the US won the space race. Choice C is incorrect because the last paragraph does not mention a second space race. Choice D is incorrect because the paragraph does not summarize what was discussed in the other paragraphs.

4. C: Choice C is the correct answer because the quote is a simile. A simile is a form of figurative language that uses either *like* or *as* to make a comparison. A metaphor does not use either of these words. This makes Choice A incorrect. Choice B is incorrect because *personification* is when human attributes are given to something nonhuman. Choice D is incorrect because *irony* is a form of humor when somebody says one thing but means another.

5. C: Choice C is the correct answer because the second paragraph describes why the Soviet Union and United States engaged in the space race. It discusses the basis of the war and why winning the space race was important. This is an explanation of the *why*. Choice A is incorrect because *who* is answered before the second paragraph. Choice B is incorrect because *how* is answered throughout the passage

206

with descriptions of what each country did. Choice *D* is incorrect because *when* is answered in the first paragraph.

6. B: Choice *B* is the correct answer because each paragraph in this passage gives general information about the Seven Wonders. This includes the date it was built, why it was built, and how it was destroyed. Choice *A* is incorrect because the ancient world and the modern world are never compared in this passage. Choice *C* is incorrect because the Seven Wonders of the Natural World are never mentioned. Choice *D* is incorrect because there are no persuasive qualities in the passage, and readers are not encouraged to visit the Seven Wonders (of which most are destroyed).

7. D: Choice *D* is the correct answer because this passage gives general information about each of the Seven Wonders. Choice *A* is incorrect because the Seven Wonders are not listed in the order that they were built. Choice *B* is incorrect because the Seven Wonders are not listed in the order that they were destroyed. Choice *C* is incorrect because the Seven Wonders are being presented separately in their own paragraphs without comparison to one another.

8. C: Choice *C* is the correct answer because each of the Seven Wonders has been destroyed except for the Great Pyramid of Giza, which has sustained terrible damage. This is the common theme among all of the Seven Wonders. Choice *A* is incorrect because only one of the Seven Wonders still exists today, making that statement false. Choice *B* is incorrect because the Seven Wonders were built in a variety of locations over hundreds of years, meaning that they were not built by the same people. Choice *D* is incorrect because the common theme is the destruction and damage that they have faced.

9. C: Choice *C* is correct because *immense* and *huge* are similar words. *Immense* means extremely large, which is also the definition of *huge*. Choice *A* is incorrect because *small* means the opposite of *immense*. Choice *B* is incorrect because *insignificant* means not important, which does not match the meaning of *immense*. Choice *D* is incorrect because *noticeable* means easily seen, which does not match the meaning of *immense*.

10. A: Choice *A* is the correct answer since three of the Seven Wonders were built with a god or goddess in mind. Choice *B* is incorrect since two of the Seven Wonders were built in modern Turkey. Choice *C* is a false statement because two of the Seven Wonders were destroyed by earthquakes, not tornadoes. Choice *D* is incorrect because in the second paragraph of the passage, it states that the Great Pyramid of Giza still stands today and can be visited in Egypt.

11. B: Choice *B* is the correct answer because Henry is the main character in this story. The word *protagonist* refers to the most prominent character that the text focuses on. Although Marty is a main character, he is not the focus of the entire text like Henry is. This makes Choice *A* incorrect. Choice *C* is incorrect because the other students are not discussed at length other than as a source of conflict for Henry. Choice *D* is incorrect because the teacher is also not mentioned much.

12. A: Choice *A* is the correct answer because Henry's story is full of hope and encouragement. Marty encouraged him to use his newfound ability and to continue to follow his dreams. At the end of the story, Henry feels confident and is encouraged about his future singing. Choice *B* is incorrect because although Henry feels disappointed at first, it is not the primary emotion displayed throughout the text. Choice *C* is not correct because there is nothing overly annoying in this story. Choice *D* is incorrect because there is no romance between any of the characters in this story.

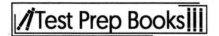

13. A: Choice *A* is the correct answer because the quote makes a comparison without the words *like* or *as*. A *metaphor* is when an object or idea is referred to something else for comparison or symbolic meaning. In this case, Henry is not actually going to roar. It is a *metaphor* for how he is going to use his newfound voice in a strong and powerful manner. Choice *B* is incorrect because a *simile* makes a direct comparison with the use of *like* or *as*. If you said, "her hair was as bright as sunshine," that is a simile. Choice *C* is incorrect because personification is when an inanimate object is given human-like qualities. Choice *D* is incorrect because an oxymoron is when a phrase seems contradictory, such as in the term *humblebrag*, since bragging is not humble.

14. C: Choice *C* is the correct answer because Henry had a strength that he didn't even know about. At school he was disappointed that he could not sing like the other birds. However, once he learned more about how he was different, he realized that it was actually a blessing in disguise. This is the moral of the story. Choice *A* is incorrect because at the end of the story, Henry is practicing and specifically mentions that his voice is not perfect. That cannot be the moral of the story since it is not a major focus. Choice *B* is incorrect because Henry did not have many friends, yet he still succeeded. Marty was more of a mentor role than a friend. Choice *D* is incorrect because if Henry had continued on the path he was on without learning more about himself, it is unlikely that he would have succeeded.

15. D: Choice *D* is the correct answer because *renowned* means known by many people, and *famous* means almost exactly the same thing. These two words are the most similar out of all the options. Choice *A* is incorrect because *studied* means carefully thought out. Choice *B* is incorrect because *unknown* means not known by many, which is the opposite of *renowned*. Choice *C* is incorrect because *hated* means disliked by one or more people. This is not the same meaning as *renowned*, which is a positive word.

16. A: Choice *A* is the correct answer because Roosevelt's first term is the one that was unexpected. He would not have become president at that time if the unexpected tragedy of McKinley's death had not happened. For his second term, he ran for the position and successfully won; therefore, Choice *B* is incorrect. There was no third term for Teddy Roosevelt, meaning that Choice *C* is incorrect. Choice *D* is incorrect because the first term was unexpected.

17. D: Choice *D* is the correct answer because the word *persistence* means to continue in the face of a challenge. *Determination* means to be resolute in a goal. These two words have very similar meanings. Choice *A* is incorrect because the portion of the text where persistence is mentioned is talking about Roosevelt doing something even though he was badly injured. There is no mention of him being sad. Choice *B* is incorrect because *ingenuity* means to be clever. Roosevelt's actions were brave, but they were not incredibly clever or creative. Choice *C* is incorrect because *laziness* means being unwilling to work. Roosevelt was the opposite of this since he was determined to do his job.

18. B: Choice *B* is the correct answer because environmental conservation is mentioned multiple times as being one of Roosevelt's passions. Choice *A* is incorrect because Roosevelt was vice president to William McKinley. He lost the presidency to Woodrow Wilson when he ran for a third term. Choice *C* is incorrect because Roosevelt was not responsible for saying that phrase. That famous quote was said by Abraham Lincoln. It is not mentioned anywhere in the passage, so it is safe to assume in this context that it was not something that Roosevelt became famous for. Choice *D* is incorrect because Roosevelt created the Panama Canal, not the Mississippi River.

19. C: Choice *C* is the correct answer because Roosevelt's love for the natural world is what would prevent him from harming a wild animal. As mentioned in Paragraph 2, Roosevelt loved the

environment and all the animals within it. This is why he would take issue with harming a bear. Choice *A* is incorrect because his love for the natural world came before his presidency, so it is unrelated. Choice *B* is incorrect because the decision to not harm the bear had nothing to do with foreign countries or policies. Choice *D* is incorrect because his fitness was unlikely a factor in why he would not shoot the bear.

20. B: Choice *B* is the correct answer because the second paragraph gives information about Roosevelt's life from birth until right before his time as president. It describes his birth, childhood, early political work, and tragedies he faced, all before he became vice president. Choice *A* is incorrect because the end of the passage is where retirement is mentioned, and it is not described in great detail. Choice *C* is incorrect because Roosevelt's policies are described later in the passage, in Paragraph 4. Choice *D* is incorrect because Roosevelt's contributions during the Spanish-American war are mentioned in Paragraph 3.

21. A: Choice *A* is the correct answer because this story is written in the first-person point of view. It uses the words *I* and *me* as we see the story from our narrator's perspective. Choice *B* is incorrect because second person is when the word *you* is used and the reader is being addressed. Choice *C* is incorrect because third person is when *he, she,* and *they* are used. This is when the narrator exists outside of the characters.

22. D: Choice *D* is the correct answer because the first portion of the story is quite spooky. The narrator does not know that the ghosts living in her home are friendly. She is seeing and hearing strange things at night. This is *eerie*. Choice *A* is incorrect because there is nothing to suggest that the narrator is *optimistic* about her new home. Choice *B* is incorrect because *morose* means gloomy and sad, which the narrator does not seem to be. Choice *C* is incorrect because the narrator is not joyful about her situation.

23. C: Choice *C* is the correct answer because *apprehensive* means fearful that something bad will happen, while *anxious* means worry about a possible event. These words have very similar meanings. Choice *A* is incorrect because *excited* means very eager, which is the opposite of *apprehensive*. Choice *B* is incorrect because *content* means peaceful and satisfied, which is a different meaning than *apprehensive*. Choice *D* is incorrect because *angry* means strong displeasure, which is not the same as feeling fearful.

24. B: Choice *B* is the correct answer because from the events in the story we know that the narrator is now friends with the ghosts. She also says that she enjoys the manor. From this, it is possible to assume that she will continue to happily live in the manor with her new friends. Choice *A* is incorrect because the narrator mentions that she had been struggling and lonely in the city. It is unlikely that she would move back. Choice *C* is incorrect because there is no reason that she would make the ghosts leave. They are her friends by the end of the passage. Choice *D* is incorrect because the narrator says that she enjoys the manor, so it is unlikely that she would demolish it.

25. A: Choice *A* is the correct answer because it is the best summary of the passage. It includes the key detail that the manor was inherited. The ghosts being friendly is integral to the story as well. The ending is summarized accurately by saying that they all live happily together. Choice *B* is incorrect because the narrator is not forced to live in the manor. She chose to do so. Choice *C* is incorrect because the ghosts are not trying to get the narrator to leave. Choice *D* is incorrect because the manor was never abandoned. The narrator's grandfather lived there.

Mathematics Achievement

1. D: Digits to the left of the decimal point represent the digit value times increasing multiples of 10 (first 1, then 10, 100, 1,000, and so on). Digits to the right of the decimal point represent the digit value divided by increasing multiples of 10 (first $\frac{1}{10}$, then $\frac{1}{100}$, $\frac{1}{1,000}$, and so on). So, the second digit to the right of the decimal point equals the digit value divided by 100.

2. A: The hundredths place value is located two digits to the right of the decimal point (the digit 9 in the original number). To decide whether to round up or keep the digit, examine the digit to the right, and if it is 5 or greater, round up. In this case, the digit to the right is 6, so the hundredths place is rounded up. When rounding up, if the digit to be increased is a 9, the digit to its left is increased by one and the digit in the desired place value is made a zero. Therefore, the number is rounded to 847.90.

3. D: To convert a fraction to a percent, we can first convert the fraction to a decimal. To do so, divide the numerator by the denominator: $4 \div 5 = 0.8$. To convert a decimal to a percent, multiply by 100:

$$0.8 \times 100 = 80\%$$

4. D: A given number divides evenly by each of its factors to produce an integer (no decimals). To find the factors of 12, determine what whole numbers when multiplied equal 12. 1×12, 2×6, and 3×4 are all the ways to multiply to 12 using whole numbers, so the factors of 12 are: 1, 2, 3, 4, 6, 12.

5. A: To determine the number of houses that can fit on the street, we can divide the length of the street by the width of each house's property:

$$345 \div 30 = 11.5$$

However, the construction company is not going to build half a house, so they will need to build either 11 or 12 houses. Since the width of 12 houses (360 feet) would extend past the length of the street, only 11 houses can be built.

6. C: The number line is divided into increments of .1 or $\frac{1}{10}$. The dot is located between the lines indicating .4 and .5. Therefore, the number represented cannot be Choice *A*, because the dot is between .4 and .5, not on .5. Choice *B*, $\frac{1}{4}$, would be .25, which is lower than .4, so it is also incorrect. Choice *D* is incorrect because $\frac{2}{5}$ is equivalent to .4, which is not between .4 and .5. Choice *C*, .45, falls between .4 and .5, so this is the correct answer.

7. B: The rate, 60 miles per hour, and time, 3 hours, are given for the scenario. To determine the distance traveled, the given values for the rate (r) and time (t) are substituted into the distance formula and evaluated:

$$d = r \times t$$

$$d = \left(\frac{60 \text{ mi}}{\text{h}}\right) \times (3 \text{ h})$$

$$d = 180 \text{ mi}$$

210

8. B: A polygon is a closed two-dimensional figure consisting of three or more sides. A decagon is a polygon with 10 sides. A triangle is a polygon with three sides. A rhombus is a type of polygon with 4 sides. A cone is a three-dimensional figure and is classified as a solid.

9. C: If Joan travels for 2.5 hours with a 15 minute, or .25 hour stop, her total travel time is 2.75 hours. If she leaves at 10:15 am, she should arrive 2.75 hours later which would be 1 pm.

10. A: The coordinates of a point are written as an ordered pair (x, y). To determine the x-coordinate, a line is traced directly above or below the point until reaching the x-axis. This step notes the value on the x-axis. In this case, the x-coordinate is -3. To determine the y-coordinate, a line is traced directly to the right or left of the point until reaching the y-axis, which notes the value on the y-axis. In this case, the y-coordinate is 2. Therefore, the ordered pair is written $(-3, 2)$.

11. C: The perimeter is found by calculating the sum of all sides of the polygon:

$$9 + 9 + 9 + 8 + 8 + s = 56$$

The s is the length of the missing side. Therefore, $43 + s = 56$. The missing side length is 13 cm.

12. C: $\frac{1}{3}$ of the shirts sold were patterned. Therefore, $1 - \frac{1}{3} = \frac{2}{3}$ of the shirts sold were solid. A fraction of something is calculated with multiplication. Therefore:

$$192 \times \frac{2}{3} = \frac{192 \times 2}{3} = \frac{384}{3} = 128 \text{ solid shirts were sold.}$$

The entire expression is $192 \times \left(1 - \frac{1}{3}\right)$.

13. B: According to order of operations, multiplication and division must be completed first from left to right. Then, addition and subtraction are completed from left to right. Therefore:

$$9 \times 9 \div 9 + 9 - 9 \div 9$$

$$81 \div 9 + 9 - 9 \div 9$$

$$9 + 9 - 9 \div 9$$

$$9 + 9 - 1$$

$$18 - 1 = 17$$

14. B: Using the conversion rate, multiply the projected weight loss of 25 lb by $0.45 \frac{\text{kg}}{\text{lb}}$ to get the amount in kilograms (11.25 kg).

15. B: The commutative property states that order does not matter when adding. The associative property deals with parentheses. Therefore, the correct option is 9 + 4 + 2 = 4 + 9 + 2 because the first two values are switched, but order does not matter.

16. D: The prime factorization of a number breaks down a number into all its prime factors. The prime factorization of 54 is $3 \times 3 \times 3 \times 2$. Therefore, three 3's appear in the prime factorization.

17. B: The prime factorization of 80 is the product of all its prime factors. 80 is equal to 8×10, 8 can be written as $2 \times 2 \times 2$, and 10 can be written as 5×2, so 80 is equal to $2 \times 2 \times 2 \times 2 \times 5$.

18: C: The correct answer has a 4 in the ten million place, 625 in the thousands places, a 9 in the hundreds place, and a 9 in the tens place. The correct answer is 40,625,909.

19. A: The problem gives us the percentage and the part. We are missing the whole. Set up a proportion to solve for the missing value.

$$\frac{150}{whole} = \frac{25}{100}$$

Cross multiply to get $150 \times 100 = 25 \times whole$. Multiply the left side and then divide both sides by 25 to find that the whole is equal to 600.

20. B: To find the percentage, divide 20 by 800. $\frac{20}{800} = 0.025$. Then, multiply 0.025 times 100 and attach the percent symbol to get 2.5%.

21. B: To find the sum, first find the common denominator. The common denominator is 18 because it is the least common multiple of the denominators 6 and 9. To change $\frac{1}{6}$ to have a denominator of 18, multiply both the numerator and denominator times 3 to obtain $\frac{3}{18}$. To change $\frac{4}{9}$ to have a denominator of 18, multiply both the numerator and denominator times 2 to obtain $\frac{8}{18}$. Then, add the numerators together and write this over the common denominator. Therefore, the answer is $\frac{11}{18}$.

22. D: To find the difference, first find the common denominator. The common denominator is 10 because it is the least common multiple of the denominators 2 and 10. To change $\frac{1}{2}$ into a denominator of 10, multiply both the numerator and denominator times 5 to obtain $\frac{5}{10}$. $\frac{7}{10}$ remains as is since it has a denominator of 10. Then, subtract the numerators and write this over the common denominator. The result is $\frac{2}{10}$. Divide a 2 from both the numerator and denominator to obtain the simplified answer of $\frac{1}{5}$.

23. C: The common factor between $18x$ and $9y$ is just the constant 9. Factoring a 9 out of each term results in a $2x$ and a y. The result is $9(2x + y)$.

24. C: Plugging 3 in for x results in $5(3) + 10 = 25$.

25. A: Each previous term is multiplied times 3 to obtain the next term in the sequence. Therefore, the missing term is $3 \times 6 = 18$.

26. B: To find the missing value, first multiply both sides times 2. The result is $(\blacksquare \times 4) = 160$. Then, divide both sides by 4 to obtain $\blacksquare = 40$.

27. C: A scatter plot is a chart that uses dots to plot values for two variables in a data set. A scatter plot is the only chart listed that shows individual data points. Therefore, it is the best option to show both the minimum and maximum values of the data set.

28. D: On Friday, 70 hot dogs were sold. On Tuesday, 30 hot dogs were sold. Therefore, the difference is $70 - 30 = 40$ hot dogs. There were 40 more hot dogs sold on Friday.

29. C: The data values in the data set {100, 100, 100, 100, 100} are all the same. Therefore, there is no variability in the data, and the standard deviation is equal to 0. The other options have nonzero standard deviation since the data values vary within the sets.

30. B: Because the coin has two sides, either heads or tails, the probability that heads is obtained on one coin flip is $\frac{1}{2}$. Therefore, 50% of the time the coin is expected to land on heads. Fifty percent of 40 coin flips is $0.5(40) = 20$.

ISEE Lower Practice Test #4

To keep the size of this book manageable, save paper, and provide a digital test-taking experience, the 4th practice test can be found online. Scan the QR code or go to this link to access it:

testprepbooks.com/bonus/isee-lower

The first time you access the tests, you will need to register as a "new user" and verify your email address.

If you have any issues, please email support@testprepbooks.com.

Dear Parent or Teacher,

Thank you for purchasing this study guide for your child or student. We hope that we exceeded your expectations.

Our goal in creating this study guide was to introduce the student to the types of questions that will be found on their test. We also strove to make our practice questions as similar as possible to what the student will encounter on test day. With that being said, if you found something that you feel was not up to your standards, please send us an email and let us know.

We have study guides in a wide variety of fields. If you're interested in one for yourself or another one for your child, try searching for it on Amazon or send us an email.

Thanks Again and Happy Testing!
Product Development Team
info@studyguideteam.com

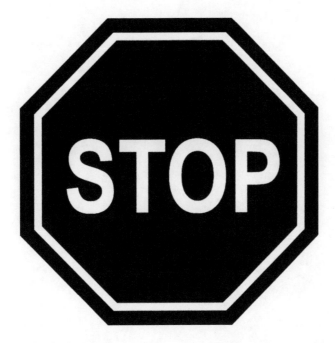

FREE Test Taking Tips Video/DVD Offer

To better serve you, we created videos covering test taking tips that we want to give you for FREE. **These videos cover world-class tips that will help your child or student succeed on their test.**

We just ask that you send us feedback about this product. Please let us know what you thought about it—whether good, bad, or indifferent.

To get your **FREE videos**, you can use the QR code below or email freevideos@studyguideteam.com with "Free Videos" in the subject line and the following information in the body of the email:

   a. The title of your product

   b. Your product rating on a scale of 1-5, with 5 being the highest

   c. Your feedback about the product

If you have any questions or concerns, please don't hesitate to contact us at info@studyguideteam.com.

Thank you!

Printed in the USA
CPSIA information can be obtained
at www.ICGtesting.com
CBHW080020251024
16392CB00008B/355